This book is dedicated to my three children.

CHAPTER 1

The Orange Poofy

IT HAPPENED IN the very early hours of Friday morning—2 a.m., to be precise. I was sitting on my front porch … well, I say *porch*, but more like a very small enclave, with only room for one, that holds the door to my electricity box. The box beeps a lot when your electric is low; when I hear this, in my head I hear it saying *money money money money money money*.

I was sitting on the ground with five cushions from the living room, reading a book with the brand-new pair of spectacles I had gotten that day, and smoking a doobie as I loved to when I was reading. Suddenly, there was a bright orange flash, so close and so powerful it turned my grass orange for a split second. At first, I thought it was the lamplight flickering off my new lenses, but when I looked up, what I saw I can only describe as an orange poofy-shaped thing with a trail of light in the middle. It happened so fast, I wasn't sure.

It really grabbed my attention. It went so fast in an outward direction—straight over my house and away across the road—in what really was quick as a flash. I started to shake just a little. I set the book down after creasing the corner of one of the pages, and then I just sat there. I had just about enough time to take a puff of the joint and think *What the frig was that?* when the same orange poofy thing flashed again.

This time, I got a better look at it. One, I was already looking up; two, it was a bit lower, level with the streetlamps; and three, it went right across the front of my garden in line with my house. This time, it was like a strong orange massive glow off everything around, but there was the same orange poofy-shaped thing in the middle, not exactly square or exactly round but in between. I could see there was light at the front and light with a trail at the back. And then it was gone. It happened so fast.

I started to tremble, but not out of fear. It was like shaking from the inside. Now I believe it was adrenaline running through me, my whole body. I quickly stubbed out the joint and kept saying to myself, *what was that? What the frig did I just see? What was that?* I repeated this for a while, in shock still, as I knew I had seen *something*. I had been a sky-watcher, starwatcher, whatever it is called all my life but had never seen anything like this ever, in all my years of looking at the night sky.

I was still in shock and shaking a little. I was alert and scanning the dark space between the two lampposts outside my house. Just as I was beginning to settle down a little, I just happened to be looking in the right direction at the right moment. It was to the right of my house, more in line with my neighbours' house. I think I was meant to see it this time. It was the same orange glow, but it had changed shape. It was a lot bigger, and it was doing something totally different.

It was like an enormous balloon, big and round at the front and smaller at the back, like a balloon tied to keep the air in. This time it was turning but twisting also. It appeared to be going up and turning right; then as it was going down, it was twisting into a turn and going left. As it did that, it spat out I think five orange things from its tail, as if it was getting extra power to go into something. At this time, I hadn't linked this with the poofy object, as they were so different in shape, though the same orange colour.

I stood in total amazement. It seemed to be getting on a right line with something, and I thought it was adjusting itself to the correct position. As I watched, five orange bits came out of the back and, one by one, they disappeared. I now was shaking in a way I had never experienced, and I had a very intense feeling about what I had just seen.

I stood there for thirty minutes, eyes scanning the sky, shaking tremendously—not in fear, but I certainly was in shock. I kept repeating to myself, "What was that?" and "What did I just see?" This was repeated many times verbally and mentality. I couldn't have counted how many times because there was so many.

I had forgotten all about my joint at this stage, but even when I did spot it lying on the ground, I couldn't smoke it (which was not like me). I was in a shocked trance about what just happened to me.

Eventually, I decided to go inside to my living room, but it was as if my feet had been glued to the ground outside. Shaking as I was, I couldn't move my feet an inch. The adrenaline was really pumping through me still, and I was still saying to myself, *what was that? What was that, Conrad?* I had never used my name to talk to myself ever, and it felt a bit weird, but I couldn't stop myself from doing this.

After about an hour, I began to settle down a bit. Well, my body did physically, but mentally, I was still buzzing and fuzzing inside my head about what had just happened to me. Then I remembered about the stubbed joint on the ground outside and went back out to smoke it, as you do. But I still never felt I ever got stoned off it. I couldn't take my eyes off the night sky. Seeing nothing coming back, I rolled another one, and this time it hit the mark. When smoking it, I never read another page of the book I was reading that night.

At this time, it was getting light, about 5:45 a.m. Birds were beginning to whistle and chirp. Once I went up to bed, I think with all the adrenaline that went me through combined with the weed, I completely knocked out to sleep. My memory is that I was very, very happy and content.

The next morning, as soon as I woke up, my mind went straight back to what happened in the early morning before. It consumed me. I knew how these things went with the public and people saying they had seen UFOs, got abducted, and things along these lines. So, I didn't tell anyone for two days.

Finally, I had to tell someone, and the only one I could trust at this time was my best matey, Colly Brown. I knew inside myself that he wouldn't say anything to anyone or think my head was away, as he knew me inside out and knew I wouldn't bullshit about things like this. It felt good to tell him, like a mental weight being lifted off my skull.

Something inside me had changed. I didn't know what it was yet, but every night from then on, I would wait for the darkness to fall with an excitement inside me that I had never felt before in my entire life. I knew, for the first time in my life, that we are not the only beings here on Earth. *We are not alone.*

As I nodded off, I did not know it at the time, but this was the early beginning of me being *awoken*, little did I know what lay ahead of me at this stage and looking back in hindsight I believe my mind couldn't have fathomed the changes that was about to enter my life.

CHAPTER 2

About Me

MY NAME IS Conrad Kirk. I was born 2 April 1976, the youngest and last-born in my family. I have three brothers and one sister currently—seven altogether including Mum and Dad. I was born in South Tyrone Hospital, and my early childhood, from what I remember, was mad but happy.

My mother left when I was just four years old, so I never really got to know her the way that a son should. But I now know that this was meant to be. We will get back to that later in the book.

I was born into the Troubles in Northern Ireland. My dad was a soldier, so of course, like any son, I wanted to be a soldier also. I am so glad that never came to fruition.

Growing up in a single-parent family amid the Troubles was a little mad, but the bond I have with my brothers and sister to this day is unbreakable. Yes, like any family we had our ups and downs, but our motto was, *if you pick on, hit, or abuse one, you hit, pick on, or abuse us all.* So, in that way, we were like glue. All that said, we maybe were a single-parent family, but we were happy within ourselves. My dad in the early days liked a tipple, maybe sometimes too much, but now, as an adult, I can understand why.

My memories of growing up at 6 Ashbeg Grove, Milltown, where we lived until I was six, are only good, bar being a little hungry at times. Then we moved to 3 Killymerron Park, which had a forest beside it called Windmill Wood. I didn't know it then, but it was a godsend: one, because it kept you out of trouble, and two, because we made so many good memories playing there.

Shortly after moving, my dad was finding it a little hard to cope, so my three brothers and I were sent off to a residential home in Portadown. My older sister, Andrea, stayed with Dad to help him. This situation only bonded us brothers closer. To get us back, Dad had to sort himself out, so it was at this time my dad met Audrey, my stepmother. She played a big role in getting us home. We also gained another brother, Dywayne, from Audrey's first marriage.

So now there were eight of us. When Dad and Audrey had their one and only child together, Mandy, there were now nine of us in total. To say the house was a bit full is an understatement, but we were all happy about this and has cemented are relationships to this day.

From an early age, we had a backs-against-the-wall mentality, always looking out for one another. When you're in that kind of situation—for me, at least—stealing something from someone or somewhere didn't feel as bad as most people would tend to think. For me, it was normal. I knew it was wrong but also that it was the only way sometimes just to eat and try to fill an empty rumbling tummy. I would come up with a few early scams to get a little money, at maybe ten, eleven years old—not sure, exactly, but certainly too young to be at it.

Back in those days, you could rent a TV, and there was a box on the back that you put pound coins in to keep it running. Then, once a month, the guy would come and empty it, take the money to pay for its rental, and leave the rest—and bingo! I would always nab a couple of pounds out of that. He always came the last Thursday of the month, 4 p.m., never late, never early, so he must have been an organized chap. So was I—waiting and organized in a different way to snap up as many nuggies as I felt I could get away with.

As the months passed, it was a good little set-up I had going. Then I noticed that Audrey would start being there when the TV rent-collector guy appeared. So, I began thinking to myself, *she knows*, but there was just no way of proving it. I think she began to realize something was up when there were a lot more pound coins left after the guy took his money, and I just couldn't let that happen again.

So, as you do when you're that young, I started engaging my brain—what else could I do? Quickly, I started examining the box itself, and I noticed it came in two pieces. Then I realized that if you got a butter knife, stuck it in the crease at the bottom of the box, and shook the TV a little, the

£1 coins would eventually fall out the bottom. Surprisingly, this worked the first time I tried it, and bingo! The scam was back on.

I remember feeling quite proud of myself after that one. I went down to the local shop, bought a niche of sweeties, and celebrated by watching Scooby Doo. That lets you know how young I was. This changed my way of thinking a little at the time—maybe stop stealing and start scamming more. Sometimes instead of sweets I would have bought twelve Weetabix and a pint of milk just to fill me up.

Another way I got a little bit of money was by finding the biscuits for my older brother Stuart. He was the first in the family to get a job, at the local Moy Park chicken factory, so had a little bit of money. Audrey had started to get creative in hiding the biscuits, because as there were so many of us, once their whereabouts was known, bingo! They were gone.

So, Stuart used to come in and ask me where they were, as I had put the time in searching for them. I would hold out my hand, and he would give me 10p. Then I told him where the goods were, and the deal was done. Got so good at this I used to change the hiding place of Audreys original placement myself and keep the real biscuit cache hidden. Once Stuart took his fill, I would put whatever he left back in the ever-more-creative hiding places Audrey had for the stash. I had to always keep one step ahead of Audrey on my little clandestine operations and two steps ahead of my brother on the private concealment. You could say a mini scam within a scam.

Writing this reminds me of the time I just couldn't find those biscuits anywhere. I searched high and low, every nook and cranny of the house, but the biscuits eluded me for the first time ever ... or so I thought. I was in Dad and Audrey's room and got so fed up searching that I just slumped down onto their bed deflated at my defeat—only to hear the crunch and rattle of the biscuit packets under both their pillows. Boom, jackpot! I remember lying there laughing about how inventive Audrey was getting as I shovelled down a packet of McVities Chocolate Homewheat and basked in my glory, nearly defeated but not just yet.

In the houses back then, you paid for the electricity with a 50p piece. When that ran out, the electric would shut down. This was happening regularly, and as I was the first home from school, I couldn't watch cartoons, as nothing—not even the lights—worked.

Across from our house in Killymerron Park was the loveliest, kindest old woman, called Miss Cullen. She was just so nice all the time. I look back now, and she reminds me of a living angel. But I was beginning to get fed up with having no electricity, so I had a brainwave as I looked out my living room window and saw Miss Cullen go into her house. I plucked up the courage to go over and ask for a 50p so I could get the electric back on, and she kindly and with her lovely smile—she always had a lovely smile—gave it to me.

When Dad got home from work, I would get the 50p off him, call over, and give it straight back. I would never let my dad get away with not giving the 50p back to her. I even have a memory of shouting at my dad when he said he didn't have 50p on him so, I then had to go to the shop and change £1 coin for two 50ps so I could give her the money back.

At that moment, I wasn't even thinking of this as my next scam. It was one day when all my friends at the time were going to the local coffee shop (Hedleys) to play pool also the gambling and arcade game systems at the back of the shop, and I just didn't have the money to go. So, I stayed home, went to my bedroom, and played with my soldiers, which I just loved anyway, as my dad was a soldier. I even used to dress up in his combat fatigues, play army, then get it all off folded up and back in the wardrobe before he got home. Bob's your uncle, no one ever knew.

Then the brainwave hit me, and as much as the electric was on, I made sure to turn all the lights off and the TV, everything electric. Then I dandered over to Miss Cullen, asked for the 50p, got it, and went straight up to Hedleys to join my friends, 50p in my pocket.

There were numerous games there, but I always played Shinobi Ninja and got that good at it. It was 10p a go, and I had 50p, so that was five goes. I was so good, it would last me a couple of hours, because that's all I used my money for. Even when we played pool, we would wait on the proprietor's son to leave the change booth to get himself a cup of coffee, biscuits, whatever, and we would tip the whole pool table and have a free game, always making sure to put it back down on the dents in the carpet so as not to raise suspicion. I think just by us always having a full game ready every single time he came back raised them anyway. We were just too quick and good at it, so it could never be proved.

Back home, I couldn't ask my dad for the 50p back, as we hadn't run out. So, for the first time, Miss Cullen wasn't getting her money back. This went on for quite a while, but sometimes I would give her £1 at a time back out of my own money from a bottle scam we used to do on the local shops.

You would gather ten bottles, 10p a bottle, unless it was the early Lucozade bottles; they were only worth 7p a bottle. You'd bring them to a local shop, cash them in, get your £1 for the 10 bottle or 97p for the Lucozade one, watch the shop assistant leave the bottles down in the store, steal the same bottles, bring them to another shop, do the same again, and vice-versa on that shop too. So sometimes, you were getting £5 a day. Normally, between two of us, sometimes three, with the same ten bottles just putting in the miles walking to different shops.

This was how I could pay Miss Cullen back some of the 50p that I was getting through my scam. She was the only one I did this for with my earnings. That's how I looked at it, because she really was the nicest woman I knew and the kindest.

Me and my brother Deane were walking home from youth club one night, and at that time you used to get your chips from the local chippy in a cone-shaped container. As they were all gone, we came up with the bright idea as we were walking past the Convent of Mercy building (local nunnery) of knocking on the front door and saying we were collecting for cancer research. Blunt as it sounds, we were just asking for money.

So, a nun came to the door, we said our bit, and she said hold on a minute. We must have waited for five minutes; it felt like an hour. We even thought she was phoning the police on us and were just about to do a runner with she appeared and dropped £2 in the tub. Bingo bongo, a nuggie each.

This progressed to writing out sponsor sheets for all types of things. I look back now as an adult and realize we were quite creative: fun runs, swimming a mile for charity, cancer research, Barnardo's, heart foundation, loads and loads of different ones. At the time, we didn't feel so good about doing this, as it was always based on lies and deceit.

So, we came up with what I thought was a more honest way of knocking on people's doors and getting money: carol singing, Deane didn't like singing that much, so he didn't do a big pile of it, but my mates at the time—Ingy, Duckbill, and JB—were up to the task. Well, I say all, but JB hadn't a note in his head. Still, we were friends and couldn't leave him out. He did get better as the seasons progressed, as we could only do it at Christmas.

The original song we sang was "We Wish You a Merry Christmas," and if the parents said, "Wait until I get my children," we had "Jingle Bells" as a backup. The good thing about this was when they asked us what charity the money was for, we all agreed to be truthful and just tell them it was for ourselves, and nobody seemed to mind—probably thought fair play to these young boys for even having the balls in the first place just to knock on the door and start singing away. That's what I thought to myself at the time.

Just for the record, Duckbill was the best singer of us all. That's a hard one to admit, even with my vocals, but he was good, and we couldn't have done it without him. We made a lot of money doing this. Then, it was up to the local Chinese restaurant at the end of the evening to get ourselves a well-earned sausage supper with curry and a can of Coke as our reward and split the money between us for Hedleys the next day.

There were loads of funny times doing this, like darting out of the way at the very last second when you noticed a local girl you fancied from about the town, but never knew where she lived until that point of just about to start singing, and dropping from four guys to an automatic two who then had to do it alone from that point on, but still shared the money, as it was swings and roundabouts as to the different girls we fancied.

The funniest, most adventurous, and most profitable singing sessions were two days I think before Christmas. We were drinking a bottle of strawberry Concord each, and we came upon a massive house at the top of Manor Court where all the rich people lived, with loads of fancy cars outside and noise coming out of the house. We knew it was a Christmas party of some sort. Normally we wouldn't have bothered with such a house, but the Concord wine helped calm our nerves a little.

We plunked the bottles down by the two big pillars as we entered the garden and knocked on the door. A woman opened and away we went with "We Wish You a Merry Christmas," like a well-attuned choir at this stage, as we had done it so many times. The woman was so excited to see us, genuinely surprised. She asked if we could sing for the children, so she went away to get them. We got ourselves ready with "Jingle Bells," ready to rock. They loved it so much; she invited us in to sing for the whole party.

Oh crap. In we went, into a big, massive room. Their faces were blurry at the start but then it was "Oh, hello, Antony!" It was Ingy's dentist. Then, "Hello, Conrad!" My doctor. Holy crap. That's when I was thankful that

9

we'd had a wee drink before we got there. But when in Rome, so off we went: "We Wish You a Merry Christmas" and "Jingle Bells." And as they themselves were drinking, feeling jolly in the moment they asked for one more just in the same way you would ask a DJ at the end of a night.

This was when Duckbill shined, as we had learnt only one verse of "Silent Night, Holy Night," but not us all. JB hadn't a clue. So off we went, and without Duckbill singing on this one, we would have gotten exposed as amateurs. I remember to this day the clapping and howling and laughter of children, and just at that moment, everybody in that room was happy.

The lovely lady did a walk around the room and rounded up all the money, and one of the men asked, "What charity is it for?" And me being the spokesman said it was for ourselves. They really loved this.

Once we got outside, we scooped our bottles of Concorde up and swigged a mouthful like never before. We counted the money altogether, and it was £45—our biggest lift ever. We really did think our Christmas had come early. We didn't sing another note that night, as £45 was like getting £1000 to us.

The next year, we got inventive and started a little earlier, at Halloween, singing away: "Halloween is coming, the goose is getting fat, please put a penny in the old man's hat. If you haven't got a penny, a ha'penny will do, if you haven't got a ha'penny, God bless you," and at that everyone put one hand behind his back, the other out in front, as if to say drop the money in the hands. It was just as good as the Christmas carol singing. It wasn't even a scam anymore it was at times hard work.

Wow, so many good memories of this, so much fun we had. I could probably write a book just about the scams we did over the early years. But back to growing up a little more. Just before I move on from those years, if we didn't do these things, we wouldn't have had a penny, because our families had no spare money to give us. So, I have no remorse or regrets about any of this, as it was for our own survival, happiness, and food. I loved it all, looking back in hindsight.

School, we went through in a flash and learnt nothing—but looking back now as an adult, I realize I loved it. I just didn't know it at the time. Even the dinner pass I bought off Duckbill for 50p was worth 75p, so I made 25p every day, as he needed it for cigarettes, and I didn't smoke at the time.

O.K., sorry, no more scam talk, but it did get me three mashed potatoes, two sausages, beans, and butter with a drink and quelled my tummy.

I left school with my GCSEs—didn't do great but didn't fail any either. Certainly, wasn't an angel at school but wasn't that bad either, probably a wee bit cheeky, and always trying to be funny. Left school straight away; going to college or university didn't even as much as enter my head. I wouldn't have wanted it anyway.

Went into the YTP scheme (Youth Training Program), did joinery for three months, couldn't saw straight not one bit, so left and at sixteen went to work in a local abattoir, Oakdale Meats. Hated every bit of it. Lovely bunch of lads working there, but I got the job through my mate at the time, Darren Rooney. He was so small, smaller than even a hobbit from the Shire, so being the only two Protestants in the whole factory, physically I was on my own. But truthfully, all the Catholics were such a good bunch of lads it didn't matter. It was a place where, if you pulled your weight, you got the respect you deserved.

Worked there for a year and a half, £60 a week. Just felt like working for buttons, but only good memories I have of that time, except for the recurring nightmares I had of cows and especially a big bull chasing me in my dreams. This nightmare went on for quite a while, but when you work somewhere like this, you can do any job, as the only way is up. Especially when you've done your stint in the green offal, smelling of shite no matter how many showers you took, embarrassing with the girls so to speak.

As I worked there, I became a lover of dance music. (Oh, and I forgot to say I had done kickboxing since I was fourteen years old with my big brother Staurt, but I'll get back to that later.) So, I was what you would have called "a little raver," and some drugs went with that scene, so to say I dabbled a little; sometimes quite a lot would be an understatement. Ecstasy tablets, LSD tabs, smoking weed, magic mushrooms, and speed were the drugs of choice, but not all together, of course.

Let's just say I had to get inventive to hide this sort of shenanigans from Staurt, as he was as straight as a flagpole, and we always trained together. Eventually, we would both become training coaches at kickboxing. So, through my double act as a raver and a kickboxer, I did live a very active life, and I was even in a band called Storm HQ (had to give it a mention). I was very busy, but as you should be at that time of your life, thinking you could take on the world.

Now at this stage of my kickboxing career, I had already had about twelve fights: won ten, lost one, drawn one. Also, I had been to Switzerland with an international fight under my belt, and it just so happens out of the five fighters that fought for Northern Ireland, I was the only one who won my fight. I know my brother was so proud of me doing this; I could see it in his eyes even now. But due to this, my brother and I got picked to fight for our country, Northern Ireland. We went on to fight the English, Scottish, French, and even my brother went to America and fought a champion over there, so yes, amazing time and amazing memories.

So, at this stage, around seventeen years old, it was the year of fighting and dancing all at the same time. The thing about it was that I loved both, but if I had to choose one, it would always be kickboxing. I went on to win the Ulster Title, and then at eighteen progressed to fighting Mick Bulger, who was the Irish champion at my weight. Both of us had sixteen fights apiece, with only one loss apiece. It was for the All-Ireland title, which meant the best length and breadth of this island. It was one of the toughest fights of my life. I went on to win the fight and become champion.

Next was British, then European, then world champion. I had finally started believing and dreaming toward this. I was so eager, I was down training three days after the fight at the Bush Crossroads, where we had the club. I had done a couple of star jumps, and something went *pop* in my left knee. Little did I know it then, but my fighting days were over. Even three operations on my knee didn't help.

I was devastated beyond comprehension. It really affected me to the core. Mentally, I wasn't finished yet, but physically my knee was saying *that's it, buddy*. Took me a few years to get over that one, as I really thought I would become world champion. It still hurts a little, my knee, but memories of it all too.

So, I think my raving days from then on were sort of filling the void from not being able to do something I absolutely loved. That is not to say I didn't have a good time clubbing, because I certainly did. My life was flashing by at this stage. I had a couple of different girlfriends, as one does, but there was one I was with at this time who I thought maybe was the one. But at the time, I was living a very mad life. I had moved out of the family home at seventeen, which in hindsight maybe was a bit early. But that was the way it was at the time.

I worked a couple of jobs over the years. There was a bit of labouring, road works, greenkeeping, salesman, and factory work, but I always loved working outside. Then I became a tree surgeon for five or six years and loved not only being outside but the job also. I ended up losing two of my ribs in an accident at work and couldn't do it from that point on. As much as I tried, it was just too painful.

So as this was all happening, I had three children, all girls, with my partner at the time. We eventually split up after eighteen years together, and I now bring the children up myself. I had met her years before in my early days of raving, but we were with other partners at the time. Little did I know then that I would go on to have three beautiful children with her.

We would eventually fade apart from each other, with different factors on both sides, eventually going our separate ways. At the time, I wished it had been a bit smoother than it was, but you cannot turn back time.

There's so much more in life I could write about—funny things, bad things, fights, quarrels, laughs, loves, late nights, even jobs—but maybe for another time. Let's just see how this book goes. I've finally caught up with myself and my story, just thought I had to tell you a little about myself before my life took a very different and unexpected direction and one that I couldn't have contemplated in a million years.

CHAPTER 3

The Nights That Followed the Orange Poofy Experience

I WOULD COME home from work and make dinner for the kids, always with an excitement of the darkness to fall. I would roll a joint and have it ready for later that night. I didn't know it at the time, but this was a common factor. The only thing that changed was me rolling two joints, as I would stay outside for quite a while. As soon as I got my children to bed—well, I say *bed*, what I really mean is that I got them upstairs and into the bedroom, certainly not to sleep, as they loved staying up late and still do to this day, once this was done it was outside.

For the first time in my life, I started to follow different weather apps on my phone to see if it was going to be a clear or cloudy night. I didn't know it at this point, but soon it wouldn't matter, as I would come to love a cloudy night just as much as a clear night. I'll tell you a bit later about the reason why. It started with me just scanning the skies with my eyes looking for something, sometimes expecting something to show up the way it did before. So, for the next couple of nights, I was watching the night sky.

6 August 2023
11:10 p.m.

Fact

I stopped writing earlier tonight. I just went outside for the first time on a clear night and saw what looked to be an orange UFO going fast across the sky, then coming back again, and I just started writing about it again. I'm flabbergasted—so happy, but it's so surreal. What's going on? I thought it could be the orange poofy, but it was high up and came from the bottom of the saucepan.

I love my new life. I feel I am being watched over, I think—don't know for sure, my hand is still shaking a little. It seems it can disappear and reappear when it wants. I was in shock a bit.

WOW! WOW! WOW! WOW! WOW!
UNREAL! SO AMAZING FOR ME.

7 August 2023
11:21 p.m.

That's two nights in a row now. I've only seen it once tonight.

On the third night, I stayed out that bit later—the same time as I saw the orange one—and at about 1:45 a.m., a big luminous rectangle went flashing by, with a white force of light (cloudy light) in front of it and a white trail behind it. And it was right where I was looking, about two times the height of my house, right in front of me.

It was so bright and happened so fast, about one to two seconds, maybe one, but enough time to let me know something solid of bright light was in the middle. I phoned my best matey Colin Brown—Colly B we'll call him from now on—and told him about it, and as he was coming home from Scotland, he said he would come to my house on Saturday night.

So, skip to Saturday, 1:30 a.m., when he arrived. We both went outside. I had a reefer rolled for me; Colly B wouldn't smoke it, as it would have put him to bed (he can't handle it; does his head in). We were probably outside for about thirty minutes, and secretly in my head I was wishing for something to happen, just so one, Colly B didn't think I was bullshitting, and two, some confirmation of what I had been telling him all week.

I was beginning to feel less excited, and just as I was about to sit down, *whoosh!* A small rectangle of light zoomed passed out a wee bit from us but close enough for us to see it clearly. Colly B was so excited, and deep down so was I—but I was even happier that he had seen one too. So as the two of us were bouncing with joy, I turned and said, "So far, one comes shortly after the other."

So just as we began to look up again, *whoosh!* Another one looking the exact same as the first flew by, only this time it was in a different direction. We both by now were jumping for joy, and I could see Colly was a bit gobsmacked about what he had just seen. I was so happy for him to see them and for me to get some confirmation that what I was relaying to him was true. At that moment, I knew he was a believer. We had seen shooting stars before, but this was no shooting star. It was too low in the atmosphere.

I finished off the joint and tried to offer him a drag, but I knew he wasn't falling for that one. Both of us couldn't stop talking, and it took us a while to settle down, as it is a very surreal experience. I don't care who you are, when you see something like that, your perspective changes a little, and it sparks some part of your brain that was never sparked in that way before. He and I were now believers, and nothing could change us. I personally was so happy that I got to experience it with my best matey.

I was hooked from that moment on. But little did I know at this point what was next. I told my children that I had seen UFO outside, and they weren't ready for it, or even ready to listen to me on the subject. So, I didn't pursue it too much, as they were still young. Also, I put myself in their position, and at their age, I probably would have reacted the same. So, I let it go and felt they weren't ready for the knowledge of my sightings just yet.

I was beginning to scan the night sky every night, even before darkness fell. I was spotting the stars while I waited; some nights I could see ten stars, next night only two, next night maybe twenty, and so on. It was never fully clear, but there were a couple of nights where it was clear, and I began to realize how many there actually were—ton and tons of them.

So, as you do this from one viewpoint, you begin to know what stars are where. I got better over time. At this time, my favourite was the one I called the upside-down pyramid with two stars at the top. My second favourite was the frying pan and its handle. Doing this night after night you really do begin to question what you were taught about at school about being on a spinning ball hurtling through the cosmos, through my observation its absolute bullshit.

Some of the bright ones were planets; I just didn't know that yet. But I began to build up a picture of where they would be and how the world turned on an axis, our was it the stars that went round just due to the stars always being in the same place night after night. As you can tell, I was no astrologer in the making but was for the first time in my life beginning to ask questions.

As time progressed, but only on a clear night, I noticed a bunch of stars all together. I didn't know at this time, but I came to find out it was what they call the Pleiades. I found this out by out by watching an *Ancient Aliens* episode about finding a drawing of them in an old cave in Australia that the ancient aborigines had made.

I don't know what made me think about doing a telescope with my hands, but my memory says it had to do with the sky being so patchy with the clouds, and with not being able to see many stars. I wanted to concentrate on the ones I could just about see, and my hands blocked the glare from the two streetlamps outside my house, left and right, giving me a better view of the stars and planets.

As I was scanning the sky through my hand telescope, I stopped at a star for a few seconds, and the star started to move up and down and side to side, with no great rhythm or pattern. It seemed a little strange at first, but I had now put my tenting fold-up chair outside on my porch rather than the six cushions from my living room sofa, so I was comfortable to say the least. I'd already consumed half a joint, so maybe *happy comfortable* is a better phrase to use.

I followed this star as it jumped, sometimes small, sometimes big, up and down it went, also from side to side again, sometimes to the left and sometimes to the right. As I pulled back and stopped it, I realized I was so far away from the star that it was static before I started to follow it. Fascinated by this, I did it again, and it happened again. The only difference was I ended up even higher in the night sky, but miles away from where I started.

This phenomenon really began to get my attention, so I started doing it with other stars in the night sky. I would put my hand telescope together at a few stars that were close to each other, and after a few seconds, it would start again. They would go to different angles and heights but stay together all the same. Even on a cloudy patchy night, these stars, I felt, were dancing for me in a weird type of way.

Then one night, the sky was a little clearer, but still with clouds in the sky, when to my left was the Pleiades star system. This was the first time they were so visible to me, as they must be farther away. When I turned my hand telescope on them, they truly lit up the night sky, like a mini fireworks display a way out where they were. They were jumping every direction up and down, all at different levels. It was amazing to watch. They all stayed tightly bunched, but as one was going up, another two were coming down, another two going left and right. The clouds that were between me and them were glowing like I'd never seen in my life. It truly was an amazing show of starlight dancing, was what I was thinking in my head at the time.

When I opened my hands again, the stars must have travelled at least a mile from where I started. I had to move my head so far left to see them all there, as if they hadn't moved an inch. To say I was astounded at this is an inner statement. I was mesmerised by it.

I must have done it about three times that night before the clouds got too thick for me to see them anymore. Each time, they would do it, but never the same way. I was just so amazed at the way the clouds lit up and glowed, illuminating the shapes of the stars so brightly.

The very next night, I had run out of cellophane but kept the cardboard tube to act as a telescope along with a bog-roll one. As excited as I was when I used these the next night, I found that nothing would move. It was just static stars. But when I set the tubes down and used my hands, they would start to dance all over again. Now, I don't know why it happened this way, but that's what went down, I have an inkling, but even now, I'm still not fully sure. The only thing I know for sure is that these stars, I felt, were dancing for me.

For the next few nights, the cloud cover started to get thick. Only if there was a break in them or a hole in the middle would I get a glimpse at the odd star in the night sky. It still didn't put me off from rolling my doobie and sitting there stargazing, but it really was more like cloud gazing.

Then, out of the blue, I began to see lights—some bright, some quite dim, shining behind the odd cloud here and there. At the start, I thought nothing of it. Then it started to get more frequent, which in turn got more of my attention.

Now throughout my life, mostly either in the early morning or throughout the day, I would see shapes of different animals in the clouds. I know this is nothing new, but this was exactly what was beginning to happen to me, only at night-time. I probably wouldn't have thought anything of it if it was the odd one, but the sightings were on a whole new scale never before had I ever witnessed. It began to feel magical to me and hard to believe at times even though it was me doing the watching.

The first ones I began to see were birds, but the thing was, there were many different types. I know it was cloud shapes, but I could make out crows, robins, eagles, owls, sparrows, flamingos, ducks … it just kept happening on a scale where I thought I was smoking some type of bird weed. At least, this was my first thought: owl skunk, eagle chronic, duck haze—jokes aside, I just didn't know at this stage. But as these shapes continued, it became clear to me that some of them were dimly lit through the clouds.

It progressed to other animals, and I'm going to go through just what ones I did see. There were crocodiles and wolves. Sometimes it was just the wolf's head, and others it was the whole wolf, paws and all. With the crocodiles, I have always watched nature shows, and I could even see the caiman crocodiles, as they had a different shape to its head. It was quite detailed for being a cloud formation. There was even a platypus with its duck-shaped beak sticking out really clear at night. There were two of them beside each other.

On, the same night, it started to show me lots of different fish shapes, with some I didn't even know. Then sharks started to appear, and dolphins—loads of them across the sky at different levels and sizes. It was the same with the sharks. There weren't as many, but they too were detailed.

One night, I saw a big great white. The dying sun must have been behind but low down on the horizon; the underside of the cloud was white and the top of the great white dark blue. Ten to fifteen minutes after this sighting, I was astonished to see a tiger shark with the detailed scales on it—that's how I knew it was a tiger shark—and even a detailed fin and tail. That one to witness was truly amazing at the time.

Then the sting rays showed up, and of all the shapes I had seen, the sting rays were multiple and had more light to them. I thought some of them were moving at this point. I say this because I saw one and, as other clouds passed in front, it lit up more intensely, and the lights started to move along a horizontal line behind the cloud going dim and bright depending on the thickness of the cloud in front of it. That was another one that left my mind flabbergasted as it looked to be alive. Amazed, astonished dumbfounded, truly I was blown away. What is going on I kept thinking to myself, my brain was rattled, and my voice was speechless, but my eyes were locked open.

This was beginning to happen on an unprecedented scale every night, that much I had forgotten about the stars and the clear night skies—even to the point where I would get excited during the day when I would check my phone weather app and see that there was thick cloud all over. The cloudier the better. The whole thing had gone 360 degrees in my mind.

Soon after this, I saw my first massive blue whale—the one that opened its mouth at the top of the water to gather whole shoals of fish in one go, also plankton. This was the scene that greeted me one night just as the sun had disappeared completely. It truly was on a massive scale. It was so big, I never made it out for quite a while, but when I did, it was unmissable, a truly magnificent sight. That one really got me, and I think I shed a tear about what I was seeing.

As it was still so early in the evening, once it dissipated (and it took a while), on the other side of the sky I started witnessing deer, mostly in twos and threes. Then bigger deer. I think these were antelope, although I wasn't sure, but they had these funny horns. Buffalo heads and whole buffaloes followed.

Sometimes there was no rhyme or reason to it all. A fish would appear, then a cow, then a lizard, snakes, honestly everything showed up at one time or another. It was amazing to my eyes at the time. There were also a couple of horses that showed up one night, their silhouettes completely detailed. Little did I know what this was all for at the time. Later in the book, I will explain what happened. It was so wild even to imagine what was going to go down.

Then I started to see lions. It was lion faces at first, some big and others so small, then it progressed to seeing a couple at a time, full-bodied: the lion's hairy big mane, legs, paws, even the tail on one of them. There were tigers, too. Then a zebra turned up. I only ever saw one zebra, but you couldn't have mistaken it for a horse, as it had the zebra stripes, and all this made from the cloud.

It was just mind-boggling at the time of seeing it. Reindeer showed up on the same night. There were mice, rats, hedgehogs, beavers, and walruses. It was so crazy for me to see all these, but the craziest was yet to come.

At first, they were hard to make out, but I began seeing what was shaped like little dragons. They began to get bigger and more defined in shape.

The difference with the dragons was, there seemed to be a tint of purplish, turquoise glow to them, but not the whole cloud-shaped dragon—just around the outside. That is why I think I began to see them so clearly. There weren't tons of them like I'd seen the dolphins or stingrays before, but I can't exactly say how many, maybe five or six, all in the one night. It was truly, truly amazing.

The biggest was yet to come, and yes, this was all on the same night. At the time of seeing this, I didn't know its proper name, but I have gained the knowledge and read up to learn it was a sauropod. I knew it as the gentle leaf-eating dinosaur from *Jurassic Park* movies, the biggest one with the long neck. When I first made it out, I saw the head of it sticking above another cloud; it even looked like it was turning its head a little, I kid you not. But as I looked down, I could make out the big body and the bottoms of his big stumpy legs with a big tail out the back. I didn't get looking at it for a long time, as the clouds became thicker and the light behind it was fading rapidly in the night sky.

As the night began to grow on me, I don't know why, but I started to call them my Cloud Angels. It just popped into my head one day at work, when mentally I was saying to myself, *I wonder if the Cloud Angels will show up tonight.* That's just how excited I was to see these clouds at night. It really did give me a strange excitement, as I began to feel they were coming out for me. I often wondered at the time if anybody else saw them too.

CHAPTER 4

Stop Talking Shit

ONE NIGHT A week, sometimes two, I would call over to my Italian buddy, Enzo Di Maio, for a couple of joints, to have a laugh, talk a little crap, and put the world to right, at least the one I knew about at this point. My best matey Colly B happened to be over on this night. When I look back, he was meant to be there. The universe made sure of it.

It was just the normal run-of-the-mill passing the doobie to the left-hand side and being forever observant as to which one of us would try to hog the joints, as the night was still young, and Enzo's cupboards were still full of biscuits. As we were smoking outside, Enzo just came out with these words: "Have you ever heard of the Anunnaki?"

As I was in the middle of taking a drag, I'll never forget it, I turned to him and said, "I'm trying to smoke my joint. Stop talking shit in my ear and give my head peace." Little did I know at the time what was going to transpire from that moment on, but I would soon find out. At this point I hadn't even told Enzo what I was witnessing outside my home in the night sky.

Now Colly B had always been on to me about secret societies, dark occults, the elites running the world with the big corporations, which in turn were run by the bankers, and how we were all getting scammed with everything, and the government was behind it all too, and how the whole thing just was just a big façade. So that night, the more the two of them went on about it, the more I began to listen a wee bit more intently. Enzo had a book called *The Anunnaki*, so gave it to me, and I took it home to read.

I told Colly B I would start looking into all the things he'd been talking about—who ran the world. Again, I didn't really know what I was getting myself into, but from that point on, it was the beginning of me becoming truly *awoken*. I have looked back on this moment later in my life as a kind of renaissance in my mentality.

I did read all the book, and by the end, I was fascinated by what I read. Every bit was mind-altering, mind-boggling, and mind-over-matter. I really started to gain more knowledge of it all, and all the unwritten history that was available through research, and quickly realized that the history taught to me at school was so little it felt like I was duped on nearly all of it.

So as the nights rolled on and my research on it all picked up, I realized that the more I investigated certain subjects, the more my phone would pop up related content on the matters I was reading about. I knew this happened, but the scale it was happening now was like my phone was reading my mind and putting things in order as a way of learning this bit by bit. I felt I was guided in some mysterious way. That's how I felt at the time.

Some nights I would stay up late, always learning new things, and then in an instant, everything changed from the inside. What I mean about this was what I've called *the light bulb moment*. I was deeply into researching the government tax and how it works, banks, the strawman, mortgages, money circulation, schools and who runs them, food industries, water infiltration, and how it all looked from my personal perspective.

Light bulb after light bulb went off in my head, just like the way you would turn the lights on in the car or when entering a dark room. Bang bang bang! All the dots connected so quickly; it was as if I was being shocked by electricity. I had never felt these feelings before in my entire life—up to this point, anyhow. I began shaking from the inside. My heart began pounding to where I could hear it. Like an adrenaline rush flowing through my body, hot flushes came over me as my brain started catching up to my thoughts, it felt like bubbles bursting inside my head instead of above it.

I'll never forget that night. Everything that I had been teaching myself about kicked in on the one go, like an epiphany. The feeling of absolute devastation of lies, deceit, darkness, money control—I truly felt my whole life was a swindle right at that moment. I still remember the feeling. I would never be the same person ever again, and as much as I thought I was awoken before, this was the night and moment when it all came together, and now I was truly *awoken*. So Colly B and Enzo, I can't thank you enough for all your early knowledge that you told me and got me jump-started on my journey.

You know when you find this stuff out in life, it's hard to take, especially when you come from a life with so much struggle and so much trauma, and then you realize it was never gonna be any other way, as it was set up this way. All you want to do is help in some way, but how can you help when you're just a normal guy working a JOB (which stands for Just Over Broke in my world and many others across the globe). But you begin to at least think. It's the sowing of the seed, and the planting of a root, a very deep root.

When I said I was truly awoken, I meant it—but from a third-dimension perspective. Now I was about to get awoken on a whole new level, a whole new world, a whole new existence, a whole new dimension, a whole new life, and especially a whole new meaning to this way of life, one I had never experienced before.

So that was the research I had been doing about the living facts of life, but the other part of my research took me down a different path altogether. This was the first time I came across Billy Carson. I'd never had an inkling who he was, but he popped onto my social feed one evening, and from that moment on, this took a different turn, and I had discovered a different set of rules to life. I understood how it was lived, inner stood (according to my research, *understanding* was spell-casting the English language that meant *subdued slave* in old Spanish language).

Billy's page was full of knowledge that I knew nothing of, and it started with all the ancient readings he had taken from the tablets and scrolls, about early life on Earth and how everything was changed a little, and how everything was more or less left out, and if it wasn't, then it was twisted to suit this modern-day living, which had accumulated to modern-day slavery. The knowledge that this man bestowed was overwhelming at first, mind-boggling, informative. He was a modern-day genius in my eyes, and in his character and demeanour.

He wasn't one who minced words to suit a certain directive or achieve high status in some way. He was a truth-teller, knowledge-spreader, and certainly the one person who didn't give a root and toot about what anybody said, as he'd done his research. The more I began to follow him, the more I was learning every day, but also learning a bit about him personally, and his experience with his own ET moment in his life, while sitting on his sofa at his home. His brain or skull got rattled a bit, I think, and I believe that was his purpose, to start gaining all the knowledge and as a living angel spread it to the world.

True is a word I began to learn from him. Well, really, it was *truth*— human DNA and how to change it from the inside out. At that moment, I didn't know how much of a yo-yo, spaghetti-junction rollercoaster ride it was going to be, but it wasn't long before I'd find out.

I didn't know what exactly these things meant at the time. Experiencing it with hindsight, I really didn't have a clue. But I had such a strong desire to follow the guidance and the experience of all these levels on a day-to-day basis, while at the same time bringing up my three children. It's not as much as hiding it from them; they just weren't ready to innerstand it all, and still aren't, at least at the time I'm writing this.

Sound, vibration, frequency, DNA Meditating, Universal, Cosmic, internal, external, Reiki, Dimensions, Realms, Emerald Tablets, 144 Thousand Thoth, Amen, Zeus, Titans Thoth Enki, Enil, Enoch, Arcturian, Pleiades, quantum mechanics, the Black Knight, Reptilians, Draconians, Lemurians, Syrians, Atlanteans, Andromedans, Spirits, demi-gods, Spirituality, Spirit Guides, guardian Angels, Ancestors, Ascended Masters, Christos, Yeshua, Elohim, Nephilim Falling Angels, God (that was a name I already knew, but not cosmic birther, source, prime creator, The One, the most high, nor Yeshua for that matter)—so many names. People, I noticed, had picked the one that felt right for them. I got to calling them all at one stage my Spiritual Mother, Father, brother, sister, Granny, Granda, just everything, the law of one, souls over souls, Mother Earth, Gaia, Moon, the Sun, Avatars, Demons, Darkness, inner work, LIGHT, LIGHT LIGHT, Shape shifters, Celestial Entities ... the list really does go on.

But for now, these were things, some that I knew about but most of them, I had never heard of. To say I was intrigued is an innerstatement. *Fascinated* is a better word for how I felt. They just didn't teach you this in school, as it wasn't part of the indoctrination process that modern schools have become.

I had been spiritually awoken, not yet awake, but it really was the beginning of not only a new way of living but a fresh start to life at forty-six years old. That really is saying something. The changing of your DNA was the first-ever thing that popped up from Billy Carson. It really was a new, honest, forgiving way of living, because up to this point my DNA was on its own controlled path. I realized that at this point I hadn't a clue; even my memory, thoughts, feelings, and reactions were already programmed. I didn't notice it at first, but the journey I was about to go on would transmute so much shit I could have filled a quarry with it, and all on a two-strand DNA, when in truth we had twelve.

Up to this point in my life, the only thing about *frequency* I knew was different radio-station channels—Radio 1, 2, FM, showing my age a little but the one I remember growing up was Atlantic 252—and vibrations were the playing of the strings of a guitar, and of course sounds were as simple as the sound of music. Nothing was known to me about the way this affects the body, bar my ears ringing from being inside a speaker back in my raving days at the Circus Circus Nightclub (best), not my eardrums buzzing but the club. What affect these things had on my body, I was clueless.

This also is a time I was introduced to Dolores Cannon through my social feed. It took me three weeks to realize she had already shifted to a different timeline (death in most people's eyes) and that it was her daughter Julia's page where I was gaining all this knowledge of the New Earth 5D. It was then I realized how much of a latecomer to this process I was. But I had an eagerness and a desire to find truth in the total chaotic controlled world that was beginning to show itself to me.

The solar system I was taught about in school was so basic and easy to innerstand. I knew no different. The cosmos and universe I was beginning to gain knowledge of was much more complicated and packed full of races, good and bad, dark and light, electrical, magnetic plasma, filled dimensions, the quantum field, quantum mechanics, black holes, other planets, realms, races, spaceships, reptilians, draconians. All this is kept from the masses of people on this earth—it really did begin to show me that there were so many secrets kept from the public that the ones who controlled this for generation after generation were very smart, very greedy, very intelligent beings who treat the general public as slaves to a scale it still gets under my skin.

All this new knowledge inspired me to delve even deeper into this cosmic life. As I look back on my childhood, when VHS tapes were the hottest things on the go, I would babysit, and my reward was going round to the local video shops to rent out a movie. I was always attracted to sci-fi movies, even from an early age. I just don't know what brought this on, but to a point I always had to watch them alone, as my brothers would have said, "What are you watching that shite for? It's not real."

I used to say, "I know it's not real, but it's good. Just use your imagination."

Looking back now as an adult, I realize why I loved the likes of *Star Wars*—anything that was deemed to not be real I loved those movies, and I suppose it was an early form of escapism from my upbringing as a youth and the outside events that were going on as I grew up. *The Troubles* is what they named it. The video rental shop was called E.T., and no, it did not stand for extraterrestrial; its name was Entertainment Today. I loved that shop on Scotch Street. To say I had a bit of interest in sci-fi was true, but not on the scale I was acquiring as an adult through the books of Dolores Cannon and Billy Carson, and on their social platforms.

Earthing and meditation I had never done before, nor the eating of dandelions—so much new stuff. Excitement was filling up my whole body and the way I was beginning to live my life. Not once in school did, I learn about Mother Earth and how the body is electrical and the heart magnetic, nor did they ever mention the pineal gland, the chakras, your meridian lines, the magnetic field that covers every single being, and the soul that lies within your own body. Nothing, absolutely nothing—and still looking, there's nothing. Educational emptiness, I call it.

This was the next step in what I call my personal evolution, and as much as I had taken a few psychedelics in my early days, what I was about to go through was so otherworldly that it was out of this world.

In the Bible, and on billboards of churches, you would always see the caption in capital letters "Ye Must Be Born Again." I always thought or should I say was programmed in innerstanding that this meant to be saved, to become a follower, and to worship the word of God—to become a Christian. For years I thought this, but when I heard Billy Carson's take on it all, what it really is is a hacking of your programmed brain, reprogramming the brain with knowledge and wisdom of the actual multi-universes that exist within each and every one of us, and not a big entity of God light years away sitting on a big throne waiting on your prayers and worship. That's what sadly some people think, and I was one of them, but it means that not only is time an illusion, but everything is also made of light, everything.

I know someone reading this will say WTF is he on about, just as I first did or thought. I know it's deep, hard to fathom as such, but it's the truth, and once you gain this knowledge, you'll realize that you have being telling yourself a load of lies from within all your living life and have been programmed to do and think like this, and you don't even know it. I am trying to be as raw as possible in writing about this to make people go out and search for themselves, read about the truth seekers, question everything you've ever been taught. Then at least you can make your own decisions on matters of your own enlightenment in the world. I guarantee once you do, you'll never see it in the way you did before or hear it after. When you realize as a living being that everything is light, it changes everything, even your thoughts about darkness.

Let me try to explain this in more layman's terms. If you're in a dark room, at sea, in a ship where all is dark, and somebody turns on the light, the lighthouse, what happens? It lights up off-course simple thinking. But when you're in an already lit-up room and all lights are on, nothing can darken the room unless you turn the light off. You see, light always has and always will rule the darkness. Once you become conscious of this, you can never become overturned by the darkness. We are light, and light is us, and light is consciousness, and consciousness is everything, everywhere, and everyone.

I could feel my brainwaves changing, but little did I know what was ahead of me. My journey so far had certainly changed me, but what I was about to experience next not only changed me, I became a totally different person. Maybe this was the beginning of me becoming awake to everything I'd been studying and expanding my thoughts in going down every rabbit hole that my mind was falling into, bouncing around and beginning to climb out of every one with a brand new perspective to a life blinded, barricaded, and blocked from me.

CHAPTER 5

Change

Early Awakening

THE MORE I learnt, the more woke I became, the more I began to change, and I was slowly but surely becoming awake—not *open your eyes* awake, but spiritually awake. At this point, even if I wanted to stop (which I didn't), I couldn't have anyway, as the intensity of what was happening me was unstoppable.

What I'm about to tell you will sound like magic to most people who are reading this, but the few who know this path will know it as a very, very intense awakening, to even some who know. It's a miracle and was an inspiration for writing this book in the first place—to try to wake the masses up to what is happening to our world. It's so big and so global, the mind control. I thought, *how can I help?*

In *The Lord of the Rings* trilogy, the first instalment, when they are at Rivendell with the Ring of Power and the elves, dwarves, and men are arguing over who will take the Ring to Mordor, Frodo walks over to the middle, lifts the Ring, and says "I will bring the Ring to Mountain of Fire in Mordor, but *I do not know the way*. The memory I had of this scene was how I felt. I wanted to help, but I was humanly alone (bar my soul brother Colly B) and felt that with what I was going through, this could be a good way to at least try to tell my story, awaken as many souls as I possibly could, and begin to heal this world and start replacing fear with love.

Now, at forty-six years old and never into this sort of thing, I found this starting again as I sat on my porch. I just happened to close my eyes—more like a long blink—and I caught a glimpse of a tiny bit of light coming from my left hand and automatically thought that I was badly stoned. I couldn't have been more wrong. Meditation is something I knew of but never read into before, nor did I ever try it. But if it meant closing your eyes and breathing through your nose and clearing your thoughts, this is what I started to do. Very quickly, I realized that when I closed my eyes, I could see light coming from my hands.

I was not really believing what was happening, yet I would look away and up towards the sky and move my hands about, keeping them down low. Sure enough, there were these two dimly lit tubes of light going straight up past my eye line. I really didn't know how to react at first. I was mesmerized a little by what was happening. My mind was bamboozled a little at first.

I began moving my hands a lot, and the lights moved the same. I looked down, still with my eyes closed, and there was a dimly lit beam of light coming out of the middle of each of my hands. I really don't know what the human reaction should be at this point, but mine was *WTF is going on here*. Could it be a flashback from the Magic Mushrooms I took years ago? I quickly assumed no, as I was quite well within myself. Magic Mushrooms are best described as "not mind over matter, but matter over mind," and I was neither.

Still, mentally, I was trying to figure it out. I opened my eyes and was consciously thinking to myself, *wow, wow, this is a bit far out here*. With my eyes open, and it being a cloudy night, I began to see lights behind the clouds—some brighter than others, others moving faster, and some quite slow, but the way they glowed up behind the cloud was amazing me, and again, I didn't have a clue what to do.

Now, with my eyes fully closed, I could see the two beams of light coming from me moving about everywhere around the skyline, as I wasn't really keeping any logical pattern going. I don't even know how this came to me, but I soon realized I could follow the lights in the clouds with the lights in my hands. When I aimed the two beams at the lights and made them connect as one when hitting the bright clouds, the lights would slow down, and right out through the clouds a burst of light came down my two beams.

If you can imagine, I had created an X shape with them, and down this light came and into my right hand. *Holy shit*, I thought, and I'm trying to be polite. There were a lot of other words used at that moment, to mad to write down. My right hand had a small tingle for a few seconds after this.

Immediately after this happened, I tried it again, and sure enough, I placed my hand to converge on these moving lights, and once I had got the lights to slow down by following them with my points of light, the light would come from behind the cloud and down again, this time into my left hand. Same again: tingling for a few seconds.

Really, from that night on, I began to repeating this over and over, till there weren't many lights left. But it got harder, as the lights got smaller, brighter, and a hell of a lot faster to catch with my light beams. It feels a bit strange for me to write about things like this knowing most people will be thinking *WTF Conrad*, but this is what I was doing. Why I had no clue yet.

By the end of the night, my hands were tingly, to say the least. It was very hard for me to settle after this, but when I eventually calmed down and made it up to my bed, through sheer exhaustion about what I had been doing all night, I must have fallen into a deep sleep.

I woke up the next morning, and straight away I knew something was different. For starters, my ears were buzzing, not loud, not uncomfortable either, but something. My head also was tingling, not in one place (all that day it would move about different parts of my skull) but always a wee buzz from my ears. I was shivering all over my body too, but again, not all at once—back of the calves, then my back, then my arms, then neck—this went on all day. I think I was in a bit of a trance all that first day after the mad night before, just going through the motions. Then again, there was something inside me that was filled with excitement, waiting on the night to fall.

I didn't really know what to expect the next night. For one, it was a clear evening. Maybe I had too much expectation from the night before. But one thing that did happen when I was outside was that the Pleiades, through my hand telescope, did what I thought to be a dance in the night sky, and as much as there were no lights from my hands, it was amazing to watch this. Little did I know it was when I went to bed later that the whole thing would kick off in a different way.

So as far as I was concerned, this was my first proper time. I consciously sat down, legs crossed, hands clenched and did all the proper breathing to meditate. I cleared my mind fully and was breathing from stomach to spine, holding my breath and releasing it slowly. I did it for about twenty minutes. Maybe I was trying to see something, but at the start, it was just wee flashy lights. I thought I was seeing shapes, but then nothing.

I did it so long the bottom of my back got sore, and I couldn't hold my breath in for too long, as it was beginning to get very painful. So, I got pillows for support and still it was too sore to go on. So, I kind of gave up on it all and lay back down on my bed. This made it much easier and took the strain off my back.

I still had my eyes closed but had stopped concentrating on my breathing, when all off a sudden, it was as if waves of white light kept coming, wave after wave, from the bottom up to the top, waves of light is the only way I can describe it. After a while, it settled down a bit. I was still lying on my back when I started to have what seemed like little faces coming up to me, from where I did not know, but they would come into view, then get clearer and a little bigger the closer they got to my eyes. I could barely make them out, but all of them were the colour green.

One even looked to be wearing a hat, like a Stetson. It would come up and dart to the side. I could make out the shape of a head, but I couldn't see a face. Sometimes it would go over my head, which made me get up and look round at the wall, but it would disappear as quickly as I saw it.

Then all off a sudden, there was three, maybe four of them as I lay back down on the bed. This time, they were all girls. I could see their outlines clearly. Two were green, one was red, and the other was an orangey yellow. All had distinctive long hair; one had straight hair, and the others looked permed. I really could see this as they moved around in front of me; I couldn't see any bodies, though, just heads. If I'm to use a reference, I would say just a bit smaller than a grape.

My ears were really beginning to ring a lot, and at different times, my body was shivering as if I was cold. But it had nothing to do with the temperature at all. I was fully aware of what was happening. As I remember, I started concentrating on breathing again properly. They would come up close to where I could make out their little faces, and they were smiling, going round in a circle. Then one would come in close. That's when I could see they were smiling, and then back out again.

I was trying to look at them all, so my eyes were darting everywhere. Then I began to realize I had my eyes still closed. This was so magical. At this moment, it's hard to convey in words what I was feeling. I believe it was a mixture of adrenaline and emotions running wild through me, transfixed at what was in front of my face. The thing about it, though, is that they all looked so happy. This relaxed me. Well, I say *relaxed*; more awestricken and astounded, I suppose.

And then, as quickly as they were there, they were gone. I remember opening my eyes and remembering that I was lying in bed. I had forgotten all about where I was for whatever length of time that went on. I just lost track of my surroundings and time.

Then *whoosh*, right out of the blue, two heads appeared and flew right at me. They went that fast over my head and disappeared into my wall. As I tipped my head back, I could see something like a black blob of matter—a sticky glue, shiny oil–looking blob, that's what it looked like to me.

I watched as a long piece of black angle iron (that's what it looked like) came out of the wall and went right beside the long mirror that was on my wardrobe at the end of the bed on the other side of the room. I could see there were little bits of neon blue the whole way down it, and it was as straight as a dye. And now, it was just sitting above my head.

I don't know what came over me, but I raised my left hand and grabbed it, realizing I could move it from left to right. Not only did my hand start to get very tingly, I also could see my arm lighting up the same neon blue that was in this long black rectangular pole, which was now showing bits and pieces here and there on my hand and down my whole arm. I have hallucinated before this, but I just couldn't believe what was going on, so I thought at the time, *I'll try my other hand.*

So, I looked at it and my arm, and it was just normal—but when I reached up and touched it, after five to ten seconds, it too went the exact same as my other one, and I held on until the pins and needles kicked in. I think it was just because I was still on my back; gravity had kicked in and was beginning to get uncomfortable.

I decided to take my hands off and sit up, but as soon as I did this, the pole disappeared in an instant back through the wall, and then there was absolutely nothing there. I was left sitting up looking at my hands and arms in wonderment. As quickly as the blue bits came, they went away. I truly was amazingly puzzled and didn't know what to make of it at this stage, but again, this was a beginning to what I'll call the next phase of my ever-evolving mind and the mind-set that went with one going through such experiences.

I remember waking up the next morning. I couldn't even remember how I got to sleep. I mean, I had no memory of lying on my back and having a think about what I had seen or done. It was like somebody just turned my switch off.

I turned my phone on, and the first thing on my social feed was a five-minute caption called "Ascending Souls." It was as if something was putting this on my social feed for me to read; actually, this would happen quite a lot for me. This fellow was talking about ascending souls, and I genuinely felt he was talking directly to me. I saved it and read it a few times, saying to myself, *if this happens to me, I'm going to try to do what this guy says in his small informative post.*

I didn't know what I was getting myself into, but I was certainly changing. So was my body. My ears rang constantly now, and my thoughts were consumed with an unparalleled feeling of excitement and unknown intrigue.

So again, my social feed popped up a woman called Rebecca James. She was a mystic tarot reader, and as much as I didn't know her from Adam, I was relating to a lot of her posts and the content in them. You must innerstand that with me, everything was all firsts. I was never into any of this before, and I could see that this woman was someone from whom I could learn about it all. To say this was getting intense for me and happening so fast is truly an innerstatement. A Formula One car, a jet plane, and a rocket couldn't keep up.

So, Rebecca James was like a shining light at that time, and I was so clueless and had no spiritual wisdom whatsoever. At the same time, another woman popped up on my feed by the name of Joanne Honey Thomas, a QHRT channeler. At this time, I had no idea what that was, but her posts were relating to a lot of the stuff that was happening to me and things that I was doing but didn't know fully what. What I mean by this is, I would do something, and the next day Joanne Honey Thomas would put up a post that told me what I had done. So, I asked to be her friend, and things from that moment began to intensify for me in more ways than one. I began to live differently.

This is when I started to learn about how we are all one from source, but most of all about peace, trust, truth, light, love, and a way of living that I had never experienced in my life up to this point. I was so eager to learn more at this stage of my now spiritual awakening, spiritual evolution, spiritual journey, spiritual messages, I fully didn't know what to call such intense experiences. This was beginning to happen daily, filling me with excitement as I waited for the evening to come. I was still working out mentally how to come to terms with it all, as it was getting so intense.

Throughout the day, I was really beginning to go with it and trying to get the "We are all one" concept into my way of thinking. It was proving more difficult than I thought it would be, but not as much as actually falling in love with myself. That was even harder, but Rome wasn't built in a day as the crow flies—whatever it takes, I was telling myself.

How deep I had to go was the deepest I'd ever gone, I had to basically pull myself inside out, is the best way to explain it. It was like being on a rollercoaster in the middle of a spaghetti junction while trying to play with a Rubik's cube as a spinning yo-yo. I hope that makes sense, because my memories of this time are so emotional, it's hard to describe.

Raising my vibrations to make myself happier and more positive is what I was trying to do, but you see, a couple of weeks before, I hadn't even known we all vibrate at a certain frequency. Just realized I really hadn't a clue what I was at, but it didn't deter me from seeking out more wisdom, and as Billy Carson puts it, it's only a mystery if you have no knowledge. So, at this point, everything was a bunch of mysteries to me, though ones I was willing to delve deeper inside me to at least solve some of them.

At one point, I felt like Conrad Sherlock Kirk Holmes with the reading I was doing. I had sent away for my first Dolores Cannon book, *The Three Waves of Volunteers and the New Earth*, and was eagerly awaiting its arrival. But the intensity of my awakening wasn't waiting on any book coming, and later as I was sitting outside, I was seeing a lot of light behind the clouds, as if the clouds themselves were like the sea, but instead of waves of water, it was waves of light, and in the form of what looked light sting rays and loads of them.

I know as I read back on what I've written that it all sounds very surreal, but I couldn't be any clearer. It was that intense. Reading the posts of Joanne Honey Thomas and Rebecca James (I was now a very proud member of Rebecca's Soul Tribe), I could see that people would meditate, and I would read their comments about dreams they vaguely remembered and trying to connect to the universal things and beings, talking about places out in the galaxy, and here I was—sometimes all I had to do was close my eyes. Even that I didn't have to do, as I would see more than enough with them wide open.

35

That's when I had to fight with my ego and not say too much, as we are all on our own journey and in our own timeline. It was out of respect that I did this and would privately message them instead. As I would read back, it did sound boastful, my own words, even though that was not my intention. It truly was an awakening, and so intensely active at this time.

Later, that night, another amazing thing happened. When I got to my room, I fully intended to meditate. But in truth, I closed my eyes for only about thirty seconds to one minute, and off I went. I could see these two women darting around in front of me with wee tiny wings on them, and as I looked down, I thought I saw one come out of my right hand. Then there were three, four. I don't know where she came from, but I thought to myself for the first time that they came out of the middle of the palms of my hands.

My eyes were certainly closed, but not my third eye, as I could see them so clearly. I would put my hand out as if to gently touch them, and they would fly around it and me right up close to my forehead. One of the little angels (that's what I was calling them, because that's what they looked like) would come right up to my forehead, and right at that moment, an intense ringing in both my ears would erupt. There was no pain, but I certainly felt it. They would sprinkle … at first, I thought it was dust of some sort, but I soon come to realize it was sprinkles of light onto my head and my eyes, even though my eyes were firmly shut at this stage.

When this happened, my face—bits of it anyway—would tingle, and a lovely tingling would start at my head and go to my nose, down my cheeks, and across my lips. Even my eyelashes tingled. It truly was breathtakingly amazing.

At this point, I was happy. I mean, it felt good. I was now beginning to relax a tiny bit and forget about the magnitude of what was happening in front of me.

Out of nowhere, I was taken by the hand, not out through my bedroom roof or anything—it went from lying in my bed to being flown across space in a see-through wobbly watery tube, but wide. What was holding my hand or, sorry, felt like I was holding on to more was a sting ray as bright as a torch flying along. There was also one to my left and another two out in front on my left and right, so it was four of them and me gliding through space, and fast, too. I remember looking out both sides and seeing stars and planets of all colours going by me fast.

I don't know how long we were flying, but it was by now super-fast, where everything seemed like it was zooming by. All off a sudden, for the first time, it slowed down a little and broke off to the left and went for another while. I saw this small very bright light coming into view. As we got closer, it all slowed down, and we were beginning to circle the light. Not once did I seem to come out of this tube thing, nor could I even see myself.

I began speaking, not with my mouth but with my mind. I remember asking was this my home, but there was never any sound. They were sting rays, sure—they don't talk. Then *bang*, I was back on my bed looking up at my bedroom ceiling, wondering, pondering, *what was that?* They were showing me something, but I had no idea at this stage. I was feeling tired and had lost track of time, and out I went like a stone.

When experiencing things like this, I always wondered how I got to sleep. It was either all the inner work that I was doing, or they had a way of subconsciously putting me to sleep. I remember waking up the next morning and straight away phoning Colly B in Scotland to tell him, as I had nobody else, I could be so open with about the new reality I was going through. With further knowledge, it could have been astral travelling, but I was still not fully sure.

The very next night, I was out on my porch, and as you do as a smoker, I had just lit up a wee doobie. What I should say is, I was raking it and smoking it as fast as I could so I could close my eyes. I was beginning to feel stuff was happening already. I never finished it. I think for the first time in my life, I wasn't getting the same fulfilment from the joints anymore. I didn't know it at that moment, but my smoking days were numbered.

I could already see strange shapes behind the clouds, shadows swirling as my two streetlamps showed the whites on some of the low clouds, but things visually were moving behind them, again fast and slow. So, I eventually got to closing my eyes, and for the first time, I don't know why, but I put my two hands together and was gently rubbing them to see what would happen. When I slowly pulled them apart, I could see the light now coming from both.

I could see the little girls coming out of my palms. There were four of them to begin with, and then another two appeared, I don't know where from. As I concentrated, they were all swirling around the front of me, and as I was sitting down, they began to settle around me. There was one on each shoulder, one at each of my sides close to my hips, and two above me, I really had to look around to see them all.

In about thirty to forty seconds, my face started going all nervy and tingly, especially my eyes and nose. It took me a while to catch on, but it was the two above my head sprinkling light on me. Once I noticed them, if you can picture me sitting down, palms of my hands open and resting on my legs, they went into one hand each. As soon as they did this, my beams of light became brighter.

Then the ones on my left and right shoulders did the same—sprinkled and went into my hands. As this was happening, the two that were down by my side came up and sat on one shoulder each. They didn't really *sit*, just *floated* on them would be a better way to say it.

I did not yet realize what was going on above me in the clouds, but when I finally caught on, I looked up and lights were darting and swirling through the clouds. My hands now had two bright beams coming out of them. They reminded me of the World War II searchlights that would penetrate the night sky looking for planes, but this was my hands. Holy crap, this sounds like crazy stuff, but there they were, and I got to work (can't believe I'm calling it that) scanning the clouds for the lights.

Some lights I could catch. Once slowed down by the beam, they came into my hand. Sometimes I could follow two at the same time with different hands and bring them down to me. This was already amazing stuff. Then there would be times where I needed both hands working together to catch it first, follow it around, and keep it in the light. When I got them with the two beams of light, eventually they would come down. As these were coming down, I was trying to see what they were. Some I thought were wee animals and others were actual people. But it was hard to see, as the more they came down, the smaller they became, and the faster they became.

As I was doing this, sometimes the little angels would float over my head, with my ears ringing. They would start sprinkling wee tiny dots of light into my eyes, and again it would go all tingly. At this point, I was beginning to feel I was either getting rewarded for what I was catching or getting more light put in to help me see better. Truthfully, I didn't really know.

As it was beginning to get cold outside, I went inside, and I remember I needed one of the longest pees of my life, as I had been dying for one for what must have been at least an hour. I had been afraid I would break off this magical work that I was beginning to see. One other thing I remember about coming in that night was that my hands were buzzing quite a bit; it was like pins and needles, just a tiny bit different. It's difficult to explain—it was like they were full of something.

Eventually, I found myself sitting up in bed, and I started to meditate just a little. Then *bang*, it was on so quick, next thing I knew, I was flying underground in like some hidden cave system. Truthfully, I didn't know whether I was levitating and everything was coming to me, or it was the other way round and I was flying through it all. I was following cracks that would appear, with me moving along the crack but always just above it.

Then it went up over two mountains, the crack always just opening in front of me, up and down. We went over these two big mountains and then out to the sea, which was full of debris, and I mean it was filled *everywhere*, as far as my eyes could see.

Next thing, I'm straight back down underneath the earth. It's all rocky now and moving oh so fast—lefts, rights, ups, downs. But always underneath, I can see my hands out in front of me, still lit up.

Then I started too slightly slow down. I was picking my way through the rocks, which seemed to be closing on me and around me as everything began to shake. It felt to me like I was seeing an earthquake, but seeing it underground, as everything began shaking and vibrating, even my hand. Everything began to fall in around me. As much as I tried, it always got to a point where it would become such a small hole, I just couldn't get through. The lights in my hands were making a path through for me, but it was as if it was building in front of me. I couldn't get out.

From that to the very next thing: I'm back in my bedroom, and there are lights flying about in front of me, darting in and out, coming up real close to my face. At this point, to say I was scared a little is an innerstatement. I was bricking it, to be honest. For the first time, I broke it off and jumped out of bed to run to the toilet, as this time, I was going to pee myself. I had just lost track of time.

As soon as I came back, I lay back down on my bed and closed my eyes, and *boom!* They were still there but had slowed down a bit. I noticed these lights were people—some just heads, others with wee tiny bodies. There was one that was bigger than the rest. He looked like a cowboy, Stetson and all. He was coming up to my face the closest. Something clicked in my napper;

call it intuition, I really don't know, because no-one told me to do it, but the "Ascending Souls" caption was flashing in my head.

So, I turned and said with my mind, not my mouth, *I release you from this earthly plain and thank you for your service. You are free to go home to your family from whatever galaxy you came to help from.* Not word for word, but this is what this guy had said to say when you think it's looking ascended. What happened next, I can never forget, and it will always stay with me.

Everything stopped coming in and annoying me but faded back a little from my view. Then, all of a sudden, right above my head, this guy with the Stetson came from behind me, looking directly at me as he started to go up but facing me as he did it, and for the first time I could see he had swarthy skin; not only that, he was sitting down, on what looked an old saloon poker table, cigar in his mouth. I could see the smoke swirling up, and he had the biggest happiest smile I ever did see. He looked so happy, and as he went up still looking at me, he gave me a wink.

I began to shake as if someone had given me a shot of adrenaline. It felt so good doing this, but again so magical to get to do it, was what I was thinking. Then next, I didn't know if it was a Viking—he had horns coming out of his helmet and it was only his face. He began to come closer. You see, as I'm doing these, my hands are out in front of me, like ten lighthouses keeping ships off the rocks. I said the same thing to him, and he gave me a wry smile—I could see it under his blond beard, as he was a yellow-coloured light. He turned his head and off he too went. That was when I caught on that they were going into my two beams of light.

The next one was a dog with massive ears hanging down, and I freed him/her too. Then came an Indian with a big, feathered headdress. He was a green light and had been swirling about, but he had never come up close. I could see he was saying something to me, but there was never any sound. I said to him, *you are free from this earth, thank you so much and your family is waiting with love, go and be free.* He also smiled, but no-one smiled as much as the first cowboy.

I was absolutely drained at this point. The last thing I remember was the little angels flying into my hands. Either they knocked me straight to sleep or I just naturally conked out.

I woke up the next morning and noticed my ears were screaming so loud, it reminded me of the angel girls sprinkling light on my face, so I put the pillow over my face. I had only just awakened, and there was another Indian right up close to my face, and he had only one feather at the back of his head. I remember saying to him, *I'm so sorry*. I must have missed ascending him the night before. Then I said again the same thing I'd learnt. I didn't even use my hands; he just went up to go through my roof and was gone. As soon as this happened, my ears stopped ringing straight away.

I flicked the pillow back off my face and must have said *wow wow wow* twenty times about what had just happened as I woke up. I really did think for the first time that I had been given some sort of gift to do this. I look back now and can't even think how I came up with it, but I did, and I got very good at my little paragraph of what to say to souls where you have the privilege to release them. Whether they had been trapped, I just didn't know, but with what was still to come, I sure as hell was going to find out.

Throughout the day I was really beginning to live differently. With all the information I was receiving from different posts of Joanne Honey Thomas, Julia Cannon, and Rebbeca James, my mind was linking and resonating with me so much. *Resonating* is a word I had never used in my life up to this point. Now daily I'm using it. This is just a few of the new words that were becoming active in my conscious new life: awareness, alignment, manifestation, source, divinity, love, love, love. *Love* was the biggest.

I really could keep going and fill a whole page with new words, but it was not the words themselves but the meaning of them and then living your life ultimately to your enlightenment with your higher self with the help of your spirit guides, guardians, soul-family angels, ascended masters, and teachers—all helping you on your ascension back to source, with the purpose of learning all your soul's lessons and contracts and authentically living your life with the intention of creating your heaven on earth.

Anybody who knows me, reading this I'm sure is thinking, *Wow, Con, what's all this?* That's exactly what I thought as I was gaining knowledge of it all. It's the secret to life. The law of one—what's better in a world than to live by truth and love? It's so simple, but as generation after generation has proved, it's not that simple when you've been through the crap, I've been through in my life. The small simple things were what I sought to get pleasure from, and the search for true love.

CHAPTER 6

The Day I Found Out
I Have a Twin Flame

Eagle or Falcon

IT WAS AN ordinary Saturday—actually, nothing was ordinary in those days, but domestic Conrad had to do his weekly shopping at the local Sainsbury's Supermarket. All was going to plan, the same as I had done for the past two years, but when I was exiting with my shopping trolley, the sun was so bright, it was blinding me. I couldn't look at it for to long. No matter what way I turned in my car, the sun seemed to be following me. What I mean by this is no matter what angle I was at on the road, it was beaming down on me. I got the feeling it was watching me.

As soon as I got home, I left the shopping in the kitchen for my three children to put away. It cost me three cans of fizzy pop. They didn't do it for nothing. That said, it was me who made the deal.

I grabbed my camping chair and went outside in the sun. I was sitting there sun-gazing. It was so bright—shimmering, really—even through the small bit of cloud that was there, lightly blocked my view a little after about two minutes it split into two. In the forty-six years previous in basking in the sun this had never happened. It quickly blew my mind. One was white, the other orange, and the orange one was shaking vibrating, you could say. I was sitting with my two hands down, palms open. This position was becoming quite regular in my life now.

Then my neighbour said hello, and I thought to myself, *oh shit, he must be looking at me and wondering what I'm doing*. I didn't ask, but that was what I thought at the time. So, I upped sticks, ran into the house, ran upstairs and into my bedroom, shut the door, opened my window, grabbed a pillow from my bed, sat my dodgy knees onto it, and got back into my meditating position: hands open and facing the sun.

Next thing, my ears started ringing, the loudest ever, with different tones to the ringing in both ears. I *felt* the ringing. I'm just trying to give you an idea of how loud it was in my ears. The orange sun now seemed to be pulsating, like a heartbeat pumping in the air, and then through my squinted eyes I could see a massive green bird coming straight from the sun. As it got closer, I could see that it was an eagle, but with a woman's head as plain as day. In the back of my mind, I could hear my thoughts speaking to me and saying "what is going on, what is happening right now" even so I was still shockingly fascinated about what was flying directly towards me. I just want to stop and tell you how this made me feel other than the feeling of adrenaline rushed excitement. Uncontrollable shaking from head to toe, captivated in that exact second right until that very moment with an emotion I don't think I had ever encountered before.

Now, I had my eyes still closed at this stage, so I knew it was my third eye that was seeing this. She began to get smaller the closer she got to me and at the same time was turning red. As I had my hands out, she went to my right hand, stayed there for a while, then went to my left hand and did the same. What she was doing I didn't know. I was thinking at the time that of all the gear I ever took in my life, I had never experienced something so magical and so real. The shape shifting was instantaneous, from balls of red back to green with no visual transition bang, bang so quick.

Then she moved back, and that's when I could see it was undoubtedly a women looking at me, smiling away. She had turned back to green and had what looked like a costume on. She was wearing an eagle headdress, but it was clear to me that it was a part of her. With the wings folded around her, she was the prettiest woman I had ever seen and shining like a green glowing star.

As quickly as she had appeared, she was gone. No flying away just disappeared in a micro-second. I was left in shock, as this was only two o'clock on a Saturday afternoon. My mind was blown yet again. That's when

I could hear the children arguing over sweets downstairs. A totally mind-boggling moment, and it was only the beginning. Things were only getting started. I opened my eyes and closed them fast just to check. My two hands were lit up like searchlights.

To say my awakening was intense—I truly do not have any words to describe all these things happening. Also, I didn't know where it was going to take me. But it was a journey I was willing and eager to participate in. Amazing, far-fetched to some, but to me as real as brushing your teeth. (Fluoride-free, may I say also.)

Little did I know what the night would bring. It started like a normal night, but it was the clearest it had been in over a fortnight, so there was no struggling to see all the star formations—at least out the front of my house. It was always my point of reference. Sometimes I went out my back door, but I always had a feeling of being drawn to the front.

I could see a few planets. They looked like stars, really, only brighter, with more flashing colours. I had my own names for some of them, like the frying pan and handle, and the upside-down pyramid with a star on the top. One of two things I noticed that night was that every single star, close and far away, always formed a triangle of some sort—some uneven, some small and others massive, but always a triangle to be found.

The Pleiades, also known as the Seven Sisters, were the clearest and brightest I had ever seen, with no clouds at all in sight. Scanning them with my ever-more-useful hand telescope, as I was watching them for about a minute, my ears started an intensely powerful ringing, it was so loud I couldn't hear anything else, and in my head, there was a strange zinging and buzzing, which I could feel. But what was even more crazy was what I can only describe as a watery beam that came straight from the Pleiades to my right eye that I was using to look through. What I mean is that I could see through it right to the stars themselves, and I could see what was going to be hard to describe for the reader—a big swirly ball of greyish, watery shiny smoke with bits and pieces of lights coming out of it but again still inside some sort of watery beam like the one I was in before.

When I say a *ball*, I don't mean a round, spherical shape. There was no shape to it, really, but it was big. I broke the hand telescope off, eyes always open. It got closer and closer, and I'm not afraid to admit it: I was beginning to shit my pants a little, even though it didn't seem evil or aggressive in any way.

You must inner stand: My ears were ringing so loud, this thing was coming at a rate of knots, and here I am sitting on my camping chair bricking it. As it got closer, it did seem to be getting smaller and smaller. It came down just on top of my garden gate at the bottom of my path and started rolling, swirling up my path towards me, still greyish and with different-coloured lights through it everywhere.

It was at this stage that I began to see the lights of my hands cross my eye line. I wasn't looking down to see it, but as this thing was approaching, it must have activated my hands in some way. I just didn't know, but my intuition told me to lay them down flat on my two knees, and that's what I did. Suddenly, out of this smoky haze, a small light appeared—a blond-haired man wearing Robin Hood–style clothing, but shiny and glowy green. To say I was getting an adrenaline rush out of this … it was spectacular, and once he got into my beam of light, he went straight into my right hand, didn't stop to say hello or nothing, just straight in he went.

All jokes aside, once he went in my hands, they started to dim down. I realized my eyes were open the whole time, so I closed them to see what I could see. There was nothing, just blackness—what everybody sees. The only thing was, my right hand was tingling, or buzzing is probably a better word. So, there I was sitting there gobsmacked, staring at my feet now in wonderment and realizing I had seen everything.

I thought, *there's now a man inside me who looked like Legolas out of the* Lord of the Rings, *in my hand, on my chair at my porch, just normal old me.* What was going on? *This is abracadabra stuff,* I thought. *Magic, mysterious, mystical me.* That was the night I don't think I ignited the joint again, because something, a creeping feeling, was instinctively telling me it wasn't right.

So now I had a couple of wee girls with wings in different colours inside me, and now a light being with blond hair inside me also, who looked a bit like me too. From this moment on, things began to happen on a scale that to a normal reader will seem like fiction, but to me that couldn't be further from the truth.

I had done all my meditation up in my bedroom at this point, but my daughter Ameila was doing stuff in my room, so I decided to go down to my living room. It was probably meant to be, as I was soon to realize I needed lots of room and to be standing for what was about to begin.

Now throughout my mornings at work and in the middle of the day, I was always trying to find things out and read up as much as I could, but I couldn't find much time, as with three children, things are quite busy. Following Joanne Honey Thomas and Rebbeca James, and judging by what I was reading about meditation, mine was altogether quite something else. I mean, I didn't need to get into a zone at this point or follow much of a breathing pattern. It was ears buzzing and let's go. Sometimes I had to rush into my living room in a hurry to see what was going on in my head as the ringing was so intense.

But just to go back a little first: I as a human being up to this point was like everybody else, not aware of anything on a spiritual side, certainly knowing nothing of a soul's contract and their life learning from lessons. I certainly was changing rapidly daily now. I had started to heal stuff I didn't know I had been ignoring for years, and it was making me see all the traumas in my life, from childhood to a boy then a teenager and now as an adult. There was quite a lot that I'd never addressed or even thought of addressing before. Love and light were entering my life for the first time ever, and I in turn was beginning to become someone new even to myself.

Truth had entered my life in a way, as I was experiencing it daily. What I mean by this is being true to myself. I had come to realize how much I put myself down, jokingly at times, but I was still doing it without even knowing I was. So, for the first time, I became aware of it and started to change and make a lot of the wrongs right.

I wasn't sure where this was going to lead me, but at this point, I certainly had nothing to lose. And it is never too late to learn something new. I didn't know it was going to be as immensely magical, intensely instrumental, or emotionally mental as it would soon become, but I knew deep inside me it was the right thing to do.

These ladies I was following on my socials were like shining stars in a dark tunnel, but I don't think they knew how much, as they had known about the Cosmic Universal Energies that is already built into the fabric of the Cosmos. I became part of their social feed. This is when another woman popped up on my feed. Her name was Ellen Redd, and her page was called

Twin Flame Initiates. As I had been trying to find more information on twin flames, at this time, I felt my angels had found her for me.

Joanne Honey Thomas was a QHRT channeler; Rebbeca James was a soul trooper, and I was part of her tribe; but Ellen was a different kettle of fish. This woman was to me a spiritual warrior who worked daily with the good and the bad spirits, the dark and the light, but specialized in the field of twin flames.

So, when I put these ladies together for me, I had a formidable force of information, honesty, truth, love, spirituality, cosmic knowledge, emotional awareness, love of oneself, law of one knowledge of realms portals, energy, and the list goes on. To me, they are legends, early wayshowers for human beings who put themselves out there with no judgment for others, and only to help the collective as a species.

Sometimes in speaking to them, I wondered if they thought I was dumb because I asked so many questions. But I soon realized they didn't care about that. They only wanted to help, and I'm sure if you're enjoying this read so far, I really could have been doing with a little help at this stage in my journey of being awoken.

Joanne Honey Thomas had asked me about the Dolores Cannon book, *The Three Waves of Volunteers and the New Earth*, so I had ordered it online. As soon as I read that book, it connected so many dots. It felt like, you know the old colouring in books you would have gotten at Christmas as a child maybe numbered from one to ninety, so you drew a line and a perfect picture would form, and away you went colouring it in. This is how I felt when reading this book. Judging by my age, I had volunteered to be here at this time to help the world heal in some way, and I learned about the metaphysical team you have with you to call upon for help.

So now not only had I these three ladies helping me with different angles of knowledge, I had my higher self, my spirit guides, guardian angels, ascended master teachers, soul family, the sun, the moon, Mother Earth herself, and now the divine creator, the cosmic birther, the one of truth and love, what most people in our world would call God, but this was not the God you read about in the modern-day Bible, of judgment, jealousy, war, death, religion, putting down of women—a greedy, malevolent entity. This is the prime creator of truth and love.

For years, I had never believed in God and had made lots of fun of him in the way I had talked of him, even to call him *him*. In my head, I had him down as a man, but this creator is no man or woman; it is the cosmic source of sound, magnetic frequency and vibrational light that is everything and is made of pure love for everyone, everything, everybody, and every place, ever evolving as a vibrational frequency, wave after wave of infinite love for all, in the quantum physical field of what people call *space*. Thank you, Billy Carson; I learnt a lot of that from you, another early wayshower for us all and a man I have the biggest respect for. I've never even met him, nor have I met any of the ladies of my socials.

This is the power of social media that has backfired on the elites of this world, which is firstly set up to control everything but not everybody. There is no doubt that the infection of Artificial intelligence is going to make this a lot harder depending on how much poison the programmers of it get away with, as there's a very big grey area around its usage and laws, may I say it's been purposefully set up this way from the beginning, by our own fraudulent governments worldwide. Lies and deceit will always fail. It might take a while, but the wheel of karma always keeps turning, if you live that sort of life, until you pay for your own Karma, you will forever be stuck on that wheel.

I still didn't know fully why I was going through so much intensity in my inner work. I was nowhere near connecting all the dots just quite yet, but I was beginning to live in a way that I never had before. At this point, I had said to my children that I was spiritual, but as kids do, they would ridicule and say it wasn't real. Just the normal things kids say. I knew I couldn't tell them all the cosmic and universal stuff I was doing and about 5D new earth. I remember trying to explain the different dimensions to them, but they weren't having it one bit, so I didn't push it any further than that.

Loving yourself was so hard for me to do, but it is vital in a journey of ascension. This took a while; I began to realize at this point the power of your thoughts and the power of a programmed mind over years and years of doubts and fears, never really knowing it was there in the first place. Once you are aware of ego, trying to solve that part of the brain and fill it with not only unconditional love for yourself but for everybody else too, even the people who did really bad things to you, it is the hardest and longest battle one can have with oneself.

I had always lived by "If you did me wrong and I didn't deserve it, or you were sneaky about it and I caught you, I will get my revenge, even if it takes extreme aggressive violence." This was something that I knew I had to let go, but having done this for years, it was proving more difficult than I thought. I made it an emotional mission that I would change this and started doing things mentally to prepare myself. I began reaching out more to Joanne Honey Thomas at this point, and she started helping me more than I think she even knew. I also talked to people on her socials, like-minded people struggling at different levels with different things, on different timelines in their own journeys.

I began to pick up different titbits of knowledge, not only on how to forgive but also to be forgiven. I went deep on this and had to go way back and apologize for every wrongdoing I thought I had done. It was becoming obvious to me there were quite a lot. If I was to tell you them all, I could write a whole book on that alone just the same way though I could write a whole book on the good things that I'd done, but I certainly will tell you some things.

But let's get back to my inner work and the next stage of my journey into and up to the vast abyss of space and down to the vast shadowland that lay deep within me and my soul, and the chapter would start when I was making my tea for my children and myself.

As I said, I had started to meditate down in my living room. I say *meditate*; this was inner work, I mean real work, hours and hours of it night after night, getting into my bed drunk with fatigue on nearly every occasion. But I truly loved doing this, because deep down I knew I was beginning to help in some way, and I was putting a lot of trust and faith into what I was doing (my soul's mission). Truthfully, I just wanted to help everybody.

CHAPTER 7

Meeting a Version of Myself

MY MORNING ROUTINE for the last two weeks was getting up at six a.m., getting breakfast, listening to a couple of songs, and having a little dance to raise my vibration for that day to make me feel good. I had a couple of favourite songs that I did this to, as I was trying to love myself a bit more each day. This is how I started. You really do feel better when you start your day like this, and I felt it was working. Releasing endorphins first thing set a good tone, even before my children were up.

I had a walk in my local forest. Never in my life had I ever done this before getting the children ready for school and getting myself ready for work. It was the evening after Legolas went into my right hand. I was making spaghetti bolognese for the girls, and I was dancing away. About halfway through cooking, there was a point in the song where I got carried away and thought that my vocals were coming back from my early escapades of carol-singing. I closed my eyes, just to hit that lovely note I knew I had somewhere, when I noticed a full shadow of myself right in front of me. At first, I was taken aback a little, as I just thought it was my shadow. I opened my eyes quick to see how this could be happening.

I'll never forgot it: "Different Shades of Love" was playing on YouTube. As quick as I opened my eyes, I closed them again, and there he was, stilled, startled, and surprised. I started dancing again, and he did the exact same moves as me, right at the exact same time as me. I was gobsmacked at this, as I had my own way of dancing. It just had to be a shadow of some sort, but then he started doing his own moves. I apologise for my language beforehand, but it was a what-the-fuck moment. This really did get my attention. Now I'm not saying his moves were better than mine, but he certainly was more elegant in the way he moved. There was no jumping about, the way I was popping at the time.

All jokes aside, I truly had a conversation with him. He didn't speak at all but was a shadow of exactly me. The only difference was I had my hair in a ponytail, and he didn't, so I knew from that point on he was no shadow. As mad as this sounds, I said to him, "I'm cooking dinner here, but I'll go into the living room later on and put some music on, and then we can dance." Never have I served dinner so quickly and eaten it so fast, nor did I get cleaned up until about eleven thirty later that night.

After gobbling the food down, I bolted into the living room, turned on my phone, put on the music, closed my eyes, and *boom!* There he was, waiting for me. I have my favourite songs on a list, and off we went dancing away together. You must inner stand: this was amazing, and I was buzzing like a bumblebee.

As the night progressed, he began to light up more, and I could make out some features—some of his face, his hair, his hands, and his legs. He looked just like me, but he was a yellowy goldy colour and stayed that way. He would go between dim in some parts and brighter in others at different times.

At this stage, I had my top off and could see I was lit up a bit, plus wee bits of light here and there all over me. This amazed my mind even more. Just as I could hear my children beginning to shout to turn the music down, my phone went dead anyway, and as this was happening, he began changing from dancing to doing some sort of routine with his hands and turning 360 degrees while doing it. It was like some kind artistic thing, and my intuition was telling me he wanted me to copy him. So, this went on for a while, doing different things with our hands and arms. Sometimes he would stop and put his hands to mine, and each time he did this, it seemed to me he would reward me with some of his light.

What I mean by this is, I would start to get brighter in parts, like full on, not bits and pieces. It was frustrating for me at times, as I couldn't fully see what he was doing. Remember, I had my eyes closed now. I didn't need to concentrate on my breathing. I seemed to be doing it naturally now. I didn't need to think about it anymore. There were so many things I was doing for the first time at this point, so it was hard. But by the end of the night, I was well lit up nearly all over. The only place I couldn't see was my face. When I would open my eyes, it was just me in the dark, but when I closed them, I could see my body was lit up.

I was sweating at the time, and I also wanted to have a look, so I took off my trousers off and sure enough: my legs were lit up too. Socks off next— and yes, feet and all. This was getting trippy at this stage. Don't ask me how I was so relaxed; I don't know, as it was such out-of-this-world stuff. Maybe the drugs I had taken in my life had helped me stay calm. I just didn't know, but deep in my head, I was thinking *wow wow wow!*

That's when he kinda disappeared on me, but it was probably all the yawning I was doing. I believed he could tell I was wrecked. That's when I realized it was eleven thirty, and I had been in there from about six o'clock— five and a half hours, and it felt like an hour. I did the dishes smiling like a Cheshire cat; I could see my reflection on my kitchen window. I remember opening and closing my eyes to see if he was there, but no, I didn't see him again that night.

I went straight up to bed. I lay down on my bed and closed my eyes to go to sleep, but to my amazement, a woman came out of my left hand as I was lying down, and she looked just like the woman who came down from the sun. She was smaller but lit up with very white outlines, and it looked like the same clothes on—just no headdress. She levitated a little above my hand and then lay gently on my palm. I think I cupped my hand a little. That's when I could see she looked so happy smiling away at me, and I was now doing it back. I don't know, but tears were now streaming down my face. I felt her presence even though she was so small in my hand.

Next thing I knew, I was waking up the next morning. My Messenger went *ding*, and it was my Italian mate Enzo, who had sent me a message the night before about things you do with your hands—signals of some sort that send different messages like harmony, creation, truth, and power. At that moment, first thing, I connected it straight away to what I had been doing the night before with Legolas. I was beginning to wonder if I should call him Conrad Two, but Legolas sounded better.

Sure enough, I put my music on the next morning, closed my eyes, and *bang!* There he was, as if waiting on me. Off we went, and it was amazing, I just know if I was reading this and hadn't experienced anything even close to what I was going though, I would think it to be fiction, but trust me: Every morning for at least two weeks, we were dancing together, but it had progressed in a way that at the beginning I found hard to comprehend.

It was like we were building something together. I will try to explain this a little. Just before I explain it any further, it had nearly gone 180 degrees as I began to copy what he was doing most of the time, and we would work at it. The move I mastered first was this: He would flip or flick his arms and hands like a bird flying up and down, up and down, then with one hand up to the roof and the other hand to the floor, arms out straight, we would do a 360-degree circle. Sometimes we would go round twice, and it would be like a wave filling the room with a white light. Other times, we would turn the other direction. Experiencing these visions daily with him was just breathtaking, mind-blowingly amazing.

Another move was like we would both crouch down, nearly like a squat position, two hands straight behind the back, and at a certain part of the song we would both rise together, arms outward, and again a wave of light would fill up the room. I didn't know at this stage if it kept going or not, but it was enough for me. There were dance moves I would do, and he would incorporate it into the dance, but it would be the same outcome, like waves of light. That's the best way I can explain it to you.

At this stage, my children were wondering why Dad had begun dancing in the living room at night. I tried to tell them little titbits, but they told me to wise up, which I totally inner stood as I looked at it from their side. I didn't push it any further, or they would have thought I was losing the nut, noddle (head), a bit. Deep down, I knew they weren't ready for the truth at this stage—maybe not at any stage. But if they read this book someday (yes, that's not a bad idea), it could be a good way of them finding out. Might be on to something here.

So as much as there was dancing in the morning, in the evening it was getting a bit more serious, yet it was always fun to do. Ever since Enzo had given me the clip-on Messenger, I had practised my hand and finger patterns. I just paused the clip and had mastered most of them. Some were very intricate placing of fingers together. After four or five days, I'm not sure exactly, I was realizing the stuff we were going to do and had gotten better at it. I really felt like he was training me, and now I was getting brighter in my work.

At the beginning, there were bits of me glowing, but now the more we had been doing this together, the more I was glowing all over. I was progressing at something, but little did I know at this point what he was getting me ready for. With hindsight, that's why I think it was training, learning, for something. I was totally captivated at this point, because it felt like magic to me.

I felt special in a funny sort of way. I wanted to do it now, but still so much was unknown to me. It was beginning to feel like once we started, after we had done a small routine of different patterns, we would end up in some sort of hall or room. I had to do some work to light myself up, and once this was done, we would progress to another room/hall type place, and that's when I would be lit up all over—not completely bright, but dimly lit up.

You must inner stand, I was completely aware that I was in my living room, and at this stage had the room cleared and everything out of my way, as my eyes were closed and I was always moving around, using my third eye, it certainly didn't look at all like my living room. To give you an idea how long this went on for, I would have to go to the toilet at least twice if not three times, so yeah, it was a remarkable experience every evening doing this.

I would get things wrong and not do it right the first time; maybe it was the first ten times until I mastered it, if not twenty. But in the end, when you do something enough times, you eventually get it. Honestly, sometimes I felt he was getting fed up, even laughing at me when I fell over, which I did quite a lot. But in the end, I could just make enough of him out to see he was smiling. I was getting better each time. My hands by this stage were the brightest they had ever been—I mean, like two torches coming out.

As quickly as he was there that night, he was away, and I was left in this room, I felt, by myself. Then, out of the blue, I just took off and started flying, you could say floating, but I didn't have my hands out like Superman in the movies. I was just floating along.

I seemed to be underground somehow. Up ahead, I saw two big doors, and as I got close, they opened for me. I couldn't really stop myself from going in even if I had wanted to, but I didn't. When I got in, everything slowed down, and I was in a big room with loads of people fighting fast— like you would hit $x2$ on a video recorder, that type of speed. They were all wearing either Viking clothing or Saxon outfits; I could never really tell, as they were dimly lit and moving fast. As I levitated above them, I could see a table with six men at it. One of them was so much brighter than the rest at the table. I mean, I could go right up and float above this table. They would never look up at me, only the one that was brightest.

On the first night entering this room, I was a bit shaky, as there looked to be a lot of hacking going on with blades between everybody. Then I would get to the table with the bright guy at it. I truly didn't know where I was at or what it was, I had to do, so I went on from the table to the back of this big medieval-looking hall and into what I would call the kitchen, and as much as they weren't fighting in there, it was just a dead end. So, I would go back to the table to the man who was brightest.

This happened for a couple of nights, until I thought I was becoming stuck a little. So, on the third night of getting to this hall, I went as close as I'd ever done, put my hands towards the brightest man at the table and said, *I release you from this place, go back to your family, they are waiting on your arrival and love and miss you so much.* At this, the whole table went into my hands and disappeared. And as soon as this happened, I was flying away somewhere different. It felt good to me like, the small passing of a test but again I wasn't fully sure.

There was no going back out the doors I came in. It was just me flying, and as I was flying, there were rocks and crevices everywhere, turning left and right, up and down. There were wee bits of light hidden here and there, so when I stopped with them, I pointed my hands at them. Eventually, they would go up into my hands. This kicked off something in my brain, so when I saw the light, wherever it was, I would stop and collect it.

The thing was, some of it was not only hard to find but also hard to catch. Sometimes I was flying so fast I would miss turns, and other times I had the choice to go left or right, up or down. After a few nights of this, I had begun to build up a map in my head and realized it was the same place, but with so many ways to go, you could say like a maze, but not one that you would think of automatically with big green hedges. It was the same idea, but underground in the dark, with different ways to go, with loads of different rock formations.

Night after night, I would go through these tunnels in search of light and collect it with my hands. The more this went on, the deeper it got, until one night I got to a ring of light with a hole in it and went through. When that happened, I was out above the ground, floating over a big open plain, until I came to some sort of camp. I thought it was an Indian camp, but I'm still not sure. What I do know is it was some sort of open prison camp, where everybody was female but for the guards, who were standing around here and there.

So many of the women had light beaming from them. I would point my hands at them and eventually they would go into my hands as wee dots of light. As these women were going into my hands, on the moment of going in, they would downsize to a pinhead dot of light and disappear. I am just trying to tell you everything here as I remember.

As I floated on into the more densely packed part of the camp, I saw a woman so bright when compared to the rest, just like the Viking or Saxon at the table, only she was being dragged by two guards by her hands, facing upwards, with her bum and legs dragging across the ground. I would go up to her; the guards could not seem to see me as I floated up, but she could. No matter what I did with my hands, they would not let her go. The same thing happened a couple of nights in a row without any leeway going through the same ring of light every time.

I would have to start from scratch at the outskirts of the camp, picking up light from the same women from the night before, but it would always lead up to the brightest woman being dragged. Then, I think out of frustration, I shouted as loud as I could within my mind, *let her go*, and they did straight away. I couldn't believe my luck. Verbally no sound, but mentally I was roaring.

When this happened, she too went into my hands, but it took a while, as she seemed to have an endless amount of light inside her. It truly was amazing to me, as I had been trying for a couple of nights at least. The next thing I knew, I was floating back up to the big doors where the fighting had been going on. In I floated, and in fast-forward mode they were hacking with blades. I would see the odd hatchet blade with the brightest guy back on the table.

I had thought this part was over. I couldn't believe I was back in the big hall as if nothing had changed at all. Inner work or not, at that moment, I think I got down a little, as I didn't know what to do. I never really did anyways. So, I transmuted that shit so quickly and started thinking of what I should do. I went back up to the table and do not know why I said it, but

56

what I said was, *everybody in this hall, I release you from this life and go to the next, as all your families are waiting with love for you all.*

Well, oh my goodness! At that very moment, they all turned into an assortment of tiny different-coloured lights, but instead of going into my hands, they went up through the roof of the hall inside a tubular type of watery tunnel. There were so many at once, it just looked like a surge of a solid cluster of light moving at once through it creating a glowing wave of illuminous light.

The only one left was the bright one, and he floated off his chair. This time, I really could see his beard and all his features. He also looked more like a gold colour this time, and again, he was smiling at me. My ears and eyes started to get very tingly at this, and that's when I realized the wee angels were sprinkling light onto my face.

At this point, I had a real good feeling inside, like I had accomplished something even though I didn't know what it was. To me, it felt at the time that I was setting them free, as if they had been trapped by something and were stuck themselves, but I just wasn't sure. I trusted I was at least doing something good for them, as my wee angels had showed up, and I hadn't even seen where they came from, but I had a strong belief now they were coming from me.

That was the last time I was ever in that hall and at the women's prison camp, but it wouldn't be the last time I would be under the ground, searching. A lot had changed since I experienced the orange poofy thing that seemed to kick-start all of this. I was getting more used to doing my inner work. I truly loved this magical time in my life but often wondered at the time, *why me?*

CHAPTER 8

The Ant Colony and the Beehive Nest

Nature

SO, IT WAS time to do a bit of outer work.

Throughout my day, I was beginning to connect to nature in a closer way. It had started off by getting up early and going for a walk in the forest. As my knowledge was beginning to pick up, I began earthing in my front garden every day, connecting to Mother Earth daily—sunshine, hail, rain, or snow. I would go out and take my socks and shoes off and sit for at least thirty minutes every day. OK, not so much in the snow, but there was never really a big pile of snowfall in Northern Ireland anyways.

I was working with a lot of animals in my inner work, which was not only giving me a little more respect for them but even insects and the micro-world they lived in. In my line of work as a painter, I would come across spiders, daddy-longlegs, wood lice, centipedes, ants, nearly all of what some people would call creepy-crawlies, and I would have just squashed them and not given them a moment's notice. If I painted over one, there was no feeling I got as if I had just done something wrong. I felt nothing; I would have gone out of my way to kill a wasp in case it was going to sting me. *Prevention is better than cure* is almost certainly how I thought at this time. No regrets, no remorse.

But now that I was spiritually awoken, things were beginning to change how I would look at these creatures from here on in. My children were very scared of spiders, and I would have always gone in and killed the spiders for them, but I had started to feel bad within myself for doing this. Things like setting mousetraps were beginning to annoy me, to the point I didn't want to set them anymore. So slowly but surely, my attitude was going 180 degrees on this. I started looking back through my life when I had done bad things to insects, and there were two incidents that stuck out in my mind. It was about to go a full 360 degrees.

I was a tree surgeon for a short time, and we were working on some tightly bunched monkey trees with a beehive stuck right in the middle. As my coworkers were getting stung the closer, they got to the nest especially with the noise of the chainsaws going, we had to stop.

That's when I volunteered to get suited up, meaning making myself airtight, or should I say bee-tight, on all my clothing and helmet and face mask so no bees could sting me. Armed with a chainsaw and can of two-stroke petrol, I plunged in. As I got closer, the bees covered me from top to bottom, trying to get to some part of exposed flesh so they could sting me. There were so many of them, but cutting a long story short, I got to the beehive and burnt it straight away. Job done. At that time, I was kind of proud of achieving this, as no-one else would do it. It certainly didn't as much as enter my mind the bees were only defending their home and their queen.

Fast forward twenty years, I was outside my front door meditating and remembering this moment from the past and tearfully asking for forgiveness from the Most High for what I saw as a cruel act. This is what becoming aware, and awakening was doing for me: it was changing my whole perspective, right down to the smallest thing.

As I was lying in my garden meditating on this, a bumblebee buzzed so loudly in my ear, my first reaction was to swipe it away. Unreal, really, and defies all my thinking right at that moment, but it was a reactive thing I'd been doing for years. As soon as I did it, I regretted it and immediately said with my mind, *Sorry, come back, and I won't bring you any harm.* I swear as soon as I thought it, I heard *BUZZ BUZZ,* a buzzing so loud. This time I didn't panic or swipe. The bumblebee landed on my chin stayed for about five seconds, then buzzed off. It was so loud. About thirty seconds later, I felt a delayed tickly sensation where the bee had landed, and it didn't go away for about twenty minutes. The feeling I got was amazing, and it kind of verified to my conscience that my apology was accepted. To not only be in touch with nature but having a belief in now an emotional connection to it, filled me with a sense of jubilation.

The other time I destroyed a colony of insects was when I was on holiday in Faliraki in Greece with an ex-girlfriend. We had gotten the oldest room in the hotel, and just adding to our misery, the view from our wooden (no glass) window was a sewage works. The view was blocked by a big tree that was practically touching our walls right at the open window.

That is where the ants came from. Not ten minutes in that room, we had ants everywhere, and I mean *everywhere*. You had to swipe your glass, so you didn't drink any of them. First night in that bed, they were crawling over us all night. There were no rooms available to get moved to, so the owner offered us free pizza to quiet us down surreal offer but one I didn't turn down either.

Next morning, we got up and went down to the pool, not to relax, but to get away from the ants. When I went back up to the room, the glasses of Coke we had been drinking out of were moving because there were so many ants on them. They certainly had a sweet tooth, but this would prove to be their downfall—although nothing to the extent I had even thought. I devised a plan to go to the supermarket, buy a two-litre bottle of Coke, and pour it on the floor of our room. We grabbed our beach towels and went to the beach for about four or five hours.

Well, when we came back, the scene that greeted us was that the whole floor looked to be moving with millions of ants intoxicated in guzzling up the Coca-Cola. I jumped onto the bed, grabbed my girlfriend's Harmony hairspray and my lighter, combined the two, and began burning the colony. When I ran out of hairspray, I grabbed my BO spray (Lynx Africa) and finished the job. I said to my girlfriend at the time, "I did the dirty work— you can clean it up."

One hour later she came down and told me she couldn't clean it up. That's when we realized the floor was made up of a laminated cork. The ants were burnt in. We went down to the local market and bought two massive rugs to cover the floor. Bob's your uncle, job done.

Again, fast forward twenty years, and here I was sincerely apologizing for this mad cruel act I had done when all I can say is I was spiritually snoring. No ants came to my chin, but I felt at least on a metaphysical plane that my apology was accepted.

Reconnecting with nature is such an important thing. People just are not aware how much, and I was one of them. When you start to look for the truth in everything instead of fearing everything, you become enlightened to so many things that are around you every day. You just are too busy to notice because you've got bills to pay and jobs to fulfil, worrying about everything in a hectic programmed life that they call the matrix. Not only do you not give nature a second thought, but you also don't even see it.

My go-to place was my local forest, Windmill Wood. From going just for a walk to begin with, it had now changed completely. I was feeding the squirrels. The forest itself is not that big, but it had some ancient trees amongst it. It was a popular forest for dog-walkers, and I for one would have loved a dog, but my eldest daughter was anaphylactic and had an allergy to cat and dog hair, so it was a no-no from the off.

The choice of food for the squirrels started with beef mini chips, because that's what I happened to be eating one day. I left a few piles, and they gobbled them up like it was a treat. Then it progressed to Beef Monster Munch. Same again—they loved it, as they'd probably had enough of the auld nuts. As time went by, I started to make them work a little. I would get Beef Hula Hoops and jam them on the end of branches and make them work for their food. I absolutely loved doing this.

At this stage, I had already bought a bird feeder for outside my back garden and fed the birds with local produce from the pet shop. But when I went to the forest, there were so many, and the noise levels of singing, tweeting, and humming really began to go through me. It just began to sound so natural to me. Each time I would go I had such a belief in whistling to them, and they certainly would do it back. It felt amazing, really. It filled me with a lot of joy every time I went.

In the forest near where I grew up, there was one tree at the bottom beside the pond, and as children we called it *the big tree*. Many good days were spent around that tree. An old friend of mine who sadly was taken away too young in life was Darren Rooney, and one day when we were kids, we both climbed that tree to the very top.

As an adult I know I wouldn't do it, but as kids, we either had some balls or were just foolishly too young. As he was so small and the tree got so thin at the top, he went the last ten feet by himself, touched the top, came back down to me, and I did the same. Never have I forgotten that moment. So, it was at this tree I would go to remember him instead of his gravestone. But now this big tree meant so much more to me on my spiritual journey. It was a magnificent big tree, one big thick trunk with fourteen big limbs sticking out in all directions.

Watching movies as I grew up, there would be the odd one whereas a viewer, you would come across tree-huggers, and I remember I used to laugh at them. It just seemed so silly to me at that time. Now it had gone full circle, and I was the one hugging the tree. I loved it, too, as my knowledge had grown, and I realized that not only had certain trees souls, but they were there holding space for us all.

Each tree in that forest was connected to the next and next and so on. They were all connected as one. So, when I was talking and hugging that tree, I was mindfully and emotionally hugging them all. That tree gave me so much energy and answered so many questions. I'll love it forever.

I have dreamed about that tree many times since, and it has always looked after me just the way it did when I was young and climbed it with Darren. The connection I was beginning to get with nature, I could see when I was at the tree. Birds would come and land at the top—not every time, but often enough to make me realize they were saying hello in some sort of way. Squirrels too would come and sit up a bit and watch, but they probably were only coming for the crisps.

When you take a little more time for yourself, you learn a little more about certain aspects of life. Once you see it, once you notice, once you spot the programming, the realization of the matrix hits you on the head like a freight train, and your eyes double inwards. You begin to see it all for yourself. I promise, you will never be the same from that day on.

This is when you start living and searching for your true purpose in life. It really hits you for the first time that money is just a piece of paper—bits of paper that you need to live, that's the thing, to *live*. It's the control behind the money that pisses me off. No money, no food. Live backwards spells evil?

We are the only planet in the Solar System, galaxy, universe, cosmos, that must pay for food. Children are allowed to starve as a result, and still the human programming is so strong, and the fear so high, most people look after themselves, and that's the way it is planned and meant to be, until countries as a collective wake up to the battle which is taking much longer than it should.

Certainly, one of the driving forces for me to even think of writing, never mind *write*, a book is to get it to the masses of people who are still at the snoring stage of life. Everything sounds so far-fetched to them through no fault of their own. Their unbeknownst knowledge is telling them it just can't be real.

Well, folks, I'm sorry to say it's all real. Every lie you've ever been told is just as real as the truth. Even as I write this, deep down in my head I know I'll get to a point in this book where I will need to ask for help with the punctuation, full stops, commas, paragraphing, even the placing of chapters, to the art needed for the front and back covers. But ask I will, because you get to a stage where everybody needs help, and I keep writing, as it's helping me to come to terms with the journey I am on in my life. Once you realize we are all one, then help is abundant; it's everywhere.

When you connect with nature, you connect with all, as we are all natural beings and have come from the same source. We all have a spark in us, where we are all connected as one. When you go through what I have gone through, nothing can divert you from the truth: the Law of One.

The programming is done so well by some very smart, intelligent, evil, greedy, powerful pufferfish secretive global men who keep the masses of people thinking that we are alone in this universe and that somehow Earth is at the centre of it all. The elites of this world—bankers, big corporations, occultists, and all the puppet governments with their façade of democracy—know all about this, and the ones who do get paid to shut the fuck up. Sorry for my language it just gets to me sometimes because it's the truth. While you're dealing with a small minority that has all the money at its disposal, basically, they have control of everything.

Everybody is waiting on World War III to begin when it is already going on, with food cyberwars, computer AI, water, climate, and weather manipulation. This is all done in such a way that we are already fighting World War IV, and it's called Spiritual Warfare. This war I'm finding out has never stopped.

There are those who have put themselves on the unseen and unheard front lines for years in all dimensions, spiritually fighting the light against the darkness. But the elites know, and they are that good at getting the masses of people to make fun of and ridicule the spiritual warriors, when all they do is help. But as Big Arnie says, "I'll be back."

The thing is, when you are a light worker, you've had to go to a very dark place to get it. So, to mistake their kindness for weakness would be one judgemental path I would advise not to go down. You'll find the lion inside is only sleeping, especially when the love is wide awake.

My inner work was beginning to get more intense. I don't mean that in a scary way; it was always magical to me, and I certainly felt I was lucky to be doing this every night. It was beginning to become habitual to me.

There are some people who would give an arm and a leg to be doing what I was doing, and I knew this from my different social feeds of Joanne Honey Thomas, Rebbeca James, and Ellen Redd. A lot of people were trying but finding connecting to the spiritual realm difficult. Then there would be people who couldn't handle it and found it scary and altogether overwhelming to do such things every night. Personally, I loved doing it, even though sometimes I was scared, maybe even a little afraid. Yet I always felt safe, protected in a way by my other self.

It always started the same. I would begin meditating, and after a while of clearing my mind, my little angels would come out and surround me, like they were charging me up a little for what I was about to do. Without me really noticing, I would be in a big room with wee lights zooming around, some inside the room and others round the outside.

I would begin gathering the light up with my hands until it got so bright. Then it would start I would begin to light up myself, not super-bright, but dimly lit. On this night when there were no lights left, I went forward to another room, and that's where I found a version of myself. This room was bigger, with a lot of gaps here, there, and everywhere, with lights going in all directions. I started getting to work and collecting them. After a short while, my hands were so bright that when I looked up at the roof—if I could even call it a roof—a hole seemed to be forming in it.

At first, I didn't think too much about it. There was much more light flying around me now. Don't ask me how I knew how to do this; I still don't know. But once I drew enough light in, I could tell that I couldn't hold any more, as some of the light would fly up to my hands and then fly away again. I just seemed to be getting directed up the way, so I would put my hand out, shoot them up the way, and mindfully push my light upwards. All would release from my hands and up and out through the hole. I could even see when there were no more left, and so it would start again. I would collect more light, and when my hands got tingly, I would repeat the feat and out they would go again. This light was filled with animals of all sorts and of all sizes. In my mind I was trying to connect them with all the animals in the night sky I had collected but I never knew for sure.

To get to watch visually orbs of light racing around, to then consciously draw them into your lit up hands and watch them downsize to micro dots of light was so amazing for me. I remember a whale coming in which took a long time and that it had to be released straight away as my hands were tingly like crazy, certainly they couldn't have held anything else at that moment.

It seemed at this point that everything was made of light. Sometimes, I would be in this room and then *boom!* I was flying, underground mostly. But one night I went up into space. I didn't go very far through space until I came to a big hole and flew in. At the time, I thought it was the moon, but I don't know for sure. Mostly the reason I think this is I wasn't flying for that long. When I say *flying*, I could never see myself flying. It was always from an eye view. So quite easily, it could have been everything coming to me. Again, I'm not sure, but I lean towards flying because that's how it felt.

Into this hole in the rock, I went until I came across a load of human beings, all crouched down on their haunches, and it was as if they were all chipping away at something. They were all wearing white clothes that were the same. There were men there—most of them looked old—but a lot more women than men. I could never see guards or anything, but I thought they were in captivity of some sort.

There were big black doors with lights on them. They were shiny, as if made of steel. I went to this place a couple of times. There was no one who was really lit up in there, but I had a feeling they were all trapped by something. I just couldn't see.

I would float up to the black doors. I was always above everyone, never down walking through them or anything, always that wee bit above, but I could never get the doors open or get in through them. There was nowhere else to go, as even above me was black shiny rock. The only thing that was lit up were some tools, a spade, a small hammer, a pole of some sort, and a couple of cups.

Everybody who was there had little hammers. They were never doing anything. Something told me they were hungry, and also I got the impression they couldn't see me. I don't even know if I picked any tools up. I did try, but

I couldn't see if I was picking them up, and then I would go. I tried a few times to see if I could help them get out or ascend them in some way, but it never happened.

Next thing, I'm out of the big hole in a flash. I truly mean, I didn't even travel out the same way I came in. I was just flying straight through space again. I travelled for what seemed quite a while this time and came to more people crouched over, like the ones I had just seen, only it was on some other planet that I had no clue of. They were above ground.

I remember being very close to these people, and they were looking at me as if they knew me, not at all like the other ones under the rock. I believed I was standing up at this point. I never really got to spend any time there at all.

Next thing I knew, I was scooped up off the ground and onto a ship where all the people were blue. This didn't last long. I believe I was in the middle of some battle, but I hadn't much time to think about. The only one I saw properly was the woman who had grabbed my right hand and lifted me up. She had the features of a coloured woman but was blue, with no hair. She was smiling at me.

I believed she was showing me something. I could see other small ships with blue people lined up on both sides of the ships, all hanging out the sides, and the ships themselves had wings but not like a set of aeroplane wings, like massive, feathered bird wings. I couldn't get a good look, but I always remember the look on the woman's face who was holding my hand. She was beautiful and looked to have battle gear or armoured clothing on. Next thing I knew, we started to go up the ways, as we seemed to be gliding only a few feet off the ground, and I was back in the second room where I had started.

It was so surreal—no traveling back, just from one place to another in a flash. Even at the time, I was dumbfounded. I remember opening my eyes only for an instant, and yes, I was in my living room, only with my head an inch away from my living room window. I was so aware of what had just happened, and only when I went to the toilet did I start to see things again as my normal house. It was such a magical thing to go through, but I do remember being a little puzzled as to what had just happened and why.

I personally think I was shown some sort of battle that was going on somewhere in the cosmos. I have no idea where; maybe this is where I was from, and the prisoners I was seeing were from there. I just don't know. But still now, I can see the woman who scooped me off that plateau of whatever planet it was. I have a niggling memory that she either had a tattoo or some sort of mark on her face. Even still, in my mind, I find it hard to remember. I just remember a glow of some sort lit up throughout her face.

Every day now, everything was moving in a new direction, and I for one was most definitely changing. I was learning more truths daily. I remember at this point phoning my best matey in Scotland, Colly B, and telling him about starting to change his DNA. What I meant by this is beginning to live your life in an honest and dignified way. Start by being truthful with everything, stop offending people every day, stop being judgemental, end the offending you do to yourself, stop putting yourself down, stop slagging yourself, hold no fear; even when done jokingly, you would still be doing it.

Loving myself is probably one of the hardest things I have ever had to do. Then, when you start believing in all you're doing, living right, filling your own cup, and emptying everybody else out of it, setting boundaries to everyone, raising your vibration and frequency, finding purpose and not living by the norms of a programmed society's way of living, you start realizing there is so much more to life than what you were taught. You begin to raise your consciousness to a higher level and see life in a totally different light.

So, I was starting to love myself. The emotions you begin to go through were overwhelming at that time. I now know I was meant to release so much. Truly, I didn't think it would take that long, but still now I realize it when my brain remembers something that goes straight to my now open heart. Loving myself was hard; loving everybody else—when you realize we are all one, all part of the cosmic birther, all a spark of source living in every one of us all at the same time—was even harder.

So, I kept going and forgiving, and truly meaning it, too. It hits you that we all come from one, and with accepting to love all beings as one, I have learnt about all the love from all the dimensions and all the magic I get to do with my third eye. I didn't know much about this world, only that I was doing a lot of work in it with a higher version of myself. This is when Christos Avatar popped up on my feed Marchewa My Friend (Vatos).

I really began to detach religion from spiritually in a clever sense with knowledge and information from him. This was another amazing part of my journey and made me realize where all these beings, lights, angels, and souls were all from: the 15-Dimensional Time Matrix. Even though time is an illusion, it is constructed this way to give it purpose and the different past, present, and future timelines.

So now my love had started becoming universal, as it was these places I was going in my inner work. When the synchronicities of angels come into your life through the matrix and through numbers, signs, and places, you really get a feeling that you yourself are universally loved by so many on the spiritual side of life. It is totally amazing, and in turn, this makes you become an all-around better person, an authentic true way to live your life, and how you get to experience every day.

This was the first time I really started to see the word *divine* on a regular basis. I was becoming more and more connected to the source of everything. When I started on this journey, not once did I ever set off and think about my connection to the divine, but here I was receiving all this information. For the first time, I really began to think that through my intense awakening, through what I was experiencing, I was being given a choice of something, right at this time in my life.

So, from this moment on, I began to change even more. I had never really believed much in God throughout my life. There were times when I prayed, but very few and far between. Situations sometimes got bad, and this is when I prayed, but to no avail. If anything, I would have slagged and joked about it, more often than not. I have learnt more through Billy Carson about the God in the modern Bible nowadays than throughout my whole life, and it is one of war, hierarchy, worship, death, and slavery.

God is always referred to as *he*. Always *he this* and *he that*. Yes, as much as there are a lot of truths in the Bible, there are so many lies, so much left out and changed to become one of the biggest businesses in the world. So, I would go as far as to say the Bible and the very intelligent people that structured its modern-day version did it for business, big business, cruel business. It even tells you how to be a good hardworking slave, even today. When you start your researching on King James alone the answers you find should tell you your truths. He was far from good, never mind having a bible named after him. A controlling evil nuance.

The source of everything is the complete opposite. The law of one. Truth and love—with only those two things, what else do you need? In the world we live in today, these are replaced by fear and lies. It's as simple as that. There is no free will in this way of living; it's all about control and death.

If people knew that you never actually die—we are all energy, consciousness is energy, it can't be killed, it just changes form and moves on. I am not saying I have all the answers, far from it. What I do have is a mind that can think for itself, free of the matrix that the masses believe is not even true.

Waking up is so much more than just opening your eyes; it's opening your heart, your life, your love, your lungs, and certainly your pineal gland (third eye) needs to open up, then your thoughts, your mind, your head, your emotions, your truth, your connections to the real world that's waiting for you all, just like it was for me. So, to go through such a dramatic intense awakening as I did, I know deep within myself that I will never be the same again. Maybe all the hardship and trauma I've gone through in my life, even the drugs that I've taken, have somehow helped me put this pen to paper. To write my story and bare my soul in this book is the only way that I can at least help as many people as I can raise their consciousness high enough that they can see through all the lies and deceit.

Even as I write this passage in my car at work on my break, I can't thank my mateys enough for nudging me to spark my awakening. Enzo with his "Have you ever heard of the Anunnaki?" and Colly B, who for a few years had been telling me snippets of controlled education: shite in the foods, dark occults, and truly, I just wasn't listening properly at the time. So, thank you guys—it's meant more than you will ever know. I've told Colly B everything from the orange poofy on, and soon enough, we would have a couple of experiences together that would set him on the spiritual side of his journey and change everything for the better for both of us.

I now know he is my soul brother, always was. We just didn't know or think too much about it. But once we met, we have never parted company or had any rows worth even mentioning. So yes, he is the first person I have met who I now know had at one time in our metaphysical life sat down at a table to write part of our earthly contract. Amazing, really, when this type of belief exists within our minds. I absolutely love it.

69

CHAPTER 9

Working Closer with My Higher Self

SO, A LOT had happened since I was making spaghetti bolognese in my kitchen and caught a shadow of myself. I was beginning to teach myself the things that I was being taught to do in my meditation and learning more throughout each day, so I would be ready for my inner work at night with a version of me. It's quite hard to say this in a matter-of-fact way, as it was not so. I looked forward to my inner work each evening, and sometimes it really was hard work, as I was so tired tending to everything throughout each day. Still, I was thoroughly excited, and always my day would build up to this in my mind.

Through Ellen Redd, I was beginning to realize it was called *energy work*, because there was a caption I read about light workers and shadow healers. With all I was doing, this resonated with me in a deeply conscious way, as I believed I was doing both, but I knew nothing on a cosmic level to be healing anyone. So, I broke it down for me to be a light worker and a shadow worker, and not actually healing anyone, only myself at this stage, as my knowledge was so thin.

That said, I was learning as quickly as possible. What would happen to me is I would do my energy work and, whether it was Joanne Honey Thomas, Rebbeca James, Ellen Redd, or now Christos Avatar, I would make sense of where I was at through one of their posts. This is when things went up another, should I say spiritual, level. Dancing with myself had progressed to just him and me in my living room doing movements together. He would always go first, and then I would copy him. As we would be doing this, different things would come out of my hands at different times, because of different movements—not only with my hands, but with the way we moved our bodies and changed direction. After a while. I began to get the feeling that I was building something.

I will try to explain it a little better. There was this one move, a 360-degree turn, and I would shape my hands in such a way that bringing them up to my mouth and blowing out, it would be like cloud, smoke, or fog of some sort coming out of my hands, and it would go everywhere, across space. As much as I was aware of being in my living room, I knew I was somewhere else in the universe that I didn't know. I was genuinely interacting with myself in a way, like we were brothers, and as this was happening nearly every evening, we were getting to know each other very well. There was never any sound, just lights and darkness at times everywhere.

After doing this together for about a week, we started putting animals out into space. They were all made of light, and with each set of motions we would do, I was really beginning to light up myself. I had begun to turn my hands in on myself, and it looked as if I had some sort of suit on, but only when I put my hands on myself could I see this. Truly, I felt sometimes that maybe somebody better educated in the cosmos and how this all worked would be better equipped to deal with all this, as I would make plenty of mistakes, and I mean *plenty*.

But I was a person who never gave up easily in my life, and I used this to the best of my abilities to overcome the ignorance I had of it all. Even now as a write about this, it's reminding me of the hardships of my own life and how it has gotten me to this moment. I'm beginning to feel like I'm healing even more so through my attachment to writing this book, setting out just how to go about it at the start and working and finding my own way to do it, just like my energy work.

It was about a week and a half into doing this work with a version of myself that I started to see bits of light coming from him and onto me. I realized, by watching them land on me, that I had what I deemed to be a set of light wings. This was the first time I had noticed these on me, as I was always too busy sending light out of my own hands and never really concentrated on myself. It was the same as my angels had done for me, sprinkling light on me as a reward. I seemed to be rewarding myself for my inner work and doing the same, but this light would land on me and then spread out and get brighter as it went. It was certainly different, and this really bolstered me and got me going again, like an adrenaline rush. I don't know what the human response is meant to be at finding a set of wings on your back, truly at the time this happened I had no words to describe how this felt, and know I said adrenaline rush but its so much more than that. Breathtaking, exciting inspiring eye-popping uplifting (excuse the pun) exhilarating, elation, certainty a little confusion amplified with shock. Surprised to say the least, overwhelmed a little but all of these was taken over by, happiness overjoyed lucky ecstatic with a sense of enchantment. I truly could keep on writing a list on my emotions about that very moment, but I will run out of ink.

Really, it inspired me to work even harder. I began to realize how magical it was all over again, and how lucky I was to be able to do this kind of work. It gives you an idea how much I had been doing this and got lost in the moment, and in some way my brain had begun to normalize it all. This is far from normal, and now a set of wings, wings, wings what! *Wow, wow wow, wow wow* was running around inside my mind. I can't find words to describe how I truly felt about having wings on my back. Even writing about it feels crazy to me, but there they were. I know I'm repeating I can't help it.

This moment made me remember a few conversations I had with different friends when I was young. Some of them have sadly passed away, Source rest their souls, but it always went like, "If you had a choice of a superpower, what would it be?" Some would say invisibility or super-strength, but mine was always that I wished I could fly. And here I am on a metaphysical level with a set of wings on my back. To say I was emotional is an innerstatement. The fascination of this has never left my mind since, and I think it never will.

As much as I was doing my energy work, I started to get carried away a bit and couldn't take my eyes off these wings, to the point where the version of myself would look at me sternly as if to get me back on course. I would begin to flap my arms up and down just to see them move and glisten with light and was thinking to myself at the time, *how would I use these wings to lift off?* I'm nearly sure he was laughing at me sometimes as I would stand there and flap away with my arms trying to lift off in some sort of imaginary way, to the point where I thought I would bang my head on the living-room ceiling if this actually worked.

This would maybe go on for five minutes, and then I would catch myself and get back to what we were doing. I was thinking along the lines of, *where would I fly to? How far would I go up in the sky or into space? How would I breathe up there?* But the thing is, I went down instead of going up. It wasn't as if I was flapping or anything; it was the same as before, flying low and fast, and taking the turns deep underground as they came to me.

I seemed always to have options and different routes to take, and night after night I would be down there finding pockets of light, some static and hidden from view, others flying away from me. I would chase them to try to catch them. As I was doing this, so often I would see light on the ground below. So, on one of those nights, I stopped chasing the ones that were ahead of me and slowed down. Though it was hard to fully stop, I seemed to be able to turn around using my head as a steering wheel, meaning where I pointed my head was the direction I went. If I looked up, I went up, and vice versa when looking down.

When I did this, I was finding more light pockets that were hidden from my view. When I was chasing the fast-flying light in front of me, I was turning around big rocks and going down or up through holes emitting some light with a bit of a glow showing, but when I went through it, it would radiate so much brighter. Every bit of light, I was picking up by focusing my two hands at it. Some came up straight away, and others felt like there was something holding them down, sticking them to the rock.

With these, I really had to focus my hands and mind to get them to go into my palms. I was beginning to see that the harder-to-get ones or the more-hidden ones were either two or three, sometimes seven or eight different animals clumped together. Only when I gathered them up could I see this, as they would go into my hands in single file.

I really did start getting a lot better at doing this. It's probably better to say I was more efficient at it. I started to have an even stronger belief that I was helping, I never did know how long they had been down there, but I just didn't want to leave any behind alone and trapped. It was my thinking at the time.

Then one night, I truly thought I had found them all, as it was the same underground place and as vast as it was, I truly was getting to know my way around all the places. How magical I thought to be even down here searching every nook and granny, setting free imprisoned light. I began chasing the fast-flying lights again and getting quicker at turning and looking more in front of me in the distance rather than just in front of me. For me, this is hard to describe in words, and I feel like I repeat myself a bit, but I don't know any other way to explain it. Not at any time when I was doing all this flying and searching did, I ever see my wings or have to flap in any way to move. It all happened so naturally.

I began to get to different parts of this underground maze. I started coming across volcanoes, lava flows, spitting magma, but all underground, like the underbelly of volcanoes, not the top of them. A bit like the veins of them that you can't see from the top, the common view that you would see in books with a mountain, hole at the top and spitting lava. It had to be the bottom of one.

I felt shaking and shattering underground, too, like I was seeing what an earthquake looked like way underground. I'd also come across swaths of flowing water, waves and all. It truly was amazing to see stuff like this and be aware that you are standing up in your living room, eyes closed, breathing and sweating away. I began to feel a small bit like some sort of video game, but it was so real to me at the time, even now words are hard to find to explain the emotional attachment you have when down there.

Sometimes the magnitude of what I was doing would hit me, and I would begin to think I was in over my head—and I probably was. But truthfully, I did not want it to stop, and I wouldn't have either. The attitude I had was *what's next*, but it was what happened next that affected me in my physical life and not the metaphysical realm. It was through work that I believe I was getting a reward like I'd never had before, and this was not the sprinkling or the making of my light wings or glowing body. This happened to me as I lay on my own bed at night, and nothing from that moment on would ever divert me from my now awakening soul.

CHAPTER 10

The Twenty-Year Malteser

THIS WAS ONE of the toughest days of work I'd done in quite a while. Being a painter and decorator, I was doing a full house for a woman not far from my home, but there were so many opening cracks all through this house, especially upstairs. The house was up for sale, so I had wanted to do the best job possible. The day before, I had polyfilled and gotten it all ready for rubbing the ceilings and walls with sandpaper. So, all day, I was doing this, and I was totally spent after making dinner for my children, cleaning up, then cleaning myself. I was so shattered, I just couldn't do any of my energy work, as energy was the one thing I did not have.

So, I decided to not do anything, even to the point of feeling a bit guilty, but knowing I was working the next day, it's just how I felt. I remember going outside to my porch, and the clouds were so thick I could not see any of the night sky at all. They were also so low down, so low in fact it looked like a mist on ground level. At this time, I was beginning to cut down on my smoking. I hadn't completely quit, but deep inside, I knew I was getting close.

As I neared the end of my one-skinner, I thought I saw a round bubble of light through the clouds coming from way high up. It was hard to make it out, as it was too far away, but I still followed it, and it kept shining like a small tingy green glow of what looked like a bubble of some sort. Across from the front of my house is a main road with lampposts running up and down it. So as this vertically came flying down, it stopped dead just behind one of the lampposts. It was then it began to go horizontal left to the other lamppost and left again to another.

If you can imagine, it was hard to see with all the clouds. I began thinking my eyes were playing tricks on me. Then it would go right, from lamppost to lamppost, but always behind the cloud and always hard to make out. It would disappear and then end up at another lamppost, so sometimes I didn't see it travel horizontally to the next one.

After a while, I began to think the wee doobie was really playing tricks with me, so being so tired, I went back into the house, washed myself, and went straight to bed. But not until I had a chocolate doughnut, just medically to digest the munchies and get food out of my mind. I can't even remember my head hitting the pillow straight out. I'm not fully sure, but I reckon it would have been about nine or nine thirty when I went to bed.

I don't know what time exactly I got awoken, and still to this day I don't know, but I got awoken so sharply with what felt like a jolt to the top of my shoulder just below my neck, somewhere in the middle. When I say *jolt*, I will try to give you an example. It felt like an electric shot, vibrating enough for me to wake, a fuzzy, tingly electrical feeling all at once.

The feeling itself reminded me of when I was young and me and a few mates of mine would go on a Sunday adventure. We left the house in the morning and never came back until bedtime, progging apple orchards, doing tactics, walking big hidden water pipes, and just generally messing around. As we were crossing a big field, all around the edge there was an electrical fence to keep the cattle in. My memory is the first guy would hold hands with the second and so on right down the line. Most of us had done this before bar one of my mates, so the joke was on him that day. Number one would touch the fence, and the flow would go through everybody and earth to the last man on the end, who got the brunt of the shock, and *boom!* everybody got a laugh. It was always swings and roundabouts with these sorts of pranks, as in some way or another we all got our turn.

It was this sensation that I felt on my neck as I awoke. In my head, I thought I was getting awoken to do some inner work, as I had not done any for the first night in four, maybe five months. So, in a sleepy half-awake daze, I started doing my hand motions instinctively. It kind of gives you an idea how much energy work I had been doing up to this point, because my brain went automatically into my spiritual side of work, without thinking about it too much.

I soon realized, though, that nothing was happening—no lights, no version of me, nobody and nothing but the darkness of my room. It was just the tingly feeling on the top of my shoulder, and at the time I remember thinking it must have been a trapped nerve or something. I put my head back down and went straight back to sleep, to tired to let it even bother me.

It was in the early hours of the morning that I was awoken again. This time, it had nothing to do with my shoulder but a tingly feeling on my left hand, a bit like I was sitting on it and the sensation of pins and needles. But that was far from the truth. What I began to see has stuck with me, and I can never forget it.

Sitting on my left hand was a wee see-through bubble, floating above my hand just a little. There was a greenish tinge to it, and I could see it as plain as day. To explain it properly, it was about the size of a table-tennis ball, even a wee bit smaller maybe, but what I saw inside still amazes me when I remember it in my thoughts.

There were three tiny greys (they were green, but what most people I know call greys). They were sitting down on chairs, and in front of them was a whole desk of controls, control panels everywhere, like they were at the helm of a mini ship, only it was a see-through bubble. The detail was amazing: wee joysticks, different colours of lights and buttons. I was absolutely amazed at this. My hand was illuminating up, also in green; in my other work it had always been a white, goldy colour.

The thing is, they never batted an eyelid at me. My hand didn't move, but I had raised myself up a little to get a better look, and they didn't even recognize I was watching them, not one bit. Not only that, two of them got up from their chairs, leaned forward, and were studying my hands, so attentive they didn't look up at me once, not once, just going about their business, whatever that was. I really can't tell you how I wasn't frightened by all this. I just wasn't. They didn't seem to have any malicious intentions whatsoever; in fact, they seemed to be discussing and working something out, and I took it as if they were helping with something.

It was such a bizarre experience in the middle of night, lying in my bedroom in total darkness bar this little green shiny bubble full of ETs working on my left hand. I remember lying back down, looking up one more time, and still nothing. It was as if they were on some kind of mission to get something done on me. I truly didn't know. So, I lay back down, and next thing my alarm went off for work.

It was the first thing I thought of as soon as I woke and hit the snooze button, twice lying there trying to figure out what it was all about. Eventually I got up, got everybody up and breakfast, school run done, and away to work I went. It was only when I started working, I could feel my shoulder a bit tender in the middle, as I was cutting the top line of the ceiling.

Now what you need to know is I have always had a lump on my shoulder in the middle and at the bottom of my neck. I have had this lump for over twenty years and had been to the doctors a few times when it had become sore over the years. It was about the size of a Malteser, and my doctor could never tell me what it was but said not to worry too much about it. To me, what he really was saying was, "I haven't a fooking clue what that is but what doesn't kill you only makes you stronger." He just went totally ignorant about it. I felt it didn't bother him, so he really didn't care that much.

Something clicked in my brain when I realized this was exactly where my lump was, so I stopped working and started feeling where it was tender but could not find the lump. It always took me a second to find it, but this time, I really could not feel it, I was so shocked by this, I dropped my brush in the bucket of paint and jumped around the room with so much joy. I was elated with happiness. I just kept feeling where it had been, and it wasn't there.

This is when I began to connect all the dots in my mind. I didn't do any work for at least twenty-five to thirty minutes as the shock of it began hitting me, and I became emotional, really emotional—not just tears down my cheeks but proper crying. I was glad the man and woman I was working for were away to their own work, as I don't think I could have held back those tears. It had been a long time since I'd had such a happy cry.

It all hit me at once: the small table-tennis-ball bubble with the three green greys inside, the big green bubble outside my front flying back and forth, from lamppost to lamppost. I felt it all right there—that somehow, they had come down, waited till I went to sleep, downsized to a smaller bubble, fricking worked on me as I slept, and removed the Malteser from my shoulder. I don't think *elated* is the proper word: astonished, overjoyed, shocked.

It is hard to explain the multitude of emotions I was feeling at that very moment. I just wanted to go home and celebrate in some way. It truly was a miracle what had happened. I knew for sure that is what they had done. God only knows what else they did, but physically they had come from a metaphysical other side and took a twenty-year-old lump off my shoulder. It truly amazed me. Right then, nothing could have felt better. Surely this is what unconditional love feels like.

All day, I cried on and off. I went home and couldn't wait to start my inner work and thank everybody from everywhere who had made this happen for me. And that's exactly what I did. I filled rivers with my emotions; I just couldn't stop. I really couldn't. To innerstand that something like this can happen in one's life is utterly amazing, and for me to experience it as a forty-six-year-old grown man has put me on a path of enlightenment. The song that comes to mind is "cry me a river" by Justin Timberlake. Love that song now.

I have always thought there was more to this life—or should I say, I was really thinking that something was always missing in my life. Something inside of me was really beginning to roar from within. I felt over these past few months that with what I was experiencing and the inner work that I was doing, in some way, I was meant to help. To get awoken the way I had and the intensity of it, and with the path I was beginning to choose, my thoughts had begun to consume me. How I could I fully stand up and try to make a difference? In these moments, I hadn't a notion how, just the feeling that I wanted to help change the way the masses thought and make people realize how long this trickery had been going on—not just to get people to believe, but on a conscious level, to collectively raise everybody to awaken themselves, or at the very least to become more aware.

I didn't know it yet, but shortly after this miracle, I was to embark on another level of my journey, and I just about quit every other bad habit I ever had done since I was a child. Rapidly, I was changing who I was and would leave the old Conrad behind to become the new Conrad and start aligning myself with my true purpose in life, my soul's mission, my divine calling. All the times I was alone and all the times I had felt lonely in my life, I have come to realize I was never alone and have always been loved throughout my entire life, from the moment I was born. I've never even made a mistake; they have only been lessons. The problem for me was that only now was I beginning to learn from them, because I was finally aware they all existed.

Now I don't see the problems in my life as problems, more like challenges. Also, I'm tackling these challenges with a smile on my face. It's all about remaining positive about everything no matter how hard it seems at the time, and always remembering nobody is perfect. Life has its ups and downs; it's the same for everyone. It's how you go about fixing them and in turn taking the lessons from them, learning and adapting how to do it better the next time, that matters.

To give one example, at the time of writing these couple of paragraphs, I'm on my tea break out in the car putting pen to paper. Just this morning, I got up and looked at my phone, and the time was 0707. Next time I looked, it was 0808, and then again 0909. You couldn't make these synchronicities up if you tried and went onto Google and found the meaning of all these angel numbers. From reading them, not only have I felt great with the knowledge that angels are doing this for me, but what I have learned from them changes me a little more and raises my frequency even more to align with my higher self, to evolve me even further as a person.

Once you truly believe and have maximum faith that you are a spirit inside a human body, nothing can ever be the same again. I cannot stress enough what these three numbers have meant to me that day. Once you start looking and then finally seeing, the numbers fall into your life. The mystery of the unknown leaves you, and the knowledge of knowing enters your life in a way you couldn't ever have imagined if you tried. It is an unbelievable feeling of the power of *love.*

To go from knowing practically nothing to this way of life—snoring without knowing, being awoken by my mates, having visions, meditating, inner work, lights, then darkness, then midnights, then even darker, bucketloads of tears (I am not afraid to admit it, I released so many tears that I often wondered how my body could make so many at one time)—to having such a strong belief that I have a team of spirit guides, guardian angels, ancestors that guide me, ascended masters, teachers, soul family, soulmates, but not only that they guide me, they do all of this with unconditional love for me, that alone is truly amazing. I have so much gratitude in my life towards them all. It is amazing to realize you are a soul on a mission at this time, preordained at this very moment to help humanity shift earth into a 5D consciousness to become a new earth.

I know to some reading this now it might sound so far-fetched, even mind-boggling to believe, but only seven or eight months ago, I knew nothing of it either. And here I am with knowledge given to me, gifts I've received. Claircognizance is a word that keeps popping up for me. Its meaning is knowing facts without knowing how you received the information. Surely this has to be happening to me, and as much as I do study and research some things I really have no explanation. But the most amazing thing I'm coming to terms with is to think I have a divine connection to the cosmic birther (God). It fills me with heightened emotions, I have never had and certainly never felt before, but once you realize that *earth*, when the letters are jumbled around, spells *heart*, another thing I thought I didn't have, it's a feeling of innerstanding that I have made the choice for something with love.

Since I've started to gather all this knowledge, physic Ellen Redd has taught me so much about twin flames and the journey one must go on to even consider a reunion on this earthly plain. It's hard for me to put this into words, but through Ellen's knowledge I have come to realize more about my sexual divinity and how important and powerful your seed is. Never, ever would I have thought this way but for her, so for that I will be forever grateful. I have stopped messing about with myself, is the politest way I can write this down on paper, as it's a personal thing to even talk about.

The journey I am on to find my twin flame, true love, the other half of my soul, is so important to me. I want to do it with honour, dignity, honesty, truth, and trust, so that when it happens, I will have left no stone unturned with my pursuit wholeheartedly in finding my true love. I now know she is out there somewhere, spiritually on her own unique path and journey, as we both magnetize our reunion together.

I just read back over a couple of pages that I have written tonight. The old Conrad wouldn't have written anything like this. Truthfully, I haven't written as much since I left school thirty-two years ago. I'm now changing every day, trying to be that wee bit better than the day before. It is harder than I first thought it would be, but stick-ability and hard work are slowly getting me to where I need to be. Where that is and what ceiling there is gonna be to my achievements, I just don't know at this stage of my journey.

The one thing I do know is that I am going to create my heaven on this earth, I am gonna help not only those around me who want to free themselves and start living an honest free life but also people unknown to me from all walks of life, as we are all one and always have been.

I'm beginning to write a bunch of words that I never even wrote at school. I'm also innerstanding what they mean, and how each word extends and extends a little more in their meanings. These words include the following:

- create, creation, creator, creativity
- spirit, spirited, spiritually, spirituality
- light, lighten, enlighten, enlightenment
- ascend, ascended, ascension
- manifest, manifested, manifestation
- pray, prayer, praying
- angel, angels, angelic
- divine, divinity, divinely
- aware, awareness
- mystery, mysteries, mystified
- heal, healed, healing
- forgive, forgiven, forgiveness
- thanks, thanked, thankful, thankfulness
- emotion, emotions, emotional, emotionless, emotionally
- wise, wisdom
- collect, collected, collectively. collective
- awake, awoke, awaken, awakening, awoken
- human, humanity, humanly, humanitarianism
- universe, universal, universally
- cosmic, cosmically, cosmos
- birth, birthed, birther
- resonate, resonated
- purpose, purposeful, purposefully
- intent, intention, intentionally
- limit, limiting, limited
- success, successful, successfully
- bible, biblical, biblically
- love, loved, loving, lovingly, loveliness

- trust, trustee, trusted, trustworthy
- authentic, authenticity
- truth, truths, truthful, truthfulness

Yes, there are a few of these words I have used over my lifetime, but the meaning behind them now to me is so different, important, significant, and present in my daily life. Now I incorporate them in the way I live, trying to be as authentic as I possibly can. It's only when you purposely start living authentically that you realize the programming you've been under, the ways that you must reprogram your mind. All off your thoughts are literally already implanted in your brain, with a pattern of indoctrination from the beginning of your childhood, through adolescence, and then into adulthood. Mine would still be going if I hadn't woken up, and it's in this indoctrination of the mind that you realize the habits you have—socially, privately, secretly, emotionally, intentionally, but most important of all, habitually in your daily life.

So, my mind was in the middle of freeing itself as much as possible. I had begun to privately feel guilty about smoking not only cigarettes but joints too. At the start of my inner work, I would have rolled two joints to prepare myself for it all, not knowing how addicted I was to smoke. This started to change when, on watching my social feed on Facebook, I found a guy whose page is called "5ᵗʰ Dimension," and quite matter-of-factly he said that another name for *spirit* is *breath*. It struck a chord in me and began playing heavy on my mind. I'm not saying I quit straight away, but it firmly, may I say, planted the seed.

I had smoked for thirty-two years and would have different friends call around for a joint, or me to their house, much in the same way someone would offer you a beer when visiting just to be sociable, not actually to get drunk. We did much the same, only with doobies. First, I quit the cigarettes and felt quite good about it. Then I would only have tobacco with joints, although at the same time I was gaining knowledge on how spirituality was the art of breathing, with the importance of breath work when meditating with so much clean air in the atmosphere.

Even when going to the forest, I would breathe more deeply mentally, as the air there is much fresher, having fewer pollutants because of the nature of the place. That's what I was beginning to think about smoking as a pollutant in my lungs. Even as I kept doing this, my gut feeling was not sitting well with me, and your gut feeling is a form of inner wisdom from your soul. I had started believing I was taking my purity away somehow. My thinking at this time was that my soul was saying to me, *That's enough now. You are aware about all these toxins you are putting into your body. Enough is enough, buddy.*

That very day, I had four cigarettes left in my packet while out in my garden. My thoughts were, *Will I buy another twenty-pack or not?* I remember mindfully asking my angels to show me a sign that I shouldn't. For a while, I had pondered and reasoned with myself, *O.K., weed is a plant, and it grows naturally, nor would Mother Earth let it grow if it was bad.* So, I went to the shop and never bought another twenty pack. As I was walking up my garden path on returning from the shop, at my front door where my black ashtray always was placed, there were two roaches from the night before on top, but I now could see some type of flower thing sitting on top of them.

The amazing thing was that the flowery thing was in the shape of an angel. I couldn't believe my eyes. Right at that moment, I was shocked to my inner core yet again. How could this happen in ten minutes? You know the things that fall from trees that when coming down go like the blades of a helicopter? It was one of those, and I still have it to this day. The puzzling bit about this is I still can't find the tree it came from. I can't find any near my house and around the housing estate. Having walked up and down the road, I still haven't spotted one.

This is when I knew that my angels had answered my prayers to show me a sign. Miracles really do happen. I have never smoked a cigarette again, and I never will. No patches, no gum, just enough was enough, and I broke the cycle there and then. I still had a bit of weed left over, though. So, the next two nights, I had what you call a *blunt*: a joint with only weed in it. But it was worse than smoking it with tobacco and defied the whole point of me quitting smoking. I coughed and sputtered every drag I took, and finally I decided that was it. I was going to throw it in the bin, it was then that I decided to give it away to one of my mates, and that's what I did. It felt great. And he certainly looked happy when I told him I didn't want any money for it.

A fortnight or so later, I found another lump of it that I had hidden and forgot it was there. I phoned the same mate and gave it to him. That's when I knew I had moved on from smoking everything. Truthfully, I felt so proud of myself that the very next thought that entered my head was to quit drinking alcohol.

There is a reason why spirits are called *spirits*, like whisky, vodka, and brandy—the list goes on. They numb the spirit that lies within you. In moderation, these drinks aren't totally bad for you, but they're not good for you either. There's a happy medium, but most people who are alcoholics are addicted to the bottle. Others love beer and wine, but the outcome is the same. Certainly, there's nothing wrong with having the odd one, but for me, no more sore banging headaches, and no more hangovers.

I had stopped taking magic mushrooms years ago, anyway, so was never really tempted by doing them again. Ecstasy is also a drug I had quit years before. There was the odd time here and there where I dabbled with an odd one, like at a mate's stag do or a special occasion, but they were very few and far between.

Just remembering back to my raving days, I was always fascinated with the different names of Ecstasy. There were white doves, speckled doves, postman pats, disco biscuits, double barrels, snowballs, victory V's, Mitsubishis, Rolls Royces, and the list goes on. It was the same with LSD tabs—peace trips, sonics, microdots, penguins—but my favourite was double-dipped strawberries. Whoever was the dealer that came up with that name was an astute one, because they became so popular just because somebody out of their nuts happened to say *double dipped*. Honestly, the whole rave scene at that time fell for that one. I have always pictured the makers standing over the barrel of acid and saying to one another, "Dip that strip in there again and instead of calling them *strawberries*, we'll call them *double-dipped strawberries*." Still makes me laugh, that one. So yes, the nineties rave scene was a time I'll never forget, a mad time of my life never to be repeated.

I also have dabbled with a bit of toot (cocaine), but never too much and never on a regular basis. It seemed to be a good drug at weddings, but back then it was too expensive to purchase. Don't get me wrong, I've had my fair share of it over the years, but this was probably the easiest drug ever to quit. It seemed to affect different people in different ways. Some got aggressive, some got happy, some danced, but nearly everybody would turn into stabbers. Couldn't shut them up even if you tried too. I was a wee stabber anyways, so I felt that sometimes it didn't really do anything for me.

Then there were ones who would lie a lot on it, or maybe a better word would be to *fantasize* on it. So as much as I did it over a few years, it was never an addictive drug to me, more of an occasional drug.

DMT is a drug I have only heard of recently, and I don't know anybody who has taken it. Something inside me thinks I would like to try it just to see what it's like, but then there's another side of me that says, *no, mate, it's too strong,* so I'll let that one go. I have got to a point in my life where I don't even have an energy drink anymore. Would have drunk Boost or Red Bull quite a lot, but even that has left me.

So, nothing passes through me anymore, and I have never been as busy with my life and living it in such a peaceful, honest, and loving way. Maybe the odd beer, but even that I just don't know, because my life's going in a completely different direction than it ever has, I mean entirely in a different way of living. For one, I'm writing this book. Never did I think I would ever do something like this and bare my whole soul for everyone to read, but this is what I am in the middle of doing, and if I can help somebody somewhere to change his or her way of living their lives in authentic truth and become awoken to who they really are, it will all be worth it.

CHAPTER 11

Best Matey to
Soul Brother

SO, I HADN'T seen my best matey in a while, as he lived in Scotland. You see, I had told him absolutely everything from the orange poofy evening. Then together, we experienced the fly-bys of two white UFOs. So, my memories are always good of this, as we got to do it together. In hindsight, it helped me much more than that, as not only did I get to experience it with him, but it gave him a bit of confirmation that something was out there and all the overloading information I was relaying to him at that time had some substance to it. Not once did he question me or not believe in what I was telling him. I think he was amazed by it all, just as much as I was, by experiencing the things I was beginning to go through spiritually at the beginning.

I know for sure if he was the one telling me all the stuff I had told him, I certainly would have found it very profound, so I do thank him from the bottom of my now active heart for being there and having the ears to listen to it all. I do call him *big ears* the odd time, as let's just say, they're not small in stature, but then again, he calls me Nosey in retaliation, so it's always swings and roundabouts with my best matey. I believe if you can't slag each other's stand-out stuff, hint hint nosey and earsy only for visionary purposes, and have a laugh about it, then where's the fun in it all?

Life is about having as many laughs about your faults as possible. Then you never look at them in this way. It's just a part of who you are. Isn't that right, big ears? Mind that he does live in Scotland; he used to hear the fire station alarm go off or even the police siren in Dungannon and knew something was up, just the same way I could smell his Chinese takeaway on a Friday night in his living room. As I said, it's swings and roundabouts in this game of life. O.K., Conrad, that's enough. No more slagging.

Colly was starting to ask me a lot of questions, and I could tell he wanted to learn more about it all for himself. So, we had decided that on the Saturday night, we would meditate together for the first time, as he was finding it hard to do by himself, with him listening to me about how intensifying my awakening was. Deep down, I knew he would have loved to have been experiencing the same thing, because we had already at this point put everything in motion to try to change our DNA, and we were living this new way of life to change our perspectives and becoming aware of what that entailed—the spiritual side of it all. He had told me that he was trying but to no avail. This was when I realized how lucky I was to be doing the things I was at that time.

So, it was about six o'clock on a Saturday night, and I got a phone call from a mate of mine who's a DJ. It was at this point where our plans got changed. He asked me if I could do him a favour and come down to his house to pick up some sort of massive speaker system, amplifier too, and bring it to a hotel for another DJ to use it. I knew Colly was coming round at 7:30 p.m., so I phoned another mate; I didn't want to burden Colly with it, as he was only over for the weekend. As it unfolded, my other friend couldn't do it, so I phoned Colly and asked him if he wanted to go for a spin with me to help me do it. Not only did he say yes, but he said he would drive.

So, he picked me up, and off we went to the DJ's house, which was in the opposite direction from the hotel. We were dropping it all off too, so it was a big drive. When we arrived, I could see why my DJ matey couldn't do it; he was celebrating something and was half-tight (tipsy drunk) and couldn't have driven. When we packed Colly's car, the whole back seat and boot filled completely up, so it was certainly more gear than we anticipated we had to deliver. But when he said the DJ's name was DJ X-ray, we both couldn't wipe the smiles off our faces, because he was one of our favourite DJs from our raving days. Truthfully, we couldn't believe our luck. From that point on, it had changed from *doing a favour* to *couldn't be happier to help*. Now it was a mission to finally meet X-ray after so many years.

It was one of the biggest blasts from the past any retired raver would dream of, and not only that, for being willing to do the favour in the first place, he handed me a bag of mandy for our troubles, as Colly had said he didn't want any money for fuel. Mandy is a psychedelic drug, for anybody out there that doesn't know, and it was at this stage of the night we began to come to terms with the fact that the universe was making this all happen for us to have the best night possible, one we certainly hadn't envisioned how it would go down.

The gear itself was half MDMA and half psychedelic, so it was one of feeling and visions, and I must admit not only was I excited, but we also both truly felt that it was all constructed in this way for us by the powers to be. What a belief system we were coming to have. So, I agreed there and then that metaphysically, it was magically manifested for us both.

So, all systems go. When in the car, we started chatting about meeting X-ray and how we would wait till we had dropped everything off and then we would need take some of the mandy. But I got this hint *take it now, and by the time we get there, we'll be buzzing.* Colly thought about it for a while (I say *while*, two seconds really), and then it was, "O.K., let's do it."

Sure enough, as we were pulling up to this hotel, *bang, boom, bingo*, it kicked in. X-ray was sitting in his car waiting with his girlfriend. They say sometimes when you meet your hero although he wasn't exactly our hero, he was the top DJ back in our raving days, that you get let down by what he is really like in person. In our case, that couldn't have been further from the truth. Not only him but also his girlfriend were the nicest people and couldn't have been more appreciative of us bringing all this stuff for him and helping bring it into the hotel.

I believe X-ray didn't say much for the first ten minutes, as these two retired country-ass ravers, one with a Scottish accent, began slabbering on a scale we hadn't before. And let me tell ya, we were already slabberers anyways, so it was tenfold *bang bang bang bang*, DJ this, music that, dancing this, sounds, moves, glowsticks, poppers, whistles, white gloves mixing, and even the dummy tit got a mention—anything that our now-active mandy brains could remember.

Honestly, I'll say it again, they were such a nice and bright couple, and Xray was so grateful he gives us a USB loaded with his music, in the shape of a cassette. Ironic, really, as back in the day, that's all we had. We both left as happy as two pigs in poo, buzzing away, and the night was still so young. To this day, his is the only phone number I have on my phone that begins with the letter X. Amazing, really.

So off we went like two peas in a pod, only really it was Colly B's now-empty Audi. We began to get excited about going back to the house to start meditating together. Only a couple of months back, not sure exactly as then I wasn't writing anything down with the intention of writing a book. Just for the record, with me telling Colly all my experiences, he was taken aback by it all. I remember that after I had told him some of the crazy things I was doing with my inner work, he just came out and said, "You should write a book on this." In hindsight, that probably was the seed set; I just I didn't know it at the time.

So, I remember stopping at the shop to get my children some treats, as they had been holding the fort as we were on this journey. With what I bought doubled by what Colly bought, to say they were over the moon ... spoiled, really. Let's just say, happy with what they got.

We went into my living room, put the chair over the door, took a fair bit of mandy out, and got it down our necks. As we were sitting slabbering away, I could feel it coming up, and it was the same with Colly. I said I would dim down the lights, which meant turning them off, as I had no dimmer switch. It just sounded better.

Now innerstand, we hadn't ever done this together and certainly weren't the type of spiritual practitioners who had crystals and sat down on our bottoms, legs crossed (not yet anyways). But we did begin to do our breathing work and close our eyes. I could already feel that things had started and had to think a little before closing my eyes. When I did, I just couldn't believe what I truly was witnessing—the amazing vision that was in front of me.

First, we were both in the room where I had been doing my work. There was no version of myself in the room, but it was filled up with bits of light flying around everywhere abundant with white light, you could say. This past couple of months, I had been doing my work on my feet, and this was no different. The only thing was that my best matey at the other side of the room was wearing the exact same suit that I was wearing, identical.

He was glowing up so bright it took me aback somewhat—but then, so was I. This was when I thought that the mandy really heightened the brightest of the white light, because he was so bright. The most profound thing, though, for me was he had some type of helmet mask around his face that I'd never seen before. In my inner work, I had thought they were working on some type of mask on me, but I couldn't really tell, nor could I see. What made me think this was that little angels would fly past my face and a light screen would follow them. But most of the time, they would stop at my ears.

So here I was watching my best matey, with the same white suit on as me, with beams coming from his hands and lights going in and out and all around him. I was asking him if he could see them, and he said no, but he was finding it hard to keep his eyes closed. He didn't tell me until later that he had his eyes open most of the time. I thought to myself, *Wow. If he could only see what was all around him at the time.*

I kept telling him what was happening, and especially what he was wearing. What had taken me so long to build, and here he was already fully suited and booted. I remember going over to him to get a better look. This is when I could see he was wearing a full head mask. It truly was amazing to witness.

At this moment, for me there seemed to be so much light darting everywhere, in and on the outside of this darkened room. I say *room*, but it was like a big yard, closed off by blackish matter of some sort. It's a bit hard to explain. I really began to get to work with this light. It was more animated to me than my usual work—brighter, shinier, and more of it—and so was the way I was collecting. It was happening super-fast.

The light itself had wisps of a smoky haze following it as it went into my hands, and when I had collected quite a lot, I would look up the ways and my eyes or my third eye, I just didn't know it, would form a big swirling hole, and I would let it all out with my hands and my mind. I repeated this for quite a while. Sometimes the beams of light coming out of my hand were like clouds of hula hoops made of white light, starting small and getting bigger as it left. It was truly magical at the time.

Colly and I were talking to each other all the time, and that's when he started to say he was moving a bunch of misty smoke around with his hands. I was watching him, and he was playing away with it. I could see there was a ball of fragmented light moving all around his hands. That's when he told me that his eyes were open and that he could see it better with them open. I was the opposite. I had mine closed nearly all the time.

Looking back, I remembered the work I had put into decalcifying my third eye—no fluoride toothpaste, sun-gazing all the time—and Colly hadn't really started doing this at the time. It took a while to collect all the light and release it, most of it upways, as Colly was mesmerized a little and was just content to play with it. On the other hand, I was busy, as there was so much light to be collected and released.

To experience such a thing with my best matey—this was the night he became my soul brother. To this day, we believe that we are brothers and sat at a table on the Metaphysical side of life and sorted our contracts long ago. I truly believe he is positioned in Scotland to shine his light and become a light worker.

We are all on different timelines on our journeys, and I used to be at him to do more, but you realize everybody's journey is their own, and as much as I pass him all my knowledge, ultimately, it's up to him to find and carry out his soul's purpose. I for one know that's when you practically must turn yourself inside out and relearn how to live your life with a completely new awareness, perspective, and go on an emotional rollercoaster where everything you thought was right you find out was not.

It was such an amazing night from start to finish, and still we felt it was mapped out for us by an unknown force. But I knew from then on, that Colly wanted to change his life exactly the way I had done and am still doing to this day. I now feel I am not only preparing what the rest of my life is going to be like to create my heaven on this earth, it is also getting me ready for what is going to happen in the next one, when my timeline is up on this earth and my energy is ready to move on to the next chapter of my soul's journey.

I felt at this time that I was starting to connect to a version of self on a deeper level and enter a form of spiritual wealth—an awakening to the divine realm and a stronger connection to the source of everything. Truthfully, it's a feeling of feelings never experienced. So, after we turned the light on and gathered ourselves, Colly wanted to go outside to smoke one of his rollies.

It was at this point, as we were standing outside my door, that there was a big crack, and I realized I had stepped on something. I turned on my porch light and saw that I had stepped on a snail. But something was strange about the glow coming from it. To this day, I don't know what made me say to Colly, "I'm gonna take a picture of that." Turned my flash on and took a snap. Oh, my goodness—what we were looking at was a war going on between light and dark. It was truly an amazing sight. The mandy we had consumed animated it at the time and made it so clear. Where I had trodden on the snail, it was all shiny white, and in the roughness of my path there was so many dark ghouls we could see, so many sets of eyes.

When we focused on the picture, it looked like the whole cosmos. We were gobsmacked. I'm so glad I still have the pictures, as nobody would believe such a thing.

Then suddenly, where Colly was standing, *crack*! He had stepped on one down my garden path. Straight away, the phone came out, flash on, and snap! I took another picture. As much as it was a different scene, we had a battle going on with light and dark, with patterns on the back of the snails, letters, electric lightning, everything, and on the side, at the edge of the picture, there was a green leaf, which to us looked like Mother Earth (with a flatbed nose) in shackles.

That's when we thought that Mother Earth had sacrificed these two snails to show us what was going on under the earth and in the cosmos. I know we were both on mandy; that's why I am so glad my intuition told me to take the pictures, or we would have no record of it, only in our heads. We couldn't shut up or put the phone down for at least an hour. At that moment, I could easily have become a professional photographer, but as quickly as the thought entered my head, it had already left.

What an amazing night to spend with Colly, and one I won't forget in a hurry. To begin a journey, you always must take that first step. I watched an interview with Michael J. Fox, and the words he spoke still reverberate in my mind, and I thought this would be a poignant time to use them: "With gratitude, optimism is sustainable. If you can find something to be grateful for, then you have something to look forward to, so you can carry on."

So Colly, thank you for being a rock when I was a sponge, because true growth requires the courage to release the past and step into the unknown with the welding of truth by your side.

CHAPTER 12

Soul Family and
My Dad's Ten Francs

IT WAS A Friday evening, and I was starting to get just a tiny bit comfortable working with a version of myself. As I began meditating at this active time, I had only to go to my living room and turn off the light. If it was early evening, I would pull the curtains, close my eyes, and there he was—it really was that quick—and off we would go. So, at this stage, I had been doing it for quite a while and thought I kinda knew what was coming, and for a part, that's the way it went.

There is a movie I watched called *Lucy* with Scarlett Johansson (beautiful) as the lead actress. At the end, she eventually turns into this black matter. In my inner work with a version of myself, that's what the walls, roof, and floor looked like, with a load of gaps that I could see through but not big enough to fall out or get through them. It was at this time that there were so many moving lights inside this sort of chamber but also so much flying around the outside of it, where I couldn't see anything but blackness.

So, as it started, I began to collect the lights moving in around me—some fast, some slow, but generally easy enough to collect. At this stage, there were at least five or six wee tiny angel fairies flying about my head and shoulders, and as I worked, they would come and sprinkle their lights on me. My ears would buzz and hum, at different levels of noise, and it was the same as the tingles on my face. They too would sometimes be a lot more animated and even last for quite a while all around my face. I had always thought this was some type of reward for collecting the light. It was at this time, and after experiencing seeing my best matey with a mask in our work, that one night I began to realize it was building or making some type of mask for me.

The only time I could get a gap in this matter was when I was releasing the light out through the palms of my hands. Also, I was beginning to not just use physical action in releasing the light but using the power of my mind to do it also. When I had done this, the roof would close in automatically, and it would be the black matter again—instantaneous, really. The light that was going around the outside I would have to follow with my hands just to try to get it to slow down a little. Also, I had to join my hands together for it to work, as one hand didn't seem strong enough to slow it down. Sometimes if I broke my mindful concentration on trying to catch it, it would escape and fly off, and I would have to start over again.

When you are doing something like this night after night, it's not like the magical aspects of what you're doing leave you, but you do become so focused on getting it done. You realize it's the same bits of light from the night before that you couldn't seem to catch. Then it becomes a mission to you to get it done and move on to the next stage, whatever that may be.

Then, doubled with the fact that you would forget what you were doing and often go off course and be mesmerized by it all, you start playing with the light, like a video game, and shining it on yourself to make your body glow even brighter. I must admit, I did this quite a lot. But when you do it for so long, the light would fly past you so close but so quick that it made you jump. Primarily, I think it was to get your attention back on what you were supposed to do and free this light up.

I recall there was one bit of light that was so fast and small, it took me maybe three nights just to catch it. It was on the outside of this matter. When I finally got it to slow down, hands outstretched, full concentration just to get it to come into me through the black wall and into the chamber with me, it took me maybe five minutes to get it into my hands fully. There was so much bright light within it. I was beginning to learn the concept that the smaller and hardest-to-catch bits of light were the biggest and brightest and held the most light within.

At this time, I wasn't flying anywhere and realized even the version of myself wasn't there, just me working in this chamber. At that moment, my memory is that I really needed to go to the toilet. So, I was blinking my way through the bottom of my house to get to the toilet. Eventually I made it, but I managed not to break the visions and actions I was doing in my living room. I hadn't done this before, and truthfully, I couldn't believe it worked.

It was a number two that I needed, so I did all the things you do to sit on the bowl, and with my bottom bathroom only consisting of a toilet and a very small sink, it was all very enclosed. But as soon as I was inside, I closed the door, and the lights really took off—and so many of them, too.

This was the first time I did my inner work in my downstairs bathroom, my tracksuit bottoms and boxers to my ankles, collecting light, getting sprinkled, having a dump all at the one time. It's funny when I look back on it now, but at the time, I remember I just didn't want to start from scratch again. As the toilet up the stairs was getting used by my Jasmine, Ameila, my youngest daughter, wanted to use the toilet I was in, and I told her to wait a wee while. Fifteen minutes later, she started shouting at me, "Dad, what's keeping you so long?" And before I knew what I'd said, I told her it was stuck and hard to get out.

So here I was, eyes closed, collecting light, getting light sprinkled on my face, bags to the ankles, doing a poo, and having a full conversation with my daughter about hurrying up. At this point, I just know my spirit guides were having a good old laugh at my expense.

I think I could have been in there a good half an hour, maybe more. It was as if they knew, and it began to all slow down a bit. So, it was at this time I finally cleaned myself and went back to the living room, having a laugh to myself. Such a surreal experience, and one that I had to think for a while whether I was going to write about. But I live by truth, so I just had to, embarrassing or not.

When I got back into my living room, I realized for the first time what actual time it was. It was 12.30 a.m., and I had been at it from at least seven o'clock that night. When you are doing and experiencing magical stuff like this, time is of no essence. It just seems to fly by.

It was just a few days before this that, when I was speaking to her on Facebook, Joanne Honey Thomas said something to me about my soul family trying to prepare me for something and how their love for me was so intense. That hadn't left my head since. So it was at this time that I was standing up and meditating on speaking to my soul mother. When I began doing this, I started experiencing a wave of emotion out of the blue. It was just tears rolling down my cheeks. Gradually, as I looked around my living room, I seemed to be surrounded by shiny people, all with bald heads, wearing shiny suits.

The best way to explain this is that at first, they all looked like the hitman outta the same-named movie franchise. At the start, I'll admit it was a tad frightening, as I wasn't expecting anything like that. I wasn't expecting to see anything. Right in front of me, I could make out womanly features on one of them—suit on and bald head, I could still clearly see this was a woman. All their faces were lit up at the top, but as I looked down, I couldn't see from their waist down, nor could I see the floor, just blackness.

I saw that her hands were raised a little. All their hands were raised a little and glowing white—not super-glowing, but enough that I could see them all. Hazy white is probably a better way to describe them.

Beside this woman was a man who was the same height, but I could clearly see was a man. I got the feeling, going by her hands were gesturing, that she wanted to hold mine. So, I raised mine up, and mine too were glowing just like all of theirs. We both held each other's hands, like properly holding hands, no feeling of a grip, just hands on hands. I began to calm instantly, and it was then I realized how happy I was feeling.

Looking at this woman's face, it dawned on me that this was my soul mother. She was smiling at me and looked so happy, and I began to cry uncontrollably, tears streaming, but such a happy feeling I got doing this. It was like seeing someone I knew and hadn't seen in years. That's how I felt, and it was then I realized my eyes were fully open. I could see my curtains behind them, as there was a bit of light shining through.

They all looked so happy. I went to the man next and held his hands, to try to paint this picture to you. I cried the whole time and was aware I was doing it, and I couldn't have stopped if I had tried. I went and did this with them all. My thoughts at this time were that I was seeing my soul mother, soul father, two soul sisters, and two soul brothers, and felt each of them, not physically but emotionally, as I did it in turn. When I say they were all smiling, I mean they looked so happy, so happy. I in turn couldn't have been more joyful and happy, and not one bit scared, even though here I was in my living room, experiencing such a magical moment with them all.

I was still amazed at what was going on all around me. When I got back to the start, to my soul mother, still smiling from ear to ear, that's when they all started to disappear from the room. But it wasn't like *puff,* and they just vanished; it was more of a gradual thing as they slowly, from being around me, were all standing beside each other in front of me, disappearing gradually into the blackness of my living room, till they were no more. I was just glued to the same spot, opening and closing my eyes, still in wonderment about what had just happened with my eyes half closed and half open. truly it was then I felt blessed in some way. There was never a sound, not one, just the vision of everybody smiling.

I'm still a bit dumbstruck when I think back to that moment with them. And I will be forever grateful to Joanne Honey Thomas, just for messaging me that text about my soul family, because I don't think I would have connected the dots or had the experience for that matter if she hadn't. Thank you, Joanne, always love and light.

This reminds me of the first post I did on Joanne's page:

LOVE AND LIGHT, LIGHT AND LOVE LET YOUR LOVE SHINE AND YOUR WHOLE WORLD LIGHTS UP.

Something close to that I think, and my heart.

When I turned the light on, my living room looked so bright and hazy compared to what I had been seeing all night. This is when I truly sat down and forgave my birth mother for leaving me as a four-year-old child. I filled rivers that night talking to my soul and truly forgiving my mum and asking my soul to speak to her soul and tell her that it was meant to happen that way, it was all planned before we even sat foot on this earth. At the end of the day, I wouldn't be here to live this life on earth if it wasn't for her. Even though we didn't get to spend much of it together, she'll always be my birth mum.

My dad was the only person in my family I had told I was getting spiritually awoken. He was seventy-seven years old at this stage had been set in his ways all his life. As much as he listened to me, I could see in his eyes that he didn't really believe what I was saying to him. But I could tell that he was at least happy for me, because I told him I had quit smoking cigarettes and pot, quit drinking, quit taking substances, started my own business, and was gonna be the first millionaire in the family. I was so glad that I had got it off my chest and told him, whether he believed me or not at this stage.

The next day, my brother's son had qualified for the All-Ireland Championship knockout boxing tournament down in Dublin, and I was driving with my dad to watch him fight. As I was the only one with Euros, I paid Dad into the tournament. Now as much as Blair lost his fight, it was a big learning curve for him at that stage of his career, and I could see he would go far in the boxing game.

The reason why I'm telling you about this is that I was down to my last five Euros, and I wanted a cup of tea. As I went to the toilet, I gave my father the five Euro note and asked him to get us a cup of tea each from this little kitchen window where it was being sold. I came back from the toilet, and he handed me my tea and gave me my change. Cut a long story short, I put it in my pocket and never thought any more about it.

So, when I got home and was putting the Euros back in a little tub where I kept all my Euro coins, I noticed that one of the coins was different from the rest. Under closer inspection, I realized it was ten francs, a French coin that looked like a one Euro coin. I had a little laugh, as my dad had got stroked, for what he thought was one Euro was actually ten francs.

I flicked the coin over and what was on the front was an angel with wings. I couldn't believe what I was seeing, especially as I could see it was a male angel due to its private parts showing. Now to anybody else, it maybe wouldn't have meant much more than getting stroked by a tea maker in Dublin at a boxing tournament, but for me, given what I had told my dad, to get a coin with a male angel on it seemed to mean something. Never had I ever come across a coin with an angel on it, never mind a male one. I hadn't really given much thought to angels most of my life, and somewhere in the recesses of my ignorant mind I had thought they were all women.

So, I began to delve deeper into the coin, and where else but Google would give me the answers. It was a French ten francs 1989, and the angel on the front was a representation of the génie de la liberté (in English, "the spirit of freedom"), a sculpture located at the top of the July Column in Paris, flanked by the letters R and F, initials of the French Republic. The reverse of the coin was the face value, crossed out with wide stripes, and surrounded by the French motto "Liberté, Égalité, Fraternité," meaning in English "Liberty, Equality, Fraternity" (brotherhood).

I would never have chosen even to investigate such things if it hadn't been for my dad receiving this coin on our behalf, so I just had to find out more. For the people reading this and maybe only beginning to innerstand it a little more, just like myself, I wanted to find out more of what the "spirit of freedom" was, and this is what I found.

For many people beginning to embrace an inner standing of what spirituality is, first and foremost it does not mean living your life as a hermit, alone or far off from society, in isolation and seclusion apart from all other beings, that as individual people could be presumed a recluse. The whole point of spirituality is to plant the seeds of love for all humankind. To spread peace, joy, harmony love and unity amplifying the birth of consciousness through a coherent heart and becoming one with the mind.

In the movie "Braveheart" were Mel Gibson shouts aloud "They may take our lives but there will never take are FREEDOM, but this alone does not mean freedom, it is merely mouthing the word itself. Nobody on this earth has absolute freedom. Pre-planned wars are fought Democracy and politics are formed interlaced with globalism and capitalism, then governed to liberate one country from another is what widely constitutes freedom. This is not real freedom but a consideration of it which embodies the analytical mind. A demonstration or an expression of a focused outcome. What gives meaning to freedom is unity, without it, it is equally equivalent to having no value. Freedom is not related to anything, anywhere are in any place but in divinity itself. Freedom consists in the recognition of divinity, a culmination to the inner realization of knowing your connection with everything.

Knowledge of who you truly are and where your being originates from is fundamentally essential. "As in microcosm, so in macrocosm." The microcosm being the part and macrocosm is the universe. As above so below. Through the educational emptiness of modern impractical and unhelpful deceit to the then doctrine dished out from an early age, man and woman don't fully know who their true self is. When asked "what is your name, who are you" and you answer your name. Is that truly who you are, are just a name given to you by your parents when born or is it the name of your body. Maybe it is a nameless avatar ensembled within a suit of skin. Who is it that is protected on the inside. This is truly who you are. You are the heart.

On Earth everything is different but is also the same. In the universe and within the cosmos differences can be found. Big and small, good and bad, light and dark, love and hate, truth and lies, and happiness alongside sadness. Complexities in the magic that endures at the beginning and that which will not prevail in the end, has only anything that can be acknowledged in the present and for a short period existent in the middle.

We are one we have always been one and always will be one. When unawakened to the freedom of the mind, with no explorations or questions of spiritual awareness. To that of only a logical mindset, enslaved in the usage of half the brain never deliberately questioning bondage and freedom. The servitude and subjugation of an unknown spiritual cerebrum. An intellect and psyche never able to discover oneself. Only by knowing your true self can you achieve real freedom from your soul. The human body is therefore treated as the manifestation of the mind. Within the laws of nature no-one can claim to be free to act as he pleases. To live on the laws of the land and in the laws of the sea so deceptive to the manipulation at times vigorously enforced with its only purpose secretly to control. No-one can truly be free, physically on the body and mindfully with your thoughts. Freedom contains a formulation, a declaration of what comes through the heart regarding anyone, anything, anywhere and at any time. This is true freedom, spirituality itself is freedom.

Consciousness itself is true freedom. The divinity of the divine, the self-actualization of "You are one with source and source is one with you" as the spark is enclosed within the heart. To begin to live a life that glows with the energies of kindness, warmth and honesty. To awake the awaiting soul that has been encased deep within a cocoon in the recesses of a controlled mind under a program before you were birthed in your mother's womb and not only coming to terms with the enlightenment of healing oneself, but to know that we have been evolving within a 15-dimensional time matrix for eons. Already sustained Compactified Dimensions existing upon one another in this universe where upon you must begin to inner stand the deciphering of one's spiritual principles. Vibrating on different levels and different frequencies within a holographic conscious entity and within again, truly a numberless number of dimensional layers, yet unseen on this earthly realm. To have the freedom of that given gift to open ones third eye and see through all the illusions displayed at every turn, beginning the exclusion of worship deep within our D.N.A. Realizing that source is you and you are source with a difference were there is no room for the notion of duality. This concept will then become your living reality.

The resonance of the sound of every word has greater merit and virtue, more than the common man and woman were ever taught. Truth is the life breath of speech. Your connection within the everything of the nothingness "The ether." Realizing that sheathed within your existence a spark is contained, a universe entrenched deep inside, hidden from your conscious thoughts but has been patiently waiting to be unshackled from its dormancy. Biologically and emotionally confined only then to ascend through the freedom of spirituality, to truly grasp what it means to walk in your light and with true freedom let it shine.

You cannot walk in the light of another it is up to you to consciously ignite your own spark that internally and infinitely is waiting to enlighten your soul." The spirit of freedom"

My dad doesn't even know what receiving that coin has meant to me. I have studied and received great knowledge and truly know what freedom means—not only that, but how to authentically live in this way. There are no mistakes in life, only lessons, and I truly am getting to a time in my life when I do finally love myself at least 98 per cent of the time. I don't think I'll ever get that 2 per cent made up because I'm not perfect. Truly, I don't seek perfection, and I wouldn't be me if I was 100 per cent anyways.

I have told my dad that we are all energy and never die, only change form and move on. I also told him when he goes to the other side, where his mum and dad will be waiting on him with open arms, they will tell him that Conrad was right, and he should have believed me. It's nice that I can be honest with him, but also, I would love for him to connect back to source himself and when he is an angel come back and say *Hi, Son, I love you*. Just in the same way I love him. I'll even go as far as to thank the tea maker in Dublin for offloading that coin to my dad that day.

Synchronicities from my angels are happening quite regularly nowadays, but this one, to go from the north of one country to its south and pick up this coin, not only shows me what the angels do for me and why I have so much unconditional love for and from them, it warms my heart even further knowing what is waiting for me on the other side. When you truly have no fear of death because you know within that you truly never die, this is when you really start living a life worth living.

CHAPTER 13

Ten Mes and I

BEFORE I SHARE this chapter, let me say that I'm not sure how long it took me to go through all of this. I wasn't writing anything down at the time, let alone thinking of writing a book about it all. So, I am not too sure how long it took, but if I was to do an educated guess, between two to three weeks, as that was the most active time off doing any of my inner work so far. I didn't know it back then, but what I was about to go through was the most magical, intense, consuming, tiresome, trippy, exciting, emotionally busy, dark, light, bright, practicing, crazy time of my life up to that point.

I had been doing a lot of inner work with my double for quite some time now, and each time there would always be some tasks to carry out. This past while, it seemed to be building something, though what I did not know. I was always turning and doing different things with my hands. Truthfully, I fell down a few times, as I just got well into it, and sometimes I would have done two 360-degree turns. My twin would have not gone round once. I was just so excited and found it hard to settle down at times. I was always looking at him to try to copy him exactly, so I would spin my body around and then quickly my head, so I didn't lose sight for too long.

Then it all changed forever in a way that at first, I found so shocking, it took me a while to grasp my situation. Whenever I had worked with, I will now call him my *higher self*—because I truly believe that's who he was, a version higher than me at least—the focal point was my fireplace, as that's where he would always be standing.

So, when I closed my eyes, I straight away could see that something was truly up, and as much as he was in line with my fireplace, he was so much closer to me. Not only that, but there were also loads of him. To say I was shocked is really the biggest innerstatement ever. I was so taken aback at this, my head was spinning so fast, I thought I was going to faint. Once I had come to my senses and began to settle down, if you could call it that, I stopped turning in all directions, looking at everybody. I didn't think the intensity levels could go up anymore, yet here I was.

Now the one who was always working with me was so much brighter than the rest, and I just was staring at him, and he was doing the same back, smiling away. He looked to be laughing, probably at the look on my face. I truly was taken aback, and at first, I hadn't a clue what to do. As much as the higher self in front of me was the brightest, I could see them all, each wearing the exact same clothes as the one next to him. I could see the whole figure, from head to toe, fully bodied men, the whole lot.

So, after a bit, I circled around, and I had to count them. It took me a couple of goes, but eventually, I was certain that there were ten altogether, identical to one another. All gold light in colour, gold yellowish, but more goldy—I hope that makes sense, because on the night when this first happened, I just couldn't take it all in, never mind making any sense of it, or what even I had to do.

This is when I noticed that there were no wee fairy angels flying around me, not one. I was so used to them now being a part of my energy work that I was missing them a little, and with still no clue what to do, I'd have been happier if they'd showed up. When doing this kind of work with your third eye (pineal gland), for its part, I really could have called it my first eye now and my other eyes the second and third, because that's all I was using. For someone who hadn't done this before, somehow, I wasn't the worst now, believing in myself more and more about what I was doing almost every night.

Just like my soul family, I could see the brightest me was holding his hands up a bit. I never heard anything, but I got the feeling he wanted to hold hands. Just to let you know, every time I would do a 360-degree turn, I would always stop directly where I knew was my fireplace, always. When my hands were closed, I could see that my hands were bright and had small white beams coming out. When our hands got close, there was an exchange of light. So, light would come out of his hands and into my hands, but that was it.

I really was like a fish out of water on that first night. I would start with him and then quickly do a 360-degree circle around, keeping my hands exactly still and at the same level. Once I got back to the brightest me, I would stop and exchange light. I don't know how long I had been doing this, but eventually instead of just turning in a circle, I stopped at the one who was 180 degrees in my turn and realized I could exchange light with him also. Again, I don't know how long I did this, stopping with just about every one of them and exchanging light through our hands, but there didn't really seem to be anything happening to me, for me, or to them.

Like a fish out of water, more like a whale out of the bathtub, I was so clueless at the beginning. It was at this stage that I was getting tired, so tired that when yawning, tears would drip down my cheeks. I finally broke it off, checked my phone, and saw that it was 1:30 a.m. and I had to get up for work, so I went straight to bed. I didn't know it at the time, but it was going to get hard to define which work I was doing, as it would feel as if I had two jobs soon enough. Tired and not tired, I was excited about what I was doing, even though I fully didn't know what that was yet.

The next day at work, I couldn't wait to get home just to see what awaited me in my living room. So quickly, the night would come. It was as if I was skipping through the days now. So many different things I was doing in the daytime, never mind the night.

At this stage, I was super-concentrated in trying to keep my vibration high and in good spirits as much as I could, which wasn't easy at times, trying to be positive in all the daily challenges that would crop up at unexpected moments. Just by being aware of when the overthinking mind and the programmed thoughts would arise, I was beginning to transmute that shit quickly—not all the time, but certainly more than before. Thinking about what was going to happen later, when I started my inner work, I would have gone on social media a lot in the evenings. So, this period of my life was completely consumed in trying to figure out my purpose in all of this.

I began to set a mental timetable of how my days and nights were unfolding. The more it went on, the stricter I got with myself, but I was always happy to be doing it. Excitement filled my mind daily, and I was beginning to practise with my thoughts about how the energy work would pan out later.

It was the second night with ten of me and myself, standing in the exact same position as the night before. Off I went like a madman eager to get going, but with no real rhythm or pattern to what I was doing or trying to achieve. All that deep thinking at work all day went straight out the window due to the magical exciting light show I was standing in the middle of. Though once I settled, after a while I did begin to concentrate that little bit harder. So, this started a bit like a fluke. Maybe it was intuition or inner wisdom, I don't know. It seemed to me at the time like a lucky fluke.

What I did was slow way down. I went to the second me and, with my hands lighting up (they were always lit up, so I'll not say that anymore), I pointed them at his feet and guided my hands right up his whole body, slowly. When I got to his head, something seemed to happen, like a stream of light from him to me, coming from his face and going around mine. This was something different.

When that had settled down and was less bright around my face, I went to the third one and did the same. Once I got up to his head, his light would come across to my face. To explain it better, it was a bit like a video game with screens of white light around my face. And then to the fourth to do the exact same thing.

Some of the light would go around my face, but as I progressed to number five, it started going above my head. I was still doing the exact same thing for number six and seven, but when I got to numbers eight and nine, it was all happening behind my head. Sometimes I would turn around and look, because I couldn't see what was going on, just the illumination of all the lights. I knew something was happening, but I soon realized that it was safer to look at myself in front of me.

When I got back to the very start and the brightest one, I did the same with him. As I got up to his head, my ears began buzzing loudly, with clicks and pulsing around my head, and then it stopped. That's when I really believed I had some sort of light screen in front of my eyes, or it could have been my whole face and even my whole head from the neck up. Something inside me was telling me I had just built a mask or even a helmet of some sort all around my head.

This is when somewhere in my mind, I thought I was getting somewhere. So straight away, I began to start the same process again, but when I got to his head, as much as it was lighting up, nothing came to me. There was no exchange. One thing was for sure: my line of sight was a little brighter.

I remember going to different ones of me and trying a multitude of things, and as much as they would glow up, I didn't believe much was happening. There were loads happening, but in my mind, I didn't think I was really progressing to the next thing. I never knew what that would have been, but I sure as hell was not giving up.

Frustrated at times, *confused* is another word that pops up, I was always trying. Then, when I got to number three and got a small indication that he was raising his hands up a little, and how I got this was he was looking at me and then looking down at his own hands, I just thought he was raising his eyebrows a little, like a gesture to me.

I had nothing to lose and would try anything, so I opened my hands and matched them up to his, and this light came swirling around my hands, clearly coming from his. *O.K., this is different,* I thought, and certainly better than me turning and twisting in all directions trying to make something happen. So, with a concentrated surge of energy, I went to number four. I don't know whether this is right or wrong, but for writing purposes, it certainly is much easier for me to number them like this, and I think I'll start using this format on paper. So, I did the same with number four, then five, six, seven, eight, and nine. It was when I got to ten that it got a lot quicker. The light began to move around my hands and wrists so much faster, emitting even more light and at the same time it seemed like shimmering sparkles.

Then finally, when I went to number one, like the original most bright me, I did the same, and as the light came from him, it was fast and brighter. Once it had settled down and he himself lowered his hands, I was left with a very bright radiate glow. It's better explained like a pair of gloves now. It was around my whole hands back and front, like little lines of wire mesh, something much the same as a butcher would use only the gloves were made of a numerous amount of small, very thin lines of light.

Then of course, me being me, I started playing with my newfound gloves and forgot all about what I was trying to achieve. But to me, this *was* an achievement, a magical one. My excitement was just so hard to quell at times. Also, to concentrate for so long, even at the time you're doing it, you get lost not only on the time but that you are standing in the middle of your living room physically, but mentally I'm certainly somewhere else in a blacked-out room, with no walls or ending to be seen, in the middle of a circle with ten of me, and one of them brighter than every other one. I was nearly going to start to call him *the fireplace one*, because that's where he was always standing. I truly didn't know if I was in another dimension or whether they were in my mind and coming out as total out-of-body-experience visually onto my living room floor.

Exhaustion from doing my inner work didn't really build on me gradually that much. My mind was so entwined and caught up in the moments of what I was doing that it just went *bang!* from working away to yawning, where if you didn't stop yourself and start shaking your head about a bit you would have got a locked jaw. I hope this makes at least a little bit of sense, how tired you got doing this. I knew it was time to wrap it up, and as much as there was never a squeak of sound, I would still thank them for turning up and doing this with me for me, and all around me.

Tired or not, it always took a little while to settle down after doing it, and I do remember lying in bed that night thinking, *Right, I have some sort of helmet or mask, and now I've got a pair of gloves that glow with thin lines of light, yet somehow, I must get to sleep.* Another thing I was doing was drinking a pint glass of water after all this, as you really did get so parched; the dryness made you do it. Truthfully, your tongue would have been sticking to the roof of your mouth. You were so dry, never mind the sharp sore head you would get, I think from concentrating so hard.

I always woke up the very next morning and would lie in bed and run it all through my mind about what I got up to, and only then would I lie back and let the realization and magnitude of what I was doing hit me, sometimes in a good way—I would get emotional about it—and at other times I would say, *Why me?* thinking about the mistakes I thought I was making. This is when my frustration would leave me and I would go back to *There are no mistakes, only lessons.* Thank you, Joanne.

The days seemed to be moving so fast now, and as much as I was doing a day's work, coming home, making dinner, cleaning up, washing clothes, doing all my daily chores, I knew that once I started my now-nightly process, I wouldn't stop. I would have two bottles of water, one on the fireplace and one on the table, so I knew exactly where they were sitting, and I didn't have to open my eyes to get to them.

This was the beginning of me getting prepared and ready. As a painter and decorator, I always worked on the 5P principle: Perfect Planning Prevents Pathetic Performance. I had gotten this from my sales-rep days but had incorporated it into my daily work, and now it was part of my nightly work. So, it was very useful to me throughout my working life. That said could easily add Prolonged Presence Persistence Perseverance and Passion to the list. I wasn't hyperactive or anything, I just had this renewed energy every day. Even though each day was filled with things to do, I never can remember getting too tired. It was as if something was giving me extra energy to do it all. I didn't think like this at the time, only in hindsight.

So night was upon me again and away I went, nearly down to a tee. It would basically start me off where I had ended the night before, not exactly but near enough. It was on this third night that it started to get a little different as to what would happen when I used my hands on not only the mes around me but when I directed my hands on myself. So, this was probably the first night I didn't let the moment get the best of me and was fully concentrated from the off. I had thought all day at work about what I was going to do, but like always, nothing went to plan. Well, my plan that I had tried to conjure up in my head all day—straight out it went with the kitchen sink and all.

I was at least beginning to feel a wee bit more switched on, or so I thought. I know this might sound surreal, but I was beginning to go round and welcome and thank them all for not only turning up but for trying to help me, as I believed that's what they were there to do. Truthfully, sometimes I found it so hard and confusing, I would give off a bit. Now I look back and realize that was so stupid of me, but at the time, it was hard, even though now I know they expected nothing of me. It was me who was humanly hard on myself, and that old programming of always deflecting blame from yourself onto others subconsciously. I know that now, but still it's what I did.

Slowly but surely, all these things were being brought up from the pits of my mind, and I was getting better at not only recognizing them but dealing with them with a positive attitude—something that takes a lot of practise, as unknowingly throughout your life you do it with a negative mind-set.

So, introductions out of the way, I had thought that day that I would start with number four, as I had a small inkling that there was beginning to be some sort of pattern to all of this. So as much as number four was glowing up as I ran my hands all around him, nothing seemed to be doing anything different—until, that is, I knelt over and went down to his feet. The lights began to get brighter and swirl a little faster, so I went closer with my hands, and sure enough, the exchange went down, and I felt great within myself that in some way I had worked out a small mathematical phase in my head.

I did the same with number five and so on right until I got back to number one—but with number one, nothing happened. *Oh no, here we go again.* So much for being a mathematician; that didn't last very long. Determined not to get frustrated and to try to enjoy the magic that was happening right in front of me, I went back to number four and, sure enough, scanned him all over. Not until I got to his feet did the light exchange take place. Instead of moving on to number five, I scanned four again. Still, nothing happened. So, I turned my hands on myself but started at my own feet, and *bingo, bango, bongo*, the light from my gloved-up hands went straight to my feet. *Wow!* I thought to myself. *O.K., let's do this with them all.* And so, after numbers five, six, seven, eight, nine, and then ten, eventually I got back to number one.

You must inner stand, it took quite a while to do all these energy of light exchanges with every one of me. For numbers five, six, seven, and eight, I don't think I even looked up once. It was all done bent over in the taking from their feet to mine. But something inside me started to feel I was neglecting a part of them, so I would start getting up and thanking each one after the exchange.

When I got to Mr Shiny Fireplace (original bright me), the noise kicked off within my eardrums, like a ringing gentle buzzing. I was beginning to feel it was like a completion of that circle of light collecting. When it was settled a bit, I looked down, and sure enough, up to the top of my shins was like a glowing pair of boots. It just looked like snug boots, if I'm to be honest. But they were shining much brighter than my knees and thighs. That's how I could tell the difference, that I had done something and completed it in a way.

After Mr Shiny Fireplace me, I would go to numbers two and three and do the same, and this would make them glow even brighter still. I can't wait to talk to someone who has also done this just to ask them how they got through it, how they felt about it all, and how many lessons they went through, but also how long it took them. If you truly innerstand what I was doing, it was taking ages to try to decipher it all, only at the time of doing it, you don't realize this as you're so highly concentrated in the actual magic of each phase that presents itself to you. Even to your own fascination of what your thinking, feeling, seeing, combined with your connected emotions to it all, while at the same time trying to remain calm, I will admit it wasn't easy at times.

I was so excited about my accomplishments so far, I went straight to number five, and my thought at the time was that if something happened with me and to me, I would reach the halfway mark, as there were ten of me. I didn't have to wait long, I thought at the beginning anyway. I started to scan number five of me, and straight away, as I started to, my hands followed him the whole way up to his head. It really stopped at his neck, though, and the lights were going everywhere around him. It was as if my hands had activated his whole body, and then the lights started coming over to me. But this time, it wasn't exactly through my hands; some of it was, but a lot was just coming over. Again, this was something different, so I just went with the flow of things.

Truly, the magic of all these things happening simultaneously was so exciting to me. How I was handling it all so well took even me back a little. I felt so comfortable in doing this all; I mean, I wasn't even the slightest bit frightened, and to this day I don't know why. I'm sure it could have been overwhelming to others. I'm sure even reading this, you must be thinking *If that was me, I'd be bricking it.* But there I was. It was just so magical, it truly was.

So as the light was landing on me, it was going everywhere around me, from my neck to down round to my knee. It was, yes, going round me, but on me at the same time. Mesmerized, I was watching this light grow on me. The best way to describe it was like hundreds of little ants made of light crawling and seamlessly flowing on and around me, and when there were enough, they would settle down and stop moving and just stay there. This was going on around my back too—I just couldn't see it, but I watched it crawl around. I did get to see it go round my butt, as I could arch my back and twist my head to look. It was settling there, too, so I presumed it was happening on my back also.

When there was no more moving light, I eventually went to number six, and it started all over again. Only this time, though much the same thing happened to me, a lot of the little ants of light stayed at my chest and more went down my arms and shoulders. Then number seven, and it would do the exact same thing, only stay round my belly and my sides more. As I was making my way back to the Shiny Fireplace Me (number one), the exchange got brighter, and it was only with this one of me that my ears would buzz and fuzz a little.

I was really beginning to light up from head to toe now. In writing this, I don't want to make it sound so formal, or like it was a normal thing to be doing. I knew and was well aware how magical it was. I truly was building something around me, an energized suit of some kind.

As I would always finish the process of going round the full ten mes, I went to numbers two, three, and four, and was then amazed how I looked after the hundreds of little light ants had settled and stopped. I would use my hands on myself, and for the first time to me, it really did look like a suit of armour of some sort, with hundreds of lights on it, so small that they looked like full continuous lines of light everywhere. It was only when I put my hands close to my own body that I could see the magnification of all the tiny littles packed or stacked tightly together segments of light in a now lovely pattern around me.

I was so taken aback by all this that for at least ten minutes, I couldn't stop looking at myself. When I realized this, I started looking around me, and all ten of me were smiling from ear to ear looking at me. I don't know if it was a reflection on me smiling and being so happy or they were so happy for me, but I remember at this moment getting a little emotional about the whole thing.

That didn't last long, as the tears that were rolling down my face started to become tears of tiredness. That's when the thought jumped into my mind: *What time is it?* It was 2:30 a.m. I had one last look at my brightly lit-up body and eventually broke the contact off and necked a pint glass of water. As far as my recollections go, I didn't even brush my teeth. It was up the stairs, have a sit-down pee, and straight to the sack. I remembered nothing till my alarm the next morning. I woke up that little more dazed and groggier this time, but again, up and at it was always my attitude, and that's what I did

My mind was so fresh, with me being lit up. Already, as I was having my eggs and toast, my mind was beginning to focus on what was going to happen later that night. I hadn't even left for work yet nor finished my breakfast, but I couldn't wait to quit work already. That morning, I felt for the first time in my life that I could carry my car to work instead of the opposite. Then I realized that only Chuck Norris does that shit. Food for thought: the man doesn't even have to cut his own grass; he just dares it to grow.

Buzzing all day at work, I kept thinking about what was waiting for me within my lightless living room. As much as it was my living room, it was beginning to feel like it was somewhere else in the cosmos. I didn't have to wait long to find out. With excitement running through my veins, I had all my preparation sorted, and off I went.

Once I closed my eyes and got my breathing going, straight away I could see them all standing with their hands in a different way. I don't know why I always would face my fireplace self-first, I believe because he was always the brightest and he was the one that was with me from the beginning. I was looking and smiling at him. The difference from the other nights was that when I did a 360-degree turn, all their hands were situated in a way, all with their hands raised and palms facing me. I'll try to explain this a bit better and hope you can innerstand what I mean. Instead of having their palms down, like that Oliver Twist moment: "Please, sir, can I have a little more?" It was more like a meme, a guy who was pretending to push on an invisible wall. That's what was facing me straight away.

Now that day at work, I was thinking I would start at number six, but when I started, I was right beside number two, and when I moved on to him and copied the hand movements, when they levelled up, we both seemed to move our hands together. Just remember, physically I never felt anything, but we certainly were touching palm on palm, and that's when either I was extracting the light, or you could look at it that he was giving me the light. Either way, the movement of light stayed around our hands and stopped just short of my elbows.

Once I felt it was over, we both stepped back a little, and I moved on to number three and repeated the feat. I did the same with numbers four and five. For me, it was repeating and seeing the same thing: an exchange of white goldy light going all around and settling to just below my elbows.

It was when I got to number six that the colour of the lights changed to blue. I thought to myself at the time that it resembled electricity. I have watched many science shows, documentaries, and films, and sometimes in them you would see charged-up bolts of lightning created for an experiment of some sort or another. This was what I was experiencing with number six compared to the rest so far.

I could see it moving around my hands and wrists, but again, it never went past my elbows. To be fully mindful of this, and aware that you are standing in your living room with your eyes closed, breathing in through your nose and out your mouth, naturally without thinking about anything but what's in front of you, is truly such a magical feeling. It only motivates you even more to try to innerstand what it's all about and what for.

I'm telling you this because I do remember at this time consciously thinking it as I maneuvered to number seven. Again, it was different. This time, it was more of a reddish orangey colour that flowed around once our hands met. I normally would look at the face sometimes, but I was so mesmerized by the colours settling on my hands and wrists, I truly couldn't take my eyes off them. The reddish lights were less swirly than the white ones, but suddenly, I began to see red hoops going from my wrists to my elbows. It didn't last very long, but again, that only made it more magical for me to watch. Truly amazing.

That seemed to bring an end to number seven and straight to number eight, and it all changed again. This time, the only way I can describe it was a continuous line of misty smoke. The bottom of my arms had like a foggy bit closely around them. The smoke went straight into the palms of my hands. This went on for quite a while, long enough for me to look up at number eight (I feel like calling him Smokey) and see him smiling. I sometimes had to lean my head in a bit just to see the smile, as these were not as bright as number one (Fireplace Me) and had to sometimes get closer to be seen better. Of them all so far, this one lasted the longest of all the exchanges.

I must admit that as much as I never felt anything when I was doing these exchanges, both my hands were beginning to buzz a little, like a constant tingle. I don't know whether this was me doing the same thing repeatedly or it was all these things happening with going into my hands. I could now clearly see that my hands were changing in how they looked—you could say like a new pair of gloves, different shapes and faint new colours of light—but they were certainly getting a lot brighter.

It was such a small turn to get to number nine, and sure enough, it was also different. The only way I can explain this is when you have no channels working on your TV, you're left with the static picture, and you try to programme the picture into the right frequency to get the coloured picture. That's the only way I can explain it. When the hands were touched, it was the same as the smoke; it went straight into the palms, and again it took a while. Even though I was in a darkened room, I still could see that it was black and white static going in, and this again heightened the buzzing in my hands. I couldn't figure out in my head what all was going on in my hands, bar the magical feeling I was getting just by doing it.

So, it was on to number ten, and I could see that his hands were up, as if he was ready and waiting for me. So, as I raised my hands, straight away we started to exchange light. The difference with this one is it was twisting or rolling out. It seemed to be coming out a bit like a corkscrew would look for opening a bottle of wine, and there were loads of them. Even though it didn't last long, it was so bright. As they went straight into my hands, it was nearly like a continuous line of them, but there was the odd break when it seemed to go black and there was a purple tinge at times. It seemed to be intermittent; it would be white, then change to purple, and as we stopped, I could see that his hands had also a purple tinge around them.

When I came to the original me, he was shining even brighter, and I could see him smiling. There was a glow to him and all around him. When I raised my hands, my ears would start gently ringing, and as we put hands on hands, it was the brightest show of lights so far—only this time, it didn't stop at my elbows. It went everywhere on me, even over my head. I could see lights swirling everywhere on me and all around me, and it didn't settle down for at least two minutes, which felt like half an hour as there was so much happening.

I kept moving my head around, as there were lights going around it everywhere. Slowly it began to settle down to at least where the lights stop moving, and still, I couldn't take my eyes off myself. I was shining so bright, and there was a glow off me. What I mean by this is about three to four inches outside my body was glowing with yellowy white light. It truly was amazing to witness it all. Not only that, but it was on me everywhere. I felt a bit like a lighthouse.

At the time of doing this, there was a sense of relief I felt because I had been doing it for quite some time. I'm not even sure how long it was either, but just to get to the end it felt like I had accomplished something—what, I didn't know.

Even more so, it wasn't even the end, more like the end of the beginning. In hindsight, though I do realize how magical it was just to be doing something like this, I truly was beginning to feel special and blessed for what I could now do with my hands. Especially when I thought back to the start of this episode of my life, I knew deep within myself I had come on tenfold, not only with my inner work but also in my daily life.

I had promised to myself before I wrote the first line of the first chapter that I wouldn't involve my children in this too much, but I have to say things were going so great with them most of the time. I nearly said *all* the time, but nobody's perfect. To listen to my children talking about their games, Marvel, anime, the Avengers, and the like, and next door their father was experiencing such magical stuff; if I had even dared to tell them a little, they would have just laughed it off and told me to wise up.

I remember sitting at the dinner table having tea, and they were all talking about some of these characters from the games they were playing on their tech at the time, about what different powers they had and moves they could do. I'll admit, verbally I was quiet and all ears listening, but mentally I was saying to myself, *that's what I'm doing*. But I also knew if I had tried to explain it to them, it would have been like *Wise-up, crazy lost-the-plot Daddy, yeah, right.*

These were the times when I thought to myself that maybe writing this book was not only important for me but for them also, as I thought it would be a bit easier for them to inner stand what I was going through just next door in the living room. It was a different way of telling them, and to let them know why I was changing so much. No more shouty aggressive-toned Dad anymore. No matter what I did, I'd say I was doing everything with unconditional love.

I know at first, they didn't know what to make of me. I was always like *Do this, tidy your room, get outside, clean up,* and all that in one breath. Now it was the opposite. My eldest daughter Sophie even said that to me one day: "I want the old Daddy back." I think it was because all the usual triggers weren't working, and she didn't know what to do or how to deal with it. I remember saying to her, "It ain't happening, you're not getting him back."

I'll not lie they now have me wrapped around their little fingers, and I know I spoil them too much, but I just can't help it anymore. They are my life, but this is my choice. I love them to the moon and back, then to Saturn and back, then to Pluto and back, then to the Pleiades and back, then to Neptune and back—you get the picture. My love for them has no end. It's eternal.

CHAPTER 14

The End of the Beginning and the Beginning of the Start

THE NEXT DAY, I couldn't get it out of my head how bright I had been. I know up to this point I had done quite a few things, but never had I looked so bright and glowing. I just couldn't wait to see what was in store for me when I got home.

I didn't have to wait too long. I went again straight into my inner work. The one thing I did notice was that when I looked around the ten of me, individually I could see them much easier because they were so much brighter themselves.

As I was looking around at them, something caught my vision out of the side of my eye. Wow! My wings were back. I had gotten so enthralled with doing everything with my hands, I believe I forgot about them. Once I spotted them, I began to ask myself if they were there all the time, and I honestly thought they weren't. I believe I would have seen them with the amount of turning and getting up and down I was doing. I just hadn't been aware of them, but certainly now I was.

As much as I was bright all around, it certainly had calmed down a little, and it wasn't glowing around the outside of me. Again, I was mesmerized by the wings, and they were that much bigger now. For a little while, I was playing around with them, swirling and flapping my arms a bit, and there was only a small amount of light that was coming off them—enough to see them, though, as the light that I did have on them was around the outside and right out to the two tips of them. It was truly amazing. Breathtakingly stunned in amazement I was.

I began as I normally would have done and went straight to number one (the fireplace). I started running my hands over him, and quickly I could see little bits of light coming off him and going into my hands. Instantly, I got it right, or so I thought. The first thing I did was hold out my left arm and lift it up so my wing was opened, and with my right hand, I would run it roughly from my armpit out to its point and deliver the light that I believed I had just received from number one. I did the same with my right arm held it out and ran my left hand off the exact same way. As I did this, you could see the light spreading over parts of my wings and glowing them up, not much at first, but still enough, where you could see the feathers of light move along. For me to even write about a set of wings in this way feels not only strange, but weird and hard to fathom. I have no writing to compare it too, even though it happened to me it's so difficult to put it down on paper. To write it in down in a non-boastful and egotistical way, but still trying not to take the magical way I was feeling at the time. Truly, I think I was concentrating so much and at the same time my mind was in a state of being constantly blown away by being in the centre of this amazing circle of versions of myself.

I went to number two and did the exact same thing. I just hadn't caught on to any type of pattern yet. Clearly, though, bit by bit, I realized the wings were getting brighter.

Then I went straight to number three. Just to let the reader know what I was doing with each of me, was running my hands around each one and being given light that I would run up and down and from side to side on my wings, distributing the light unto my wings. Every time, the wings would get brighter. When, I think, I got to number seven or eight—I can't fully remember—I was beginning to see a lot more of the wings now and how big they were.

Suddenly, Ameila, my youngest daughter, burst into the living room. Before I could say anything, she had the light turned on and had started to ask me about a track suit she wanted from Shein. I opened my eyes fully and could see that wee look on her face, like *What's going on, Dad? Why is the light out?* I just told her I was meditating.

We had a conversation about a few things, and she went back to her laptop. I got settled down again and turned off the light. When I closed my eyes, I couldn't believe it—it was as if it was the start of the night, déjà-vu style. Everybody was lined up, but more to the point, all the lights on my wings were just around the outside, as if it was at the beginning of the night. Oh, no! I was going to have to start from scratch.

That's exactly what I did. The only difference this time is that I was super-concentrated right from the beginning. I started at number two this time, and off I went with the same pattern, repeating as I went around in a circle: two, three, four, five, six, seven, eight, nine. As much as I write the numbers down like this, each transaction of light exchange was always a little different. I would stray and sway off course a bit as my wings got brighter and shinier. I would twirl around sometimes.

You must innerstand that as much as I knew I had to concentrate on what I was doing; I truly couldn't stop myself. It felt so magical and surreal. At the same time, even your emotions would get involved. As much as I knew it was me and fully aware what I was doing and where I was, that didn't take away from the fact that in my quickly rotating brain, there were ten of me feeling like I was either in a different dimension or on a different planet, with a set of wings on my back lit up like a Christmas tree. My mind would still get overwhelmed quite a bit.

Most of the people reading this don't really know who I am. Hopefully, this book will change that a little. To the few I do know, it must sound a little crazy and bizarre. When I'm writing this, I put myself in your shoes and think to myself how I would feel reading this about someone I have known most of my life and with family all my life. The ones who truly know me should know I wouldn't put pen to paper if it truly didn't mean something to me, to bare my inner soul in such an extreme way. I can't help or even try to convey your reactions and responses to it all, but if only a few of my readers wake up to what's going on in this world and begin the journey of healing themselves, then for me, it will all be worthwhile.

It was when I had finished with number ten that I was about to go to the first of me, but who now was really the last. He was the one who I thought in my head was like the end of a cycle of at least some bits of my inner work. This was guesswork for me at times, but my intuition, my gut feeling, was telling me it was so.

Then my phone rang and rang and kept ringing. It certainly broke my attachment to what I was doing. Deep down, I knew it was getting late, and instead of finishing, my mind thought that if someone was phoning this late, something must be up. So, I broke off, opened my eyes, turned the light on, and answered my phone. It was my ex-partner who had just come round from not feeling well. I talked to her for a while, and she seemed to calm down a bit. When we both knew she was going to be all right, we quit the call.

It was then that I realized it was only 11:45 p.m. I had thought it was going to be about one or two in the morning. It just goes to show you, once your mind is engaged in something, time is of no essence.

I turned off the light and closed my eyes, and there I was again with just a small line of light around the outside of my wings, with everybody looking at me. I judged in my head that it would be too late to start again and made the call to go to bed. I remember going around to everyone and apologizing, even though I didn't think I had to. I felt it was the right thing to do at that time.

I broke the connection off and went to my bed, and it was while lying there gathering my thoughts that I began to feel a little frustrated, not really with myself but that something was at work trying to stop me from completing this task. I thought back to when I had done all the work on my hands; it was kinda like a checkpoint in a game. To describe this a little better, in a Super Mario game, at the end of each level, you go up the steps, do a big jump at the top, and see how far up you land on the flagpole. That is like a checkpoint, because what you have done up to that point is saved.

This is how I felt now in the recesses of my mind somewhere about building or putting the light on both my wings. Maybe I had to do this all-in-one big go. Truly, I didn't know, but when you're entwined and involved in carrying out such magical tasks (I don't know what else to call it), that was how I felt when something disturbed me. I really kinda had to go back to the start and begin it all again.

All the next day, I couldn't get it out of my mind, partly because it was so intense and fresh that I couldn't. Then, on the other hand, I wanted to get it completed to see where I went next. As much as I was trying to slow myself down, we human beings want everything finished yesterday, and therein lies the problem.

Not everybody, but surely most people don't stop to enjoy the present moment anymore—the there and then, the feel of a situation, the continuance of just being at one with self. I for one was beginning to change that within myself. It's easier said than done, mind you, but if you are going to make yourself aware of the present, you must start somewhere. So, promises were made inside my noodle that day that I would try to enjoy every minute off what I was working on and achieve each mini goal as it presented itself in my work.

Later that evening, I went through my usual routine of going to the toilet, having my water strategically placed, and clearing my mind in preparation for the evening's magic. The only difference is that I said to my children that I was working on something important and unless it was an emergency, to try not to disturb me. The other thing I did was to turn my phone off, as this had begun to prove a bit of a nuisance, particularly at certain moments.

I can't stress this enough: It really was like once I got all ready and into position, my new best ten friends were standing there waiting on me. These are the present moments that I'm talking about. Normally, I would have got straight to it, but on this night, I paused in awe of them all. I don't remember how many times I thanked them for turning up. It was like a gathering of thank yous in abundance.

I stopped and looked at them all. I had talked quite a bit to them up to this point, but this night I remember saying to them, "Right, let's get this done and no distractions. I'm gonna be on the ball tonight." The last thing I said to them as I was facing my shiny fireplace number one was, "Let's light this room up tonight." Zoned in like never before, just to talk like this shows how fully immersed I truly was.

I really was living in the moment. I was shivering, not with coldness, but the hairs on my body were standing up, especially all the way up the back of me, from my calves right up to the back of my head. It felt amazing, I don't know if it was adrenaline, but what I do know is I was pumped up ready to go more than I had ever been. Excitement comes to mind. I don't know if there is a word higher than *excited*, so I'll just say quadrupled with excitement.

Anybody who has ever taken acid, microdots, amphetamines, and ecstasy—it was like having a small amount of each of them in one go, with the only difference that it wasn't taken with a load of mates at a party drinking, smacking, and tripping, and slabbering of course. Also, it was free. There was more to it than that—a very personal thing, with a magical feel to it and a reason behind it all to find who your true self is and not the person society has moulded since you became a strawbaby in this very sneakily controlled existence. When you begin to see through all the lies, deceit symbols, the following of all the money, the façade that is called democracy—when you write that word down and know the truth behind it, you can see the spell-casting demon in it.

This was altogether something different—angelic it felt like to me. I was blessed to be awoken and now fascinated to be doing this magical inner work and truly now being *wide awake* to everything, everyone, and everywhere, not only on this Earthly plane but in the multiverse, dimensions, metaphysical realms, whatever one wants to call it. It's what eludes the masses, the simple truth of this cosmic universe and the real connection to the cosmic birther, source, prime creator, God, the *Law of One*, Christ conscious Christos all that lies within duplicated with infinity.

So off I went with a feeling of purpose, strongly believing within myself with a fiercely determined attitude that I would complete this mission that had been bestowed upon me. Only this time, I was going to thoroughly enjoy every moment. Before I got underway, I started at number one and went around to each one of me with hands down by my sides. I turned and faced each one, raised my hands, and in so doing, they all raised theirs. One by one, I touched them and thanked them for what we were about to do. There was no physical feeling of touch but instead a feeling from within, of togetherness, closeness, oneness, insightfulness, but most of all, a deep awareness of happiness.

Once I got round to my shiniest self (number one), I went straight to number two and began with the little routine that had worked up to this point of gathering the lovely light of their bodies and distributing it along both of my wings with both of my hands. Each one took quite a while, and I was beginning to elegantly flow my hands across each wing in what I personally thought was a lovely way of doing it. Purposely, I was trying to do it with a bit of style or finesse now, dare I say it, but I thought to myself *I've got the hang of this now* and was feeling very good about it.

I was believing in myself that bit more and truly beginning to do it with my heart. It's hard to convey in words what I was feeling, though I felt something warm and an actual closeness to every one of these light beings that had stood before me night after night, having so much patience with and for me. For the first time, I think I was falling in love with them, and in hindsight, I have looked back and realized this is when I truly started loving myself from the inside out, eternally and unconditionally. It felt great.

I was flowing through it and had gotten to number eight and began thinking of getting to number one. You see, it was so hard to quell the human instinct to want everything yesterday. But I transmuted it quickly and was getting back to my present moment when *bang, bang, bang* went my front door knocker. I couldn't believe it and tried to ignore it. Then again, *knock knock knock*. Again, I ignored it, trying not to break my concentration or lose my connection. Then for the third time, *bang bang bang*, and the connection I think broke it off with me, as now my mind wasn't in the game.

So, I put the light on and put my T-shirt back on and answered the door fuming, but at the same time trying not to show it. It was a good mate of mine, and straight away I asked him what he was at, just calling round and not giving me a jingle before he did, which was the normal thing that would have happened. He said he did, and that's when I remembered I had turned my phone off.

As my mind was spinning internally, I couldn't get it out of my head that something was working to prevent me from completing this task. It felt to me that somebody or something knew what I was doing and used or sent different people to prevent or stop me in some way—unbeknown to them, of course.

So, I masked my true feelings at the time. But underneath, I felt like a steam train with a ton of fresh coal just thrown into my burner, face like a burnt onion. I know we had a conversation about something, I just can't recall. All I could think about was that I would have to start all over again.

Believing that night that I truly had it mastered and was lighting my wings up so naturally, not going off course, no flapping about, no thoughts of hitting my head on the living room ceiling, I began to get upset—but I quickly calmed myself down. I was beginning to do that for the first time in my life, very, very quickly, and it just wasn't from the thoughts of "There are no mistakes, just lessons." It was something else from inside me that was changing. My temper wasn't there anymore. I wasn't flying off the handle anymore.

My old nickname for a while was Morph, and after a few years that got changed to Mad Morph due to my quick temper and how instantly I would have reacted to a situation with quick aggression, mostly verbal but sometimes physical. Gone it was from me now. I would go as far as calling myself a new nickname: Gentle Morph. Then there was always the odd person who mistook my kindness for weakness and would awaken the lion that for the most part was sleeping inside, and Mad Morph would come back. It was in these moments that I would teach myself to respond rather than react, which again could inspire a new nickname: Mad Gentle Morph.

So back to the night in question. I was sitting with my mate talking, and I decided two things secretly in my mind. One was I was going to leave my inner work. energy work, magical work, out-worldly work, light work, shadow work, amazing work, and just altogether the best work I had ever done in my life to tomorrow evening, and I was thinking about starting before it even got dark. The second thing was, I was going to set a boundary with my mate.

The thing was that my mate still took a bit of gear and loved his weed still. For me, there was nothing wrong with that at all; it was just that I had quit all these things and wanted them completely out of my life. For the journey that I was now in the middle of, those things didn't serve any purpose. I had done it for long enough in my life, and the last thing I wanted was somebody coming round to my house doing what I had done for so long. It defied the purpose of what I was trying to achieve.

I was never too shy to talk about such things, and my mate took it well. I think he fully inner stood what I was saying. The worst thing for him to do was to think it was a personal thing. It wasn't even anything to do with him, and I'm so glad he recognised where I was on my journey as I told him and tried to get him into my way of thinking.

I quickly realized everybody is on their own journey, and as much as you can bring the horse to water, you cannot make him drink it, nor can you light anybody's lamp. It's completely up to them. So, after that night, I told him I would always be there if he wanted to change his ways and go about starting to heal and raise his vibration and change his DNA. I knew when I said this that I lost him there and then. I can't blame him, as it reminded me of my Anunnaki moment with my mate Enzo months earlier, but then there's that little creeping thought inside me that if I can change, anybody can change.

I know that I'll never be the same Conrad ever again, nor do I want to be. To be awoken and gain the knowledge that I have, I truly do feel blessed in some way. Never did it ever cross my mind that I would say such things about myself. My dad, who is seventy-seven years old now, was the first one I told, and as much as I try, I cannot push or preach to anyone, as it's not my purpose. I can make them aware, and they can do what they want with it.

It was tough to tell my older brother Stuart that I was spiritually awoken. He's like my father in so many ways, and in no way wants to change his ways. Same thing when I asked my brother Deane about what happens when your timeline is up (death), and he in his mind can go no further than six feet under in a wooden box, and that's it for him. I don't believe it; I truly know that it's only the beginning of the next chapter.

I have such a strong belief, and truly believe that this just falls short of a memory that I have. It was my own family that chose me to awaken first, because they deemed me the strongest and most likely to wake up. You see, for your lower self to begin to embrace your higher self, you must learn with cosmic knowledge that you have sat down with your soul family before your life has even started on earth in a different dimension and pick your family, pick your contacts, pick the life you are going to live, and pick your brothers and sisters. It sounds so mad and so far-fetched; how could it be? But therein lies the divine purpose and connection with the divine realm and your own chosen path.

The generational curse-breaker, the black sheep of the family, the karmic lessons to be learnt—it's all so interconnected in your ancestors and ancient bloodlines. To experience the magical journey, I have been on and the things I've done, which you have now read about; the things I've seen, not only with my eyes closed meditating, but with them fully opened; there is nothing that can stop my direction in life, only myself. As I know there will be many hurdles to overcome, I'll jump over each one when and where they pop up. Even if there is a high jump set even higher, up and over I will go. Now if the pole vault stands in my way, that's when I will use my wings to get over it, if I can ever finish my mission to make them. Believe me, that was proving easier said than done.

I'm solely writing this next short paragraph to take time out from writing about myself, to thank the legions of angels and spirit guides that walk with me in my daily life: the synchronicities that pop up for me, and the help with my life path, the knowledge I gain from them, their unconditional love for me. The many times I have brushed so close to my death, I now look back on those moments and know for sure it was their intervention that saved me, always giving me a few seconds to save my own life. I didn't know it at the time it happened. Only with hindsight have I come to realize this and have an unfathomable desire to honour them, as they have kept me alive for a good reason.

So, if my angels can read this, I thank you. With unconditional love from to the top, the bottom, the left and the right, the back, the front, the middle, the centre, the core. and round the whole outside of my *heart,* I give you my infinite love and gratitude cosmically, universally, spiritually, ancestrally, karmically, genetically, and finally, eternally. Love is the most powerful force in the universe. I embrace my divine love, purpose and the fulfilling of my destiny.

There have been so many doors that have been slammed shut in my face throughout my life. I have begun to open so many, and as much as some are still locked, I have the keys now to open them all. I have a big bunch of keys to open doors yet unforeseen. Once you truly become awoken, it is brought to your attention quickly that you've entered a war, but not the wars we as humans have come to wrongfully get used too. This is spiritual warfare and has been going on for longer than any of us can remember. About ten years ago I became a member of my local library. I started reading about wars, I didn't know it at the time why, but I started with wars beginning with A (which was the Algerian war) and finished with the letter Z (which was the Zulu wars) and read every war known to man in between. Only now do I at least think I know why, my soul wanted to learn what it was all about. Not just about the cruelty and bloodshed, but how each man and woman fought really for each other rather than their governments. Bravery, comradeship, family, home loved one's safety, and what they thought to be freedom and through me got to experience the emotional attachments that connects it all from an industriousness and resourcefulness earthly human perspective. In the end you find out it is the love of someone or something that gives them a will to fight on and in turn survive.

Spiritual warfare is much the same only its love for all. You realize you get attacked sometimes daily and you don't even know it, and the funny thing is, the people who are doing it sometimes don't even know about it either. You see, when you live with a low vibration, you can be manipulated easily and used to invade other people's minds and hearts. Don't get me wrong: there are people who know fine rightly what they are at. Most of these people are infected with their own greed and live in a materialistic world making judgements on others, only because they see themselves as having more.

There are so many ways to have wealth than just the financial aspect of it. There's a saying that your health is your wealth, which is very true. Spiritual wealth, abundant wealth, caring, compassion, love, kindness, and knowledge of one's inner wealth are the keys to eternal happiness.

I heard this on my phone one morning: "The more you shine, the more shadows you cast on yourself. It just goes hand on hand that's the price for all this, because some people don't like what I do. That's just the way it is." The biggest mistake a person can make is to give up. You might not reach the best version of yourself in this lifetime, but you can reach a better one than you are right now.

In life, what you see sometimes is not what you get. Most people have two faces. There's the one they want you to see, and then there's the hidden dualistic one that they try to keep for themselves. As sad as this sounds, most if not all people respect the money and not the person, and it is the ones you love the most who will hurt you the most. Only when you emotionally detach yourselves from them do you realize that it was your own energy that made that relationship special. That's when you're left with a realization of how ordinary they were. Trust means everything, but once it is broken, *sorry* means nothing. There are two things that will define you in life: your patience when you have nothing and your attitude when you have everything.

I go back to the age-old saying that "Money is the root of all evil." It's not; it's the dark side of people who love it. Money is only bits of paper that can easily be burnt. It's the people behind the money that make it truly evil. Don't get me wrong: we all need money to try to live a normal life. But it's been masterfully manipulated over time to suit the rich and consume the poor.

When I say *poor*, a more accurate term is the working-class people who get no say at all. Before you get paid for your weekly/monthly work, it's already been taken off you with the worldly tax scam, with no say in the matter. You work overtime, they scam you even more highly. Even at that they are employing robots to do some of this working-class work. Do the robots then pay taxes too? Are the private companies that run the robot scam even more into tax evasion?

The point I'm trying to make is that it's always the working class who pay. Even in all the organized world wars, the working class pay with their blood. The rich are normally officers who sit back and organize away from the killing—not all, but surely the majority. The rich fund the wars, the working-class people (civilians) die in the wars, and when the dust is settled and the blood is spilled, the rich get richer fixing and rebuilding all the damage that was caused by wars. The only thing they can't replace is the people who have been sacrificed to no end for some bullshit megalomaniac tiff between—yes, I'll say it again—greedy rich pufferfish. If the people would unite and just say no, that would be the end of it in a matter of months. To plan a war but have no one to fight in it—that's when it stops.

All these lines on maps displaying borders—I personally call them money lines, and the price to cross them is lives. We are all one: British, Chinese, Mexican, Russian, African, Indian, American, Swedish, fat, thin, short, tall, handicapped, crippled, you get what I mean. We are all one and live with the law of one, not all the bullshit laws of each so-called border. And yes, these are again made by the rich and if not then bribed by the rich. The picture is beginning to get painted. The rich get richer, and the poor stay poor. It is organized this way on a global scale.

So no, it's not the actual money that is the root of all evil. It is the people who control it. Control, control, control, fear, fear, fear, high fuel, high energy prices, and we are the energy. Again, electricity bills (and we are all made of electricity), food, homes, water, and they poison all of that too.

People who are awoken and live in a reality out of this matrix know all off what I say, so this is for the ones who yet think the matrix is a trilogy movie with Keanu Reeves or, sorry, Neo he is called in the move. Mix it around and you get the word *One*. Same as *Earth*, mix it around and you get the word *Heart*. We only get *One Heart*, and that's what they want you not to use. The fewer beating hearts in the world, the happier the rich will be. We all want to be rich, yes, but never forget that an unseen source also runs the rich, and this is where the real war is fought: spiritual warfare.

The ones on the spiritual front lines fighting in the metaphysical shadows are the light workers, light warriors, wayshowers, truth bearers, heart users, and twin flames spreading peace, love, and light instead of darkness, fear and death.

One of my main reasons for writing this book is to get that message across. It's time to stand up and be counted, to look within yourself and gain the knowledge that is needed. Then all the light bulbs will go off in one go.

People I talk to say to me, "How we can do anything? How can we mere mortals help?" But that's what lies inside each one of us. We are all Christ; Christ consciousness Billions believe we only have two eyes, but we have three. The third eye that sees all, they have calcified from birth, knowing that if enough of us as collectively awaken, that's it, it's over. That's how we can all help, but not as mere mortals: as divine beings living in our human avatars who should be creating our heaven on earth instead of creating our own hell on earth.

Pineal is another name for "pinecone." Just Google the one that is the biggest in the world, and you will find it is situated in the Vatican. They know they always have so wake up dear souls.

The good people of this world who are reading this, the Christians, the church-goers, normal folk, the ones who are waiting in fear—may I truthfully say to all who are waiting on the Messiah to come down through the clouds all shiny and bright with words of wisdom to take you home, you only need to look within and realize that Christ has always been here. You all have the spark of Christ already inside you. I don't say this lightly; I say it with the knowledge of real love, and with *One Heart*. If it offends your beliefs, I apologize, but I can only try to make you all at least aware of the truth, the whole truth, and nothing but the truth.

We truly are all one, and yes, we all look to one God wherever and whatever that shall be for us all. I am religiously spiritual. The only difference between *spirituality* and *religion* is that us spirits have learnt to detangle the lies and deceit that have been put into the Bible to control the masses. Spiritual beings who truly use their all-seeing eye cannot be controlled. All we want as a collective is to at least make you aware of all the bits of the Bible that are lies. That is where all the spirituality has been removed for the now modern generational readers to consume.

It says an eye for an eye and a tooth for a tooth. If this quite literally was carried out, the whole world would be toothless and blind. Work hard for your slave-masters is another thing that is written. To even think that a God who made this world would put that thinking into the conscious mind of the people to rule over them and subdue them to a hierarchy for worship—that alone tells me it's nothing but a controlled fear-driven lie to rule over others.

The word *amen* is another reminder of how some parts of the Bible were made by the controllers of words, spellings, casting names to ancient rulers off this world, that would deem themselves to be gods. When you do your research and gain your knowledge, you begin to realise it's all false teachings of ET that, yes, were more highly genetically advanced than the normal human beings. And that's exactly how the ones who pillaged, raped, and murdered wanted it to stay. Thoth, the writer of the Emerald Tablets, was the earliest wayshower of how there was good in this world; but his brother, Amone Ra, was the opposite. When you say *amen*, that is to whom you are referring.

So many people might hate me for saying this, but so be it. I cannot say anything else. If just all the people who said *amen* in this world stopped it and just said *thank you* instead as collective beings, that alone would in some way help raise the vibration of the whole planet and help the light come back into this world and shine so much brighter. This would be the start of the conscious revolution of the people globally to just say *no more*.

I must mention Billy Carson and his studies over the years of all the ancient texts and where the modern-day Bible derives most of its information from, because without his knowledge, I would still be saying *amen*. The biggest thing globally is not to fool everybody but to make the people of this world convince themselves that they have been fooled. I was one of those, but not anymore. They say the truth always hurts, but it always comes out in the end. This will be the case for everything, and the quicker this happens, the quicker the third-dimensional consciousness will get raised to the fifth-dimensional consciousness, and it will become what it was always meant to be: *heaven on earth*.

CHAPTER 15

Ten to One

FROM WAKING UP the very next morning, my thoughts had begun to consume my mind. If it wasn't a knock on my door, it was a call coming through to my phone. Or the one that I could most easily expect, one of my children looking for me for some reason; this just didn't seem to bother me as much as the other reasons, because I'm their father, they live with me, and I would drop anything in an instant if they were seeking my help for something, as any father would do for his children to love, help, provide, and protect.

It still didn't take the thoughts away from my mind, though, that there seemed to be an unforeseen force at work to stop me from completing this stage of my inner work. This only made me more determined to not only get it done but to enjoy it and cherish every minute of doing it, as it felt so special to me to even get the opportunity to experience such a magical moment in my life.

Of course, in life, there are many coincidences that occur at different times, but this had happened to me too many times, just as I was progressing to the completion of something major to me in my inner work, for it to be what most people would call a natural coincidence. I have now gained the knowledge that there are no coincidences. Everything happens for a reason.

Excitement began to fill my brain and my body. All my pre-organising was done and dusted, and so it began. Well, that's what I thought, but no. I closed my eyes and nothing and nobody was there. *Oh no* was instantly what I thought. My mind began racing at a rate of knots. *Are they gone? Have they left me? Where are they? Am I alone? Has the boat sailed away?* Panic had started to enter my body.

I felt it, but I began transmuting this feeling and meditating deeply. My breath work became so organized as I began settling my brainwaves down from a slight feeling of abandonment. After a while, I could feel myself beginning to relax, but still it was just me in my living room alone in the dark, with the slightest bit of light coming through the top of my pulled-shut curtains.

Then, as I stood in the middle of my living room, I began to see them appear all around me, as if coming out of the blackness of my walls. I was turning, not really focusing on one spot but twisting around with a sense of a massive realization that they were all there. Only then did I realize how panic-stricken I had been. I apologized to them all and knew that it was my human response of wanting everything yesterday. I had forgotten that patience is not just a card game, it's a virtue. I can't deny the relief I felt. Happiness now filled my mind, and I couldn't wait to get started.

There seemed to be something different, though, as I looked around at the ten beings of light who resembled me nearly to a tee. The light coming from their heads was brighter, and bits and pieces of light were moving around them closely—not loads of it, but enough to let me know that they looked just a little different. And so, it began. This time, it really did, but not before I got a wee flap of my wings, as there was still a small part of me that felt a sense of relief.

I did say I wanted to enjoy every minute. Talking in this way, I don't want to say it so matter-of-factly, as this was far from the truth. I can only imagine how it sounds to someone who hasn't gone through such moments. I can only say that this time last year, if I was reading this about someone going through this type of thing, I would have been a little sceptical without question—but here I am a year later doing it daily.

I had no spiritual background. I certainly felt unqualified at times experiencing it all, but I came round to thinking this is the way that maybe it was meant to be for me—learning as I went along, not only every night but every day, about all aspects of my life. The ups and downs, the ins and outs, the nos and the yeses, the knowledge I have gained has been so fulfilling for my life. It has changed not only how I live but the way I now look at and respect everything every single day, from the biggest tree and the highest tower to how ant colonies work and even beyond to the microscopic world that is around us every day, from head to toe, to how your cells work, how we are made of atoms, electrical, magnetic batteries in a way, even to the point of what's the right and wrong way to charge those batteries. Amazing really.

The reason I am writing these little snippets of information about my learning is that before my awakening, my mind was controlled by the matrix way of living—worrying all the time, fear of failure, given to much of a fook about what other people think. Truthfully, looking back, I had known nothing different, because unbeknown to me, I had been controlled so secretly and sneakily from birth. That just to recognize this way is such an eye-opener for me. I'm still astonished by the work that has gone on to keep us all subdued for so long, generation after generation, right up to this day.

If that doesn't give you an incentive to want to help, then nothing ever will. It's just not your time to wake up and accept the truth about how this world really works. There are not too many things that are free in this world, but one thing is the *news*. It's on in the morning, late morning, brunch, lunchtime, afternoon, midday, early evening, evening, nine o'clock, ten o'clock, midnight, and now there's even a channel for twenty-four-hour news. The news never stops, always repeating the same crap over and over, repetition, every day and every night, just to make sure it gets into your head in some form or another.

Even if you don't watch the news, or television for that fact, as you're scrolling, streaming, video watching, up pops the news out of the blue, and it's all free. That's something to think about. I'd say it's about always trying to hack and manipulate our minds with their bullshit. Sorry, rant over. It's just so hard to suppress sometimes, all the shit they feed to us daily. The way I was awoken, I am only trying to awaken others to all this manipulation.

Back to the magic of my wee living room, where something *big* was about to happen in my life. The last person I thanked for showing up was Mr Shiny Fireplace, number one. I felt it was through him and the previous work I had done that the other nine of me showed up in the first place.

So, I went straight on to number two and started off my routine, running my hands from the feet up, pointing the flats of my palms at him and working my way up his light body. When I got to the top, there seemed to be so much going on around his head, with the light moving and flashing a little, so I went that little further up to his face to collect the light that was everywhere.

That's when something new happened. I saw it, felt it, and heard it all at the same time.

As much as it felt just a tiny bit strange sticking my hands more or less into his face, my ears began to buzz and ring, my body began to shiver in different places at the same time, and as I watched, number two kept getting smaller and smaller, from his feet upwards, disappearing in front of my eyes until it was only his head, and then it too went right into my hands.

I began doing what I had always done and started to spread the light all over my two wings, one at a time. I couldn't help how amazing I felt this time doing it. So magical it felt to me, and so much light on my wings, that inside my mind I remember thinking, *Wow wow wow truly amazing.*

Once I had done this, I quickly went to number three and started the same process over again with the exact same results: ears ringing, body shaking and shivering, and the disappearing of number three eventually into my hands. To say I was buzzing is an innerstatement. I felt so high that even all the drugs combined I had taken throughout my life could never have matched it.

The light that was beginning to light up the inside of my wings was amazing. I then noticed how the outside seemed a lot dimmer compared to the inside. It was as if the lights weren't going to all off my wings at once, because they were so bright on the inside.

Bang straight unto number four already uncontrollably shaking, and away I went again. Same thing happened once he disappeared into my hands, and I started spreading the light. This is when I noticed that it was lighting my wings up from the bottom, and I could clearly now see that one half was so bright, and the moving of the feathered lights was amazing to watch. Also, I felt amazing doing it.

This is when I began to see the blackness where numbers two, three, and four had once stood. I turned my head and could see Mr Shiny Fireplace looking directly at me. It's so hard for me to describe everything that was going on. Even as I looked at myself, I could see that light was distributing unto my body and legs. It was as if the lights were crawling around on me—it truly was.

I remember as I turned to number five thinking to myself, as my adrenaline was surely now pumping around my whole body, that I was dying to stop and have a flap or a flow of my wings. As I was going up number five with my hands, my mind was making a promise to itself to stop and do it, to enjoy every moment of it. And that's exactly what I did, but it wasn't for long. When I had delivered all the light to my wings, I began turning, twisting, flowing with my arms like some sort of made-up dance I was trying to perform. My wings were so amazing I couldn't take my eyes off them; totally glued I was. They were all lit up and on my fricking *back*. On my back was a set of *wings. What?*

These were unbelievable feelings and visions. I can't describe in words how I felt—like I wasn't from here, but also not knowing where I came from. Up to this point, I was Conrad doing magical inner-energy work. But as my eyes locked on my wings, for the first time I blurted out, *who am I?* Of course, I got no answer, and I wasn't expecting one either. But my mentality began from that moment on to deeply think about who I was and where I had come from. I am me, always will be, but the spirit that dwells inside me—yes, it is my soul, and so is me. Confused? Think how I felt standing in my living room in awe with a set of light wings on my back.

Quickly I began to gather my senses and look around for number six, ready and waiting, looking straight at me, probably wondering if I was dancing or about to take off, as I was waving my arms and hands around so much. As I began looking at number six, it dawned on me that he didn't have any wings himself, nor, in fact did any of them. Whether I didn't notice or just didn't think about it until that very moment, I had a quick look about me, and yes, none of them had. As I did this, it looked so strange now, the black empty space where they had been night after night in my work. I began to think for the first time that night that I had to finish this somehow, so I snapped out of my headspace and got back down to being given more light.

I believed now that I wasn't *taking* the light anymore but being *given* it as a gift, reward, or even a blessing. I honestly still didn't know. I was beginning to feel special in some way, but not an ego special, not in the sense that I was above any one person. I believed in the law of one and how we are all one. This knowledge had now entered my mind and was becoming fully incorporated as part of my daily thinking, where I would look down on no man or woman and see everyone as equals.

Everybody's problems affect them differently—how they look, how they react, how far they are willing to go and sort them out, how long they hold on to such things. There's a multitude, an endless list of things I could jot down, but the point I'm trying to make is that as much as we are all different, we are also the same. Yes, we are on different journeys and different timelines, but still we are made up of the same things.

I will admit that my awakening was so intense and extremely active, nearly every day and night, and I was getting to a point that here I was with ten versions of myself (now five) sparkling with a set of wings on my back. I felt amazing, but at the same time, I felt I was the exact same me, just experiencing mind-warping visions with my third eye. I was sensing somehow that I had a great purpose to do in this life somehow—whether it was helping people awaken, healing, spreading my light, raising vibrations, or sending out certain frequencies.

I know some readers don't even know what a twin flame journey is. Neither did I until shortly after my orange poofy experience. Through psychic Ellen Redd, I have learnt what it means to reach my destiny and find my reunion. But even when you know you are on a twin flame journey, and deep down what you must become to even think about having a squeak for it to come to pass. As much as I long for the conclusion of such a reunion—as much as I want to make love to her morning, noon, and night and just be as one—what I truly want to do is help anchor the light in the world and ultimately light it up and awaken, arise, raise the collective consciousness, and help everybody eventually live in a world with peace, love, and harmony for all to experience their heaven on earth.

So off I went, gathering the light from the bottom to the top of number six. It just seemed to be bouncing everywhere, swirls, flashes, lit-up lines, short, long, straight, and curly. I was in awe watching this, ears fuzzing and buzzing, goose-pimpled everywhere, and then to get to spread it on my wings—yes, I said it, *my wings*—and keeping calm within myself and always trying to keep my mind on the task and at the same time my excitement under wraps. That was sometimes the hardest thing to do. I would always somehow come to my senses. I believe in the back of my mind that I was thinking I didn't want to start all over again.

So, it was straight unto number seven, always fighting with my mind not to stop for a five-minute swirling and moving my arms in waves. As number seven disappeared into my hands, I immediately started to put the light up and down my wings. They were beginning to really fill up with light everywhere now, and with it being so dark, the detail was the most magnificent sight I had ever seen, and they were on *me*. Wow. I absolutely loved it, to tell you the truth. Everything I was experiencing from minute to minute just kept getting more amazing, with each passing second.

As I turned to face number eight, I could see number nine, number ten, and number one all looking at me. At least I think they were. But I couldn't now help myself from looking at the darkness where the others had once stood. I felt lonely now in a funny sort of way, but not in the sense that I was alone, I knew I wasn't. Again, I struggle to put it into written words. It was maybe the time I had spent with them all, and now when I looked over they were missing, so I guess I sincerely missed them.

When I had finished with number eight, I immediately turned and got to work on number nine. I knew not to let my mind wander, as this too was a constant inner battle. Now not only my wings but I also was lit up like twenty Christmas trees. All my human instincts were fighting that feeling not to stop and wave and dance around my living room with these amazing light-feathered wings glowing and now lighting up the room.

Starting with number ten, I began to calm down a bit from within. I knew I was far too excited, but as much as I tried, I couldn't quell it in any way. Then suddenly a calmness then came over me as number ten gave me his light and then gave himself into my hands. There just seemed to be so much light going everywhere now, not just into my wings. I really do mean everywhere. I knew some was going behind me, but I daren't have looked, as there was just so much happening in front of me.

It was at this point I started to get a bit emotional, as I was spreading the light everywhere now on my wings. I began looking at Shiny Fireplace Me, the one who had been the first I had seen and was with me from the word go, since making my spaghetti bolognese that night and dancing for nearly two weeks together. I just couldn't stop myself from becoming emotional. As much as I talked to the other mes, this was the one who I had slabbered to the most, and I felt I knew him better. Somewhere in my head, I thought it was the same with him also.

I can't remember what I said, but there were so many *thank yous,* and *I love yous.* The gratitude I felt even before I started—there was something inside me that didn't want to take the light from him, even though I knew he wanted to give it to me. I know this probably sounds a bit deep, me talking like this about him, but if you had gone through what I had with him, I would nearly guarantee you'd be the exact same.

Believe it or not, I reluctantly started to do as I had done with the other nine. Tears were leaking from my eyes and rolling down my cheeks. I was not crying as such; there was no sound. But in hindsight, maybe I thought this could be the last time I saw him, as all the others had disappeared and become a part of me and my now-massive set of wings. And so, it began.

CHAPTER 16

Up Up and Away

THE CALMNESS I felt dissipated very quickly once I started to receive the light from me and my own metaphysical best matey. I didn't know then, and still I'm not fully sure, if this was my higher self helping me or a multitude of versions of myself. But they were trying to help me with something—I'm sure about that. I could now feel the excitement running through my veins, lights swirling up my legs, twisting and turning as they were coming up, alongside my hands, it was everywhere.

I can't describe how I felt right at this moment, because it truly was a first, and I don't know what to call it, as nothing had ever happened to me like this. But also, I'd never felt anything like this. Being caught up in this moment, I even forgot about the wings on my back. As I nearly had my hands raised all the way up to Shiny Fireplace, I paused, not for long, but long enough for us to look into each other's eyes. I was sweating, tearful, and cheerful as both of us were smiling at one another.

Then I raised my hands the way I had done with the other nine mes, up to his face. This is when, from the bottom up, they would disappear upwards and then into my hands. Not this time, though. What happened next has echoed in my mind ever since. He went right through my hands and straight into my head, straight to where my pineal gland is, right in the middle.

Shivering and shaking, I could hear my blood being pumped around my ears, then fizzling, buzzing, zinging, and ringing in my ears. Inside my skull was either shivering or vibrating. I was so taken aback. I had felt things before, but nothing so intense as this. My mind was filled with nothing. It was just there right there at that moment, the present. The feelings I was experiencing were flowing through me, and there were flashes everywhere. I couldn't make anything out but lights of every sort, everywhere around my head. It could have gone down round my body, but I couldn't see past the lights around my head.

Normally in my inner work, at this point I would have started to spread the light on both my wings, but no. *Whoosh!* I went directly up and stopped. Couldn't make much out at this point, but I knew I went up the ways or else something came down on me. *Whoosh* again. I felt like I went up some more and stopped suddenly again.

As much as my head and ears were ringing at a very vibrating pitch (it's the only way I can put it into words), I also could hear clangs and bangs like doors of some sort were opening and then closing. This is so hard for me to explain, as things began happening so fast, but it wasn't as if it was maybe your front door or car door shutting. It was a different sound of closing, louder, and as much as I couldn't see, I could hear them shut. I swear it was as if some of them were getting sealed shut or even opened— that I didn't know.

What I did know was there was a force that was making me rise up. Then it would stop, and then raise me up again. I don't know how many times this happened, but this was the first time I began to have a bit of logic, because I was making sure I was breathing right and was so afraid to open my real eyes, if I could call them that anymore. I was afraid of losing this magnificent connection I was in the middle of experiencing.

At this stage, I finally remembered my wings and eventually had a small look by twisting my head around. They were glowing, bigger and brighter than ever before. I didn't know where I was. I couldn't see out very far, as it was just blackness, but it sure didn't feel like my living room anymore. I believe I had travelled somewhere, or something had travelled to me. This is when I seemed to have stopped going upwards through some type of door that I couldn't see but could still hear. This was when I started to see all the wee angels whizzing around. I say *angels*, but I didn't know for sure.

Anybody who has ever watched Tinkerbell—they all looked about the same size as her but not as bright, because I remember Tinkerbell was very golden and bright in the movie. These were not as bright and of different colours: green, blue, red, orange, and yellow. Not as brightly lit up, but enough that I could see they were all girls, and all had a wee set of wings on their backs. They were darting around what felt like a big room. The only thing is, I couldn't see any walls—just darkness around the outside.

Suddenly, the force that had pushed or driven me upwards was now pushing me horizontally across this room. But this time, I could see a door at the end of the hallway that I was getting pushed toward, and it was massive. The door seemed to be black, but there were loads of white light in its face. That was the only reason I knew it was a door.

As this force of energy was guiding me along, it was as if my feet were about two feet off the ground, and I was floating along with my legs static. The little angels were flying about me here and there, some zooming in. Some seemed to stop and have a look at me, and others just whizzed past fast—so fast they just looked like wee orbs of different colours.

When I got up to the big doors, I heard and saw them begin to open. Compared to my height, this door was massive. I was so excited and at the same time optimistically nervous, as I really didn't know what was going to be behind the opening door. At this point, I was shaking all over and could feel the sweat trickling down my cheeks. As the door opened, at first, I didn't see much. The room itself was dark, and I again couldn't see the outer walls of this room, if that was what it was.

Then there was a light above me that grabbed my attention quickly. It was a woman floating above me, moving all around me. I wasn't glowing anymore brightly the way I was when working in my living room a minute ago. The woman had white wings on her back and was an older woman. Dare I say, not meaning in any way to sound rude, she was not only a more mature-looking woman but was a lot bigger than the rest of the ones I had seen up to this point.

I felt at ease right away, as she was smiling at me and going around me. I could see others zooming around as they would come in and out, but the woman angel looked all organized and businesslike. This is the impression I got. She was all around me, inspecting me all over. She seemed to be lifting my wings with her hands and looking at them.

I don't know why I did this, but I put my two arms straight up and out at both sides to lift my wings up and have them fully spread. This is when I began to feel things around my back and arms, like the night I got my lump removed but at the time didn't know it was being removed. What woke me up that night was a jolt of electricity, and this is what I was feeling all over my back and at different places on my back shoulders and arms, even down to my hands. It was as if I was getting touched with something that each time vibrated on the spot it touched on.

It was still hard to see it all and getting very hard to keep holding both my arms up. You can be sure there was no way I was going to drop my arms, though. My kickboxing training days kicked in, and there was no way I was going to let them drop.

In my mind, I was thinking in some way that I was getting them attached better to my body, but I didn't know for sure. It was what I was feeling physically at this point. No pain whatsoever, just different parts vibrating and buzzing. My hands began to get very fuzzy and tingly at the wrists and fingertips. At this point I didn't know if it was from me holding my arms up for so long or if something was happening to them.

Next it was my neck and the back of my head. My ears began to buzz louder. It would go from one ear to another. I could hear it, and then my two ears would go at the same time.

It really did begin to feel for me that I was getting worked on in some way, and this was the place where it happened. I don't know if that is true or not, as I could only see the older, bigger, and wider angel woman appear and disappear. Yes, there were lights around the room, but I could never see more than about one metre away from me at any time.

I was so caught up in this moment, I can't give you a time how long I had been in there, but if I was to estimate it, I'd say ten to twenty minutes. There was never any sound, bar my heavy breathing, and I could always hear my heart beating and ears ringing.

Encapsulated I was at this point, knowing that something was happening to me, but what I wasn't fully aware of. I kept thinking to myself and wondering exactly where I was and how I had magically worked so hard to get here. I could never see too much, and I think it was planned this way.

Suddenly, all the vibrating stopped, and my ears let up a bit. I could clearly see the older angel hovering above me. Then she went away from me until out of view, but always looking at me as she went. This is when I lowered my arms. When I did this, I began to look down to see what or if I was standing on something.

This was the most physical part of any of my inner work up to this point—to go through such an experience and consciously be aware of everything that's happening. You're aware of each breath you take, every movement you've made, every vision you've seen, quadrupled by all the mental thoughts zooming around your brain. I was trying to not only make sense of it all but also not lose concentration and mess it up and doing all this when I didn't know the right way or even the wrong way of doing it.

I felt inside me that this angel had given me a proper once over and done stuff to me or for me. I wasn't quite sure, but it wasn't long before I found out. When she left me, I had an actual moment to myself and began thinking *Where actually am I? Who was that? What just happened to me?* when suddenly *whoosh*, up I went, and I mean the fastest I had ever gone up and up and up some more.

I couldn't see anything around me as I went vertically at such a speed. There was no force pushing me. I believe it was me doing this. It just took me a while to catch on. As much as my mind was racing, I was doing this with my thoughts at the same time. So that's when I thought to stop, and immediately I did. It was amazing. Right at that moment, I had both my hands and arms down by my side.

That's when I began to look around me, and I was looking at myself quite a bit. Looking at the wings I truly felt magically enchanted but most of all I felt unconditionally loved. This is when I spotted what looked like a grey planet of some sort. It looked like the moon without all the crater marks, just a light grey planet. You must inner stand, I hadn't a clue what I was looking at or where I was, but to explain it better, it was me hovering in the world of space. I couldn't see any stars, and I was a wee bit away and above this grey planet.

I decided to fly down to take a closer look. Now, I don't say that lightly: "decided to fly down." It wasn't how I had imagined it would be, and I thought back to my living room when I was doing a flapping motion, when I was so enthralled as I looked at them. When I say *fly down*, I just thought it, and off I went, concentrating on the grey ball. I remember putting my hands out the way you would see in the Superman movies.

I felt a tiny bit silly doing this at the time, but it didn't last long, because in front of me, I unconsciously and unintentionally began forming a hole in the fabric of this space I was in. Quickly I pulled my hands down to stop it, but it didn't stop. Although it didn't get any wider, I was still creating

143

this hole in front of me. It's hard to put into words how I felt when this was happening in front of me.

That's when I realized I was doing it with my eyes. My mind was now going a million miles an hour over what I was doing. The hole kept getting deeper, and that's when I put my hands back up and intentionally widened the hole with them. Don't ask me how I knew how to do any of this, as I can't tell you. I just was doing it as I was going along. There was no instructions or map or anybody showing me the way; it truly was just right there in front of me, as me with wings on my back was now creating some type of portal with the use of my hands while there were light beams coming from my eyes. They just seemed to me to be burning or creating a big hole. This seemed to all be done with the combination of different light rays or beams.

What an amazing experience I was having! Even though I didn't know where I was, I thought to myself, why not just go for it? And in I went. I didn't have to move my wings in any way. I just thought about going in and in I went.

When I went through, there were now two grey planets. Again, they were below me, and again I didn't know what to do, or even if I had anything to do at all. So, I chose one and gradually kept going down and down until I reached it. I seemed to go into its atmosphere, and I saw ground and mountaintops way below. I don't remember seeing any water.

As I looked down, I could see now some type of mist—pure white mist, or you could say smoke—coming out of my hands. As I just hovered there, I raised my hands and pointed them forward. The white smoke came flying out, and I mean loads. I could see it forming loads of clouds out in the distance. The white smoke itself seemed to be going at an awful fast rate. My hands started to get a little cramped, so I started flicking my wrists and wiggling my fingers a bit just to try and take away the cramp.

There now seemed to be electricity coming out of my hands, and as it was leaving it was going so fast, I could see it in the distance flying along. The line of it didn't break right to both my hands. I didn't know what I was fully doing, but I felt I was building something on this grey planet—in the atmosphere of it, anyway.

I did this for at least ten minutes. In hindsight, I never contemplated in my head that physically I was in my living room at this point, because I was so into what I was doing and magically experiencing. My mind was so fixated on doing this, and I thought to myself I must be helping in some sort of way. Like I knew I was doing something special but didn't have the cosmic knowledge yet as to what it was. Deep down, I trusted myself that it was for the greater good of something. Through my inner energy work, I had gotten to this point of doing a lot of stuff with not only my hands but now my eyes.

This is when I started to mess around a bit and was pointing my hands in any direction and stuff would happen. I was going back to the Superman stuff in the recesses of my napper, but it was in doing this that again, accidentally, I started to form a hole right up in the atmosphere of this grey planet. Only this time, once it started, I really went with it. As I was making the hole bigger, I could see a planet coming into sight through the opening, and it just looked like Earth (Heart). As I went through, as much as it looked like Earth with green and blue, there definitely were no white clouds to be seen. I noticed this straight away.

I began flying down to have a closer look. Yes, I did say it: *flying*. Ever since I was a child, and I'm probably speaking for loads of adults now, grown-ups and children alike, I'd have loved to have flown. Yet here I was doing it. It was so magical and so surreal at the same time—mind-boggling, really.

It's so bizarre to go through something like this. It's the most intense thing I have ever done. But even more bizarre is writing about it. I've just gone and read about six or seven pages back in this old jotter, and it really sounds way out there, especially for someone who has never meditated before or had no spiritual beliefs ever brought to my attention or entering my life. I was one of those people, but here I am doing this with what I learnt to be the spark of the divine, which is inside every one of us. To get to this point in my life, I have had to practically pull myself inside out, and as much as I can't go back and change the beginning, I can certainly start where I am and change the ending.

At the start, when I said that about pulling myself inside out, my thinking was that if you did this, it would be bones, organs, blood, ligaments, intestines, etc. that you would be grabbing. But now, what I would have in my hand is a small orb of pure white light. This is what each one of us has inside, and as much as it's easy to look within, it's not so easy going through the process of healing; forgiving yourself; bringing all your fears, anger, resentment; facing judgements—the list is so long, I would fill the page with so many programmed thoughts. Not everybody's ego is willing to let them, never mind want them to go through with it and see it to its end.

I am one of those people who not only want to see it to its end, I see it as the beginning of a life filled with peace, love, and truth, with a purpose not only to embrace my soul's destiny and walk the path, but to embrace my divine purpose to awaken right at this time in order the help this world see the truth of life, and in doing so expose all the lies and deceit that we have been indoctrinated in since our childhoods.

Truthfully, anybody who knows me will have to get to know me all over again, as I am not the same Conrad, I was two years ago. I have gone through so much in my life that I don't care what others think of me. It's none of my business what they think of me. There are so many things that have not yet come to pass in my life, but I will make sure that when they do, I will enjoy each moment. To wake the masses up even to begin to ask question after question about absolutely everything they were ever told would at least be the start of the beginning of the end, and I was told from a young age that the truth always comes out in the end, and as much as it will hurt, it's still the *truth*.

So here I was flying down to a planet that looked just like Earth, though what I was going to do when I got there, I did not know. Again, there were no clouds anywhere, and I could tell it wasn't the Earth I'd seen in videos or pictures from NASA over the years as there's has become less and less reliable. Real fiction they pump out and I believe right from the start, their concept was to fool the masses around the world, with continued and deliberately constructed very intelligent lies done with the technology they have which remains hidden and unshared.

Just as I got close to it and was about to enter it, there was a *bang, bang, bang* on my front door. I couldn't believe it. Really, it was just a knock on the door, but in my mind, it was *bang, bang, bang*.

Immediately, the connection stopped, and there I was standing in the middle of my living room floor. Excuse the pun, but I was brought right back down to earth in an instant. So, I turned my light on and put my top on. I remember sinking the whole pint glass of water in one go, I was so parched, but didn't realize how parched I was until I stopped. It just took me a few seconds after I flicked the light on to get my bearings. I even twisted my head around to see if the wings were still on. That's how deep I was in the experience.

It was my mate who had called round to see if I wanted to go for a spin with him to pick up his daughter and a friend at a club about twelve miles away. I didn't want to say no so reluctantly said O.K. I asked what time it was, and I remember him saying it was 12:45 a.m. I couldn't believe it. Seven hours straight I had been in my living room, and I could not believe how the time had passed in a flash for me. In a way, I think I needed a little break, as it was so intense at the time. As I believe now, there are no mistakes. It probably was divine timing, and I really could have done with settling a bit.

So off we went, came back, and my mate smoked a doobie by himself outside on my front porch. This now was about two thirty in the early hours, and I couldn't stop yawning and wanted to go to bed and to sleep. We said our goodbyes, and I went back into my house. Going into my living room, I suddenly felt a bit strange and was a bit foggy-eyed, is the best way to explain it.

I knew something was up when my skull and ears began zinging, ringing, and vibrating all at the same time.

CHAPTER 17

The Office
and the Back of My Head

MY MIND SUDDENLY began racing in circles around my head, so I sat down on my sofa and began meditating. Within ten seconds, I went from closing my eyes to sitting in an office, an ordinary-looking office. It reminded me of an early eighties private detective's office. The thing is, I was watching it from a slightly higher position, behind I can only say myself. I thought that it was Mr Shiny Fireplace Me.

From this point on, I didn't know it yet, but I would witness this looking at the back of my head—I should say a version of myself. The long blond hair and the back of the shoulders was all I could see. It was like an out-of-body experience, of me looking at a version of me from behind.

Not once did he/me ever look around at me and acknowledge I was there. I don't even think he knew I was there. Then again, he must have, as at this point, I wasn't so deep into it and knew I was sitting on my sofa. I just did not want to open my eyes and check in order not to break the connection. Also, for the past month, I had been doing all my inner work standing up. I had to. So here I am now, I think, sitting on a chair—not me, him. It was empty at this stage, just the two of us—the back of his head and what must have been me, as I never actually got to look at myself the whole time. I remember thinking *Am I just a set of eyes here?* or was I using my third eye to make a little opening behind him to watch this all unfold? Surely, I must have been allowed to.

I was looking at a table and a chair. There were things on the table, but I couldn't make out what they were. There was something I recognized on the table to be a nametag, one that anybody would have on their desk in an office, maybe saying *Managing Director, Sales Executive,* etc. That sort of thing is what I thought was like a wee V stand, but I couldn't make out what it said. In the far-right corner, there was a filing cabinet—a very outdated one compared to modern standards. Also on the table was a dimly lit lamp that didn't give off too much light.

The most amazing thing in this little dingy office was the big rectangular window that was at the end, because out of that window you could see stars everywhere. It was like the view out of the window was space itself. I couldn't make out any constellations or anything, but I still could see a phenomenal number of stars.

So, there was all this in my vision along with the back of a head with long blond hair. Suddenly, two of what I believed to be men at first walked into the office. One was very tall with a white coat on, the type a scientist or lab technician would wear, and the other seemed to be wearing a suit, a dark suit. I never saw his face, only the back of him, but I could see the tall one's face—not clearly, but enough to see that it looked a bit like an ant's face. I know that sounds a bit far off, but it's the truth: it's what he looked like. I'll call him Antman just for writing purposes.

The more I watched these two interact with each other, I understood that it was Antman's office. He would look directly at the me in front of me and say something. I never ever heard as much as a squeak from anybody but knew that they were talking about something that seemed very serious and important, as I could see the version of myself, Shiny Fireplace Me, nodding his head sometimes up and down, as if to let me know he was agreeing with something, and other times left to right, as if saying no to something, I just didn't know, as I was definitely an observer in all off this.

I couldn't see the man clearly, or even if he was a man, but he showed characteristics like he at least was talking on my behalf, for me, or so my intuition was telling me. As much as he would turn around and must have been saying something, I could never make his facial features out or get a good look at him. Antman was holding a piece of paper on an ordinary clipboard. Again, I could never see what was on it, but it was an ordinary clipboard that we all use.

They were going through a list of something, but never a sound. There was some talking being done, though. I could clearly see a debate of some sort, and then both would look at Shiny Fireplace, and he would nod away. This went on for quite a while back and forth, and with Shiny Fireplace nodding away.

Watching all this, in some weird way, I thought I was either getting scolded or asking to get something sorted out. I had no way of knowing; at this point, I was only watching them interacting with one another and guessing really. Then Antman started writing something on the clipboard and got up from leaning on the table talking to the man in the suit (Suitman, heehee), who now I truly believed was some sort of friend of mine, or it felt that I worked for him in some sort of way. Again, guesswork. Maybe he worked for me—I had no way of telling. Antman then went over to the filing cabinet and took out what I can only describe as a long white piece of paper and handed it to Suitman.

As everybody was leaving the room, I could see Shiny Fireplace get up off his seat and start walking out of this office. It wasn't as if I had to do anything to follow him; it just happened, like I was connected to him in some way. As we went out the door, all a sudden we (well, he) were now standing in a bigger, more open space. I couldn't even tell you if it was a room or not. Right in front of me was a tall blue woman—yes, blue—and she had a serious, but kind look on her face. I even could make it out that she was an older woman, not like a granny, but you could just tell she wasn't young.

She was standing over what looked like a church pew, but a small one. She was reading something out from it, looking down at it and then at me again. I couldn't see the floor or anything. It seemed cloudy and misty in all the background, up and down. Clearly, she was instructing me about something, talking away as Shiny Fireplace nodded.

There was a serious look on her face, but also a warm look about it. It wasn't threatening in any way; it was more of instructing me about something again. Not as much as a squeak could I hear. After a while, I realized that Shiny Fireplace Me was always nodding up and down, as if agreeing all the time and saying yes to everything. Back in the office, he would shake left and right for no sometimes, but not once in front of this blue woman.

She had small white lines and light purple lines in her face. Her head was shaped a bit like a triangle, but not a pointy one, a more rounded triangle, if you can picture it. Again, she was always looking at the me in front of me, but not once did she ever look directly at *me* me. I was beginning to feel invisible, but then again, I also thought that I was meant to see all this. Truthfully, at this point, I was just fascinated by it all and was fully aware that I physically was sitting on my sofa, though consciously, mentally, and spiritually I was certainly somewhere else altogether.

Then, as suddenly as I was standing in front of this blue woman, in a flash I was back sitting in the old office with Antman and Suitman going hammer and tongs, talking away. Antman was writing away, too, on this piece of paper.

This is when something caught my eye coming through the door. It was another person, a man wearing a big drape coat and with an Inspector Gadget hat on. I don't know what you call that hat, but instantly I thought he looked like Inspector Gadget out of the cartoon, not because of his face but what he was wearing. He sat directly opposite me on a chair that I didn't even know was there, as I hadn't seen it before he sat on it. I couldn't see his full face. The hat darkened his face down, but I could see his eyes, and they were coloured between red and orange. That's all I could see and all I would ever see of him, if it was a him.

He was sitting, talking to Shiny Fireplace Me, when Antman came over and handed him a piece of paper. They shook hands, and in turn turned to Shiny Fireplace Me and shook his hand.

Look, never in my life would I ever have thought that I would be writing a line in a book about Antman, Suitman, Inspector Gadget Man, Shiny Fireplace Me, and a blue woman with a triangular head, and me looking on and feeling like the Invisible Man. I'm laughing my head off writing this paragraph. *Wow*. What a vision I was having, and what a night I was having, to see and go through all this in one night. *Wow wow wow*, I kept saying to myself.

So now it was just Shiny Fireplace Me, then actually me behind him, with only eyes to see Inspector Gadget. He was looking at the piece of paper given to him by a seven-to-eight-foot Antman. I haven't stressed his height enough. He really was so tall and skinny in the lab coat.

I could clearly see they were talking a lot about something. I could never hear as much as a note, but it was nonstop for a while. This is when I noticed that Gadget Man was holding his hand out, and Shiny Fireplace Me seemed to be giving him something. I could not see, as my vision was blocked by the version of me, but as they did this, Gadget Man kept opening his jacket and putting something in the inside coat pocket. This kept happening, but never could I see what was being handed over.

After a while, both stood up and shook hands. When this was done, it was like a quick white flash, and I found myself in what looked like some sort of special room. I mean it really was this quick. I will now try to explain what was in this room, as it was so different from the office.

Firstly, it was colourful and bright, though never could I fully see Inspector Gadget's face, only his orangey red eyes. He was sitting on a white chair, and Shiny Fireplace Me was sitting down. I couldn't see the chair, but both were sitting. To my right hand, there was like a rollercoaster rail, a big red one, but I could only see about maybe ten to twelve parts of the rails, because there were white fluffy clouds all around that side of the room. The red rails went from the floor at an angle of 45 degrees roughly pointing upwards.

Gadget Man was sitting on the white chair and seemed to have a long white pipe with red on the top right beside him coming up from the floor. I couldn't see the bottom of this floor either, but he wasn't holding the pipe in his hand, as it seemed attached to something. After looking at him for a while, he was sitting close to shiny fireplace. This place was bright, but smaller and more enclosed. I can't say much more than what I've described.

I began to think that his face was just darkness, like a light grey, with only his eyes coloured. There was nothing malicious looking about him, nor did I get a bad feeling about him. It was like he was doing a job of some sort, very matter-of-factly it seemed to me, but I was intently watching everything. Not once had Shiny Fireplace Me turned around or tried to; it always seemed to work that way. Even if he turned a little, I seemed to have turned so I stayed directly behind him all the time.

As I watched, Gadget Man put his hand on the white pole, and out of the fluffy cloud down the way came a type of compartment trolley of some sort. There also seemed to be some type of baggage or a jacket type thing lying on it. He started to pull things out of his inside pocket and put them in this type of jacket bag; I find it hard to call it anything else, because that's what I was looking at.

It didn't take me too long to realize what was now happening in front of my eyes. You see, when doing my inner work, as I progressed through different stages, as you have read in this book, I was always doing different things with my hands: gathering light, sending things out, making clouds, shining beams of light, sucking things in, pushing or shooting things out, making holes in or through stuff, sending either white or grey clouds across vast places, ascending things, animals, people of all sizes and shapes from different timelines, sharks, whales, dinosaurs, electrical jolts, lightning, hoops of beams ... there was just so much.

I was now watching these things getting put on this trolley inside this jacket bag-type thing that seemed to be affixed and already a part of this trolley apparatus. It was like all the things I had done or could do with my hands were getting put onto this. They were taken away, and my only way of knowing this was all the up-and-down nods of Shiny Fireplace Me. I couldn't see the mouth of Gadget Man, but I could tell that he was at least facing me directly on. He bent down and pulled what seemed to be a yellow jacket bag closed and zipped up the middle, and the zip was big and wide. Also, it was black.

He then hit the red button on the top of the white pole and quickly disappeared through the fluffy cloud and away. As quickly as it got shot up another trolley appeared from the clouds and came down with another empty yellow jacket bag on it. In my head at this stage, I was thinking one of two things: either I was getting these powers taken off me or in some way my work was done up to this point and I had no need for them anymore.

The more I was looking at this happening, I was rethinking and replaying in my mind all the stuff I had done night after night, day after day, all this magical stuff, traveling through space, freeing light from the recesses of some underground system on this earthly plain. I had a strong feeling I was underground on some other planetary plane, but I can't be sure also I thought about how much I had now done with my hands. It was them that had helped me do so much.

This was when I saw my pair of wings getting put into the yellow jacket on the trolley. Truthfully, I hadn't even thought about my wings through this whole ordeal until this very moment. I clearly could see them lighting, glowing, glistening, and sparkling as they were put in by Inspector Gadget. He truly was treating them very respectfully and seemed to be handling them very carefully and softly, as if they were fragile, like you would do when packing glasses or porcelain into boxes when either storing them or getting them ready for transit.

I began doubting myself a bit about why this was happening, and why I was getting to witness it somehow. All the work I had done to get them and what seemed like upgrades on them, to getting them affixed to me properly only a couple of hours ago, and here they were on a trolley rollercoaster where I could only see a couple of rungs before they went up through the clouds. All the times I got stopped when I was about to finish them—also my mate calling round when I was in the middle of it all—and I just was glad of the rest. Maybe I was meant to meditate in some way before stopping, and I just hadn't the cosmic knowledge or the know-how what to do, as it was all to raw and real to me. I truly didn't know.

When *bang*, he hit the now red button and off they went, I was a bit devastated about it. I couldn't quite work it all out in my head. Maybe *sad* would be a better description of how I felt right at that moment—but again, when you truly believe there are no mistakes, only lessons, something transmutes in your mind.

I was still getting over my wings disappearing when I witnessed the trolley come down again empty with another yellow jacket-looking thing on it. What kept me going was the back of the head of Shiny Fireplace Me always nodding in agreement with Gadget Man. This was when I saw my white glowing suit, like a full body suit of lights with a pair of gloves, and some sort of visor helmet being put in and zipped up. The red button was pushed, and up they went and disappeared into the clouds.

As my mind began to settle, I thought maybe they were being put away for safekeeping and would always be there if I needed them. It was only my intuition that was telling me this, but mostly me doing a lot of guesswork. As I thought this, Shiny Fireplace Me and Gadget Man were shaking hands. The next thing, it went all black, just pure darkness in an instant.

That's when I opened my eyes, and it was just me sitting on the sofa in my living room. As much as it seemed a little foggy, it was my eyes readjusting back to normal, as my third eye had gone straight to sleep on me. It was already up in bed out cold, through sheer exhaustion. I looked at the clock, and it was 5:15 a.m.

What an eventful, action-packed, magic-filled, and at times very emotional night! I never really got to thinking about everything in detail, as I was so drunk with fatigue. My head hit the pillow like a six-inch block.

The next morning, as soon as I awoke, if you could call it that, my mind was heavily focused on the most magically mad and eye-opening night I had ever experienced, full stop. But as bizarre and strange as it was, it was just as exciting and informative. Time did not exist when I was experiencing these magical events I had gone through, and now here I was lying in bed trying to make some rational sense of it all in my foggy fickle mind.

The knowledge I have gained over this past year has been eye-openingly phenomenal. So, I was desperately trying to figure out why I had gone through it all. The first thing that came to my mind was the normal human response that it was taken from me. I was trying to rationalize my rawness in all these universal cosmic workings of energy, not knowing how to fully protect myself, differentiating between what was good and bad, real or fake, light and shadow, because in those moments on that night I felt a bit underqualified for doing such deep inner work. At times, truly, it felt like I had been thrown in at the deep end, so to speak.

Don't get me wrong: I didn't want to slow down. I truly loved what I was doing and being shown. I accepted fully what was happening to me. Some of the things I was experiencing, I honestly went with the flow of all the moments that were presented to me. Somehow, I seemed to get things right, as much as I knew I got so much wrong. I believed that this was playing a big part in my intensely fierce awakening.

I have no memory of doing any of these things in a past life, no idea how I knew instinctively how to get so many things done. I was witnessing in some groups that some people knew they were Lemurian, Andromedan, Atlantean, Arcturian, or Pleiadian, and were in contact with their ancestors. I had read many different cases where people remembered some of their past lives or what planet they were from. I have none of these memories of places or different timelines or what race I belong to. I can guess, but I truly have no clue.

What I do know is that through the intensity of my inner work with dark and light energies, I travel to places all unknown to me, meeting and ascending animals, so many people and things, and in the most unrecognizable places. Having a natural knack for it, honestly, I truly loved what I was being given a chance to do. I felt blessed to be involved with helping, and the more I learnt about light workers, shadow workers, grid workers, early-way showers, truth seekers, and how this all helps the collective consciousness of earth itself, this alone inner-motivated me to do more.

It is good to know in some way that you are helping in this world with people who are in such a low vibrational mind-set, so much so that if you said to them about going within and healing themselves you might get laughed at. They just don't recognize that everything is vibration, frequency, and sound. I know this firsthand because I was one of them, so I could quite easily relate to the laughing, but to be awakened the way I have, it's about getting it out there, and at least you are making them aware.

I want to try to heal as many people in the world as I possibly can, and hopefully baring my soul in this book can give me a platform to at least begin with my soul's purpose and follow my divine path to spread what I know about the secrets that are purposefully hidden from the masses by very smart, generational, sneaky, greedy, controlling, rich, dark, cruel, shadowy *pufferfish*. Yes, that's what I'll call them: pufferfish. From now on I'm calling them this, because it's an insult to call them human beings. All they do is poison and manipulate the world and everything in it.

Back to the longest night of my life. So instead of thinking that somehow, I got everything taken from me, I began to think I had witnessed either the changing of my contract, the extension of my contract to a higher self, or the receiving of a brand-new contract because I not only felt I hadn't done enough but that I was only getting started.

I realized this could happen by listening to a recording of Dolores Cannon speaking that I saw on Julia Cannon's social platform. Not only did I convince myself of this, when I thought it, my ears reacted in a way that confirmed it for me. To have such faith in this is a power within itself.

This reminds me of something else Dolores Cannon said: "The key to true peace and happiness is to let go of judgement, fear, and attachment, and to live in the present moment with an open and loving heart." I couldn't have thought about anything else at this stage, and I got straight out of my bed and gave each of my children a kiss on the head and said that I loved them. Cheesy, I know.

I got so emotional that morning with thoughts of providing for and protecting my children with my life implanted in my mind forever. Also, at this moment, I felt proud that I not only refused the vaccine but also allowed none of my children to receive it either when so many around us were getting it. No matter what I said, the hive mind was working at its height around this time, and I have a memory of asking different people which pharmaceutical company they received their vaccine jab from. Not one person could tell me, not one. That alone tells me so much about the programming that goes into creating the hive mind. Maybe next time with more information shown and knowledge gained, the right questions will be asked before you find yourself in a position of having no rights to even ask questions that fall on nothing but deaf ears.

This is why I feel so much about people of faith. Normal folk go to church full of hope and faith with no experience of anything of what I was going through spiritually, although still having blind faith in the creator of all. One stands for truth and love, the other fear and control.

I truly believe the matrix programming of the school system has been happening for many years now. As much as there are periods of religious education, it is taught in such a way that they don't want you to believe in a creator of all. It's such a corruptive way of teaching, making it so far-fetched. Then alongside it all, they teach you not to believe in any of it, and they have mastered it in a way you don't even know that there is a matrix, only a Hollywood movie, but at least that proactively gets you to think about it. At least we became more aware that one exists. If you watch the Matrix movies from an observing perspective it tells you so much of what is going on within a holographic reality. So, in life much spiritual teaching is left out and replaced with teachings of a controlling mind-set for the masses to worship and to, instil a belief in a hierarchy that has its true purpose hidden within the matrix itself with systematic control at its forefront.

Once your personal consciousness sees through all of this, alarm bells should start ringing, the bubbles should begin to burst, and all the light bulbs should start going off like crazy. If not, then maybe it's time you took a moment out of your life and began to educate yourself and turn all the unknown mysteries into knowledge rather than ridicule, laugh, and put down the people whose only aim is to help in the only proper way through truth, compassion, love, and peace.

The unawoken ones, which I once was, would then begin the name-calling of *weirdos*, *Bible bashers*, and *treehuggers*. If you fall into this category of people, you are not awake. You are still snoring. When change takes place in your life, sometimes you know how to keep those old habits with all your might. By exposing yourself, by losing and suppressing yourself, you do not know other people's needs. We revolve around patterns we may have become aware of but are not yet ready to let go.

Maybe we never wondered what *releasing* means to us. How do we experience it in the body, and what is our limiting belief that this release in us can awaken? It shows you how to let go of fear and how letting it go awakens the need to cling to your relationship with your own soul. Life is not about dividing, it's about unifying. We are all one and live under the universal law of one, not the laws of the land and the laws of the sea.

The bankers have indoctrinated into the fabric of most societies on the globe, divisions between religions, races, rich, and poor. It will always be this way until, as a collective consciousness, we awake en masse and just say *no* to it all. I can't remember where I heard this next phrase or who said it, but I've always remembered it: "The magic you are looking for is in the work you are avoiding." Never were truer words ever spoken.

On a more personal level, I have taught myself to hear the call of my soul, which I know now through my oversoul is united with the soul of the universe. It tells me that when the injuries heal and the despair of past traumas begin to heal, they leave behind scars that embody the pain you have endured and show you your own resourcefulness to overcome the obstacles that have been in your way and the ones you have put there yourself. Tomorrow will go better if you use today to make a difference. It might appear a simple thing to say, but it's not.

So, when I was starting out on this journey, I decided to write a book because I thought my experiences were so raw, real, and at times magical that it would help others become more aware of the spiritual side of their own lives. I remember having a conversation with Mahoney, a close friend. When I told him that maybe I was thinking about writing a book, he replied that AI—artificial intelligence on an app he had downloaded—would write it in a couple of minutes, the whole story, just give it a title and *voilà*, job done. My thinking at this time was that *I* for intelligence and *A* for artificial were the factors that prompted me to think a little deeper. Unbeknown to me, he had helped plant a seed or even more so, the beginning of the growth of a small root.

As much as people talk about AI, the word *artificial* is seldomly spoken when referring to it. People talk more about the great things it can achieve, working out people's personal and global problems and in the shortest time thought possible. But therein lie so many unforeseen problems. Its maybe the programmers more than the AI itself that will do the most harm in the end.

Human emotions play such a big factor in each one of our lives daily, good and bad, big and small. Without them what would we be or what even would we become? *Artificial*, that's what. Yes, emotional decisions can be made wrongly, but it's 50-50 they can also be made right. At least they are made based on the perception of a real being with a spiritual human heart. Maybe that is the way it is meant to be. There are no mistakes, only lessons.

To make decisions with no attachment of human emotions aligned with the connection of living one's life, who then would stand to benefit from the emotionless artificial controlled response? The very sneakiest and brightest of all pufferfish and their-long awaited meticulously planned cruel global agenda of the depopulation of the 8.1 billion emotionally driven spiritual beings of this earth.

Without present emotions, who are we and what would we become? Just pieces of artificial data controlled by numbers, attached to nothingness. This concept will baffle some, not all, but it will never an awakened soul. There is so much global manipulation of everybody's emotions, so vast you are deemed crazy to even think such unhived thoughts, but here we are fighting religious wars generationally planned with foresight that only carefully benefits the elite pufferfish global community.

As wars are so expensive, they need public money to then be distributed to private military pufferfish companies to do with it as they please. So not only do you pay with your life but your money also. Disgusting. Everything since you were born has been designed in a way to keep you in a controlled state of just over broke. That's what *job* truly means. Prosecution in other lanugages.

You will come to realize and see you have no say in the matter; only pufferfish do. As much as there can be good things done with intelligence, *artificial* is exactly what it says.

When you become spiritually awakened, sink deep within yourself, and gain the universal truths that we are all spiritual beings of light living a human existence, you become anchored from that point on. You will never be like you were. There is no going back. They say that time makes the heart grow fonder, but for me, it makes the heart beat stronger.

I cannot stress enough how hard it must be for people to read my words about having a set of wings, traveling through space, glowing suits, powers beyond human construct, eyes that make holes in matter, blue beings, dinosaurs, people trapped on unknown planets, contracts, angels, not to talk of a twin flame, one who shares a soul with another, a metaphysical twin, a divine connection to the divine realm inside yourself ... believe me, the list goes on. To find this all out by experiencing it firsthand—and then to live it out in such magical ways, to make a choice to help, to accept you have a divine purpose—is such an extraordinary journey to go through so late in my life, or I could say early in my life, depending in how you observe it, also it's not easy especially to keep going, but it's certainly worthy not to give up.

I truly believe within myself that I was meant to tell my story and have an unfounded faith that it will consciously, unconsciously, or subconsciously help so many people raise their awareness and realize their own truths of this world. There has been so much effort globally put into this world to prevent the truth of the cosmic workings of this universe and the law of one. This is the beginning of the conscious fighting back of the truth. Through the law of one they must tell you about what they are going to do before they do it. When this is known to the masses on a global scale, it will be their downfall. The pride they take in being so sneaky about these events to appease their own egos, within songs, cartoons, movies, video games and television and on money, all done to avoid their own unstoppable relentlessly seeking cosmic karma. Subliminal masters at the low frequencies because they need it so, as their disservice to their own soul will have to wait another lifetime, to forge a different cycle of an unforeseen contract.

CHAPTER 18

I Love the Sun and
the Sun Loves Me

WRITING A BOOK—A novel, my story, an overextended essay, whatever you want to call it—is something that not only did I think I would never do, but to go ahead and actually do it, to put my pen to paper, is something I'm already looking back at amazement at the journey this has put me on, and I haven't even finished the book yet. In my head, the last chapter I wrote about was going to be my final one when I first decided to go on this journey. But as different things unfold in your life, your mind progresses, your emotional reality changes, and you realize your story is still living alongside each paragraph that you write.

I've never written as much as an essay from my GCSE history exam. Big shout-out to Mr McConnell, my old history teacher, who taught me everything needs a source. You can't have anything historical without a good source to back it all up. This has taken on a whole new meaning in my life as I look at the source of the cosmic universe, as the beginning of breath itself. There's a saying that all roads lead to Rome. For me, all life leads to the source, every heartbeat, every cell, every electrical pulse, every atom, every little vibration and sound all lead to source, whatever that may be. It is the nothing that lies connected to everything.

My life is led by knowing that I have a small spark of this inside me, a piece of the source. Every one of us does. To find it, you must look within, then look within a little more and then with an imaginary shovel dig deep down within, and with truth, honesty, peace, love, forgiveness, and gratitude, you will find what has always been there waiting and wanting to be found by you: your soul. This is what I have done, and it has led me on a journey of all journeys, and one that I now know is about creating heaven on this earth. I don't say these words lightly, as to get there I have filled the River Nile a couple of times with waterfalls of tears. O.K., fair enough, not that much, but you get the point. The built-in emotions and sense of feeling you are given as a gift makes life itself worthy of living by truth.

I find my mind beginning to think forward with thoughts of how to end this book—what my last paragraph will be. Even now, I'm thinking *What's going to be the last line.* Then *What's going to be my final written word?* I am sure authors have faced this dilemma from the very first book scroll, tablet, papyrus ever written, and here I am thousands of years later doing the exact same.

What I'm about to write involves something that I had intended to keep for myself. I don't fully know why, but it plays such a big part in my ever-evolving life now that I have changed my mind—a full U-turn to be honest—because now, I truly believe I was meant to tell it as part of my story.

I love the sun, and the sun loves me is a sentence that quite literally popped into my head as it relates to the gift that I now have and use when and where I can. Ever since I was a child, I was told to never look directly at the sun, or you will eventually go completely blind. It was programmed into my brain, mind, thoughts, and inner core beliefs. I grew up totally believing 100 per cent that it was true. Not once did I ever question it, and sure enough, as all children do, you'd look directly at it and yes, you'd blink like a faulty indicator as the white flash nearly blinded you.

Each of us has thought this at one time or another, even to the point where you would look up accidently and the sun would hit your retinas and whoever you were with would probably hear something to the effect of, "Oh shit, that nearly blinded me!" and the sunglasses would be pulled out and put on. As a self-employed painter and decorator, when outside on a sunny day painting a house with white paint, there is no doubt that the reflection of the wall, plus the wet shiny newly applied paint, would treble the strength of the glare of the sun rays on my eyes. At that moment, for sure I thought that I could certainly go blind.

As a forty-seven-year-old spirit having a human existence, I've come to realize that it was always bullshit fed to us throughout our childhood, so by the time you even become an adolescent, the program was set in motion, in a very early young form of matrix programming. It was done that well. I can't even tell you where I first heard this; it just was there, like it was purposely put there for reasons unbeknown to all of us. As you have read in some parts of this book, I have looked and stared at the sun, and amazing things it has done for me—to me and with me—but what I now can do even amazes me every time I do it.

For years, the sun has been not only a source of heat but also the source of a good suntan. Each year, you would save up the money and plan to go on a summer holiday. The most common booking would be somewhere in Spain, or if you could afford it, a tropical holiday—always with the belief that the sun shines brighter there because of the climate bar being unlucky, and 99 per cent of the time you would get sunny weather. That's exactly the way I thought it would stay, and I had no reason to think anything different.

I always loved the sunshine due to the tan I got. It was the opposite for many red-haired beings, like my stepmother, Audrey, who got burnt like a tomato and then peeled like an onion. It's like a man's make-up, because with a tan you tend to look a lot better and feel a lot better too—without the lippy, off course.

That all changed one day when what I now know to be my flame twin came down from it as I meditated in the sun. At the time, of course, I hadn't a clue what was happening. But as I have written earlier in the book, it was a truly amazing moment in my life.

As I progressed with my learning, and as more knowledge was awakening from within myself and what I read, I began getting energy from it. I would look until wee black dots would form, and my eyes would become resistant to the original glare and brightness that it gave off. That was all I had done thus far. At this point, I wasn't even doing it to decalcify my third eye. I didn't need to, as it was working or automatic at this stage.

Then one early morning I was looking out my kitchen window at the sun coming up, and I spotted what at first was a light coming out of the top of the sun. It rapidly grabbed my upmost attention. It was like a beam of light coming out the top of the sun, and my mind just couldn't get round to the fact. I thought it was some sort of glare or reflection through my kitchen window.

It seemed to work a little better when I angled my head at a certain position; out it would pop, pure white light, like diamond white, and so crystal clear. It then dawned on me that if I flicked my head forward, it would go straight back into the sun. I did this repeatedly until my neck got stiff, and my head got a little light.

I had to get my youngest daughter up for school, but as I did this, I couldn't get out of my mind what had just happened. As it was such a busy morning, I had nearly convinced myself that it was a definite reflection through my kitchen window. I drive to my work painting a woman's house, and on the ten o'clock break was sitting in my car. The sun was still out, so I got out of my car and did the exact same thing with my eyes and head and *bingo!* There it was again, only this time, it was so much clearer than it was earlier in the morning through my window.

It was so clear that I made out the shape of what it was. Dumbfounded at that moment about what I was seeing, I was amazed beyond anything, and I wasn't meditating or even trying to. Just *bingo*, there it was.

That's when I became aware of exactly where I was: in a woman's garden, looking up at the sun, eyes wide open, and at probably what seemed a very weird angle. So, I stopped immediately and went back to my work. All that morning, though, it's all I could think about right up to dinnertime.

So, I parked the car behind the brush at this woman's front drive, in such a way that I could look up without looking weird. As soon as I got into position, I looked, and sure enough, there it was popping out at the top of the sun again. I clearly could make out a man with his arms straight out, but I couldn't see his face. What I could see was that he was he and was made of pure light. It was like it was see-through and it was the shape I could make out the most, but clearly the light that was being given off was beams, rays, swirls, patterns of every type, just proceeding out and across the sky.

I didn't want to go back to work, but I had to. All day, it was all I thought about, hoping that the sun would stay out long enough after work so I could do it all again. It did, and I didn't fully know what I was doing and for what reasons at this time, but I knew at least that it was all good. I felt it: the feeling of not knowing what you were doing and at the same time doing something that made you feel great. So, this was how I felt that got me not only excited every time I did it, but visually I could see it happening right in front of me. Truly, truly amazing—I mean this from the bottom of my heart. This is so magical to do, and the only person who knew at this point was my best matey and soul brother, Colly B.

He listened to me in awe. I knew I didn't have to even try to make him believe me; he just knew that I was telling the truth. To have someone in my life at this moment like Colly was a blessing, as I had no like-minded people who would have innerstood any of it the way he did. Solid as a rock he was for me. So, thank you, Colly. There are no words that I can write about you that explain how you've helped me, as you have been on this journey right alongside me. So, with a warm heart, "I love you, matey, forever." We have a bond that cannot be broken—to infinity, bro.

I have always, throughout my life, subdued my feelings in one way or another. I got very good at hiding my true feelings, so sometimes what you got was not exactly what you saw. About 90 per cent of the time I was me, but there was always about 10 per cent I kept to myself. Even I, at times, didn't know I was doing it. To go through these experiences so rapidly has brought up emotional trauma I didn't even know I had, so even with myself, it took a while just to recognize it as trauma.

I have gone deep within myself and pulled out just about every emotion known to man, dealt with it, and healed whatever I could. Even today, I am still healing. In this journey, there has been no hiding places—and then, now, to see a man angel of light come out of the top of the sun and shine light right over my head and into the atmosphere.

As if I could not be any more amazed about what was happening, to be at your home making dinner and then going outside and in between doing this amazing magical thing with the sun, then going back in, finishing dinner, cleaning up, then back outside spreading light through this process—my intent and work on this began to intensify and snowball a little, as I was so amazed by it all. The trust and belief that I was beginning to have in what I was doing came from the feelings I got when doing it.

To explain this a little better, I would see patterns or light beams stream out from the man in the sun and spread across the sky. Sometimes later, if the conditions were right, it would show up in clouds right across the whole sky. To visually see this at the beginning filled me with a great sense of self-empowerment. Just to witness such things one, maybe two, hours after my doing this … there is a colossal stream of thoughts that comes along with it.

After three or four days and nights of doing this, the ego part of your psyche transmutes and begins to dissipate those feelings of power, and you realize that you're using your heart and mind together. Then you begin to see it as a gift. The gratitude I thought mentally and said verbally was nearly continuous. You really do begin to spiritually think about the connection to one's higher self, which also implodes your connection to the divine.

The emotional rollercoaster of all the highs and lows up to this point could surface at any time, but when doing this with the sun, my emotions were always happy ones. Inside yourself, the emotions, the good feelings, comes in wave after wave. I sometimes could do nothing but release, with so much happiness attached to it. Really, it made you feel like you were choosing to do something special for the greater good.

In doing my work with the sun, I got very tearful in the middle of it. The detail that this allowed me to see was extraordinary. I could clearly see him come out as a short shaft of light, and as I held my eyes straight on—the tears let me look closer and for longer, because they took the sharpness of the glare out of the sunlight, like a shield over my eyeball—I could see the wings through the light glowing brightly and shimmering. If I moved my eyes around and squinted at the same time, I could see the patterns on the wings. It quite literally looked like that of a peacock when it spread its wings open, and so, so magical to watch.

The more I moved my head and eyes, the more he would spread out and push the light as far as my neck would go. Sometimes when I was tearful, I could slow it right down and hold it where I wanted it, and truly watch him take shape from the top of the sun. The light that he gave off was so bright and awe-inspiring to me that I would do it so long, although my eyes and neck would begin to hurt a lot. My memories at the time were of the old saying *No pain, no gain* (old school).

This was like the pinnacle of all my energy work and light work. No meditating needed; I felt it was now implanted in my makeup, my DNA. I just didn't know all the answers, and I still don't. I wasn't thinking could this get any better. I'm only writing it down now because it did. More breathtaking magical light popped out suddenly when doing this one evening as the sun was just about to go down.

When I was doing it one night, my neck was beginning to get sore. Sometimes I would put my hands behind my head to support the weight of my napper so I could do it for longer. I moved my head forward for a little rest, and when I moved it back again, I then to my total amazement saw another light come out and spread across the sky. At first, I thought that maybe it was just my other eye playing a trick on me, as I had been doing this for so long. So, I put my head forward and did it more slowly this time.

What I saw shook my emotions to the core, and I mean to the *core*. Realizing what I had just witnessed, my body began to buzz with shivers nearly everywhere, and I couldn't help myself but burst into tears. Proper crying took hold of me.

Normally, when doing amazing life-changing new things in my life like this, I would get emotionally tearful, but rather than wipe the tears away, I would let them run down my face and feel them as they went down. Some would go into my mouth, and I could taste the tears, and there was a small part of me that liked that taste. I don't know why, I just did.

Other times, my head would be tilted back so that I could feel them run down the sides of my head, and as they got to my ear, I really did begin to feel the tears roll, so tickly and slowly, into my ears. Again, this felt good to me. I wouldn't purposely stop them from going right in. Truthfully, I loved the sensation of the feeling itself as it trickled in some were very hot.

But crying now at the moment of realizing that the other beam of light was coming out of the sun was an uncontrollable, childlike crying. The actual noise and the fact I couldn't wise myself up and stop it, that repeating of intake after intake of air shuffling into my mouth, exactly reminded me of the way you would have cried as a child.

It was clearly a woman that I saw, and she was not the same white diamond light as the man. She was just as bright, if not brighter, but it was like a goldy bronze shade. *Wow wow wow bingo bango bongo*. I couldn't get hold of my emotions at this point. My nose was filling up so fast, it was beginning to drip out of my snout. Wave after wave of emotions came over me. I don't want to sound all boogers, but I had no tissues with me, so I used my sleeve because I did not want to leave the vision for a split second just in case it disappeared somehow.

With all the tears coming out, I tilted my head forward again and could hold it at the point where the two of them came out at the same time. With the glaze and glare of my tears protecting my eyes, I would slowly bring them out and watch them both go from a shaft of light coming out of the top of the sun to two angels' side by side, with wings, and both with their hands and arms straight out in a cross position.

I was beginning to calm my emotions down to where the crying stopped—but not the tears. They kept rolling down my face. The more I tilted my head back, the more of the sky they would spread out and cover it with their light. Truly amazing, not only to be doing but to also be seeing it with my own two eyes making it happen.

At this point, my neck was really getting painful, as my head had been back for some time. It was so hard for me to stop, as the feeling I was getting about spreading light began to relay in my mind. When I tilted it back and forward, I would stop just before they went back into the sun. As much as I couldn't see both their faces clearly, as it was lines and swirls and flashes of pure light, what I did make out was that the wings on the woman looked exactly like the ones of who I knew now to be my twin flame, from the time she came down and turned into a woman that one day coming home shopping from Sainsbury's.

Away I went again. I now felt that I had no control of my emotions. I kept getting waves of heat, then they would get hotter. It's so hard for me to put into words how I felt. It felt like very hot emotions, once the penny dropped who this was. Then it began to hit me who the man angel was, and just when I went over to get a better look, the sun itself was getting surrounded by a massive cloud, and that was the end of it for that day at least.

When I went back into the house and sat down, trying to gather my thoughts, I felt a bit different about myself. It's hard to explain—just something different. Who gets to experience amazing stuff like this? I began thinking about what all twin flames are doing. I honestly had no idea. I didn't have any like-minded people I could discuss this with; only my best matey, and he got it all.

I haven't even met my twin flame yet—well, not that I know of. But here I am on a metaphysical side of my spiritual life doing all this stuff. So out of the top of the sun must be my higher self and twin flame on a different level or dimension to me doing this, and I visually get to see it through my own eyes. It's what I thought that night.

Experiences like this are so hard to fathom at the time, but when you feel emotionally connected to it all, it takes a bit of time to sink in, but the attachment to it spiritually, mindfully, and visually makes it feel right inside.

Somehow, you are meant to go through it in this way. There are probably people out there who couldn't handle it or believe it could happen—too far-fetched. I get that, because it is so otherworldly for the normal everyday rational person to begin to think about in their minds. If it wasn't happening to me, I certainly would fall into that way of thinking.

I'm writing this as living proof that it can and does happen. In this spiritual life, I have seen people who say to hide these gifts to keep them a secret, but how does that help? Humanity as a collective rise as one. Maybe it's fear that stops them; I just don't know.

Going through all of this, if you hold on to fear, you're only attaching yourself to something that's a man-made illusion. Embrace the unknown, for it is the birthplace of miracles. You are greater than the obstacle. You are stronger than the struggle. You are more powerful than the challenge. Hold your light when things get tough; the universe always has your back. Align with the cosmos and let the magic happen.

The universe always replaces what exits your life with something bigger and better. Don't be stuck holding on to the past or resisting change. Welcome new energy. Let go of what needs to be removed. There are great blessings in surrendering and allowing. As you release the old, it makes room for the new. I love that caption.

That night, I went to my bed with my mind filled with seeing my twin flame alongside my now higher self. I had thought it was a sun angel, but I felt a connection. What was I connected to? Was it my actual self, Conrad? Was that me coming out of the top of the sun?

I found it hard to fall asleep that night, as a form of excitement filled and flowed through my veins. I had been doing it by myself for a while only now I had my goldy bronze twin flame by my side. That night, through pure exhaustion and a very stiff neck, I must have eventually knocked myself off to sleep.

As soon as I awoke the next morning, my mind automatically shifted its thoughts to the night before. This was beginning to happen to me quite regularly now. I'm not saying I was getting used to it in any way, only that it was becoming more frequent as I was falling more in love with myself and the work I was doing.

That morning was the first time I thought about my twin flame in a different way. (I get a lot these first times in my ever-evolving life.) I have songs I would listen to that linked or recoiled my mind to think about her. You must inner stand, with all these thoughts and feelings of being emotionally linked, I had no memory of being with her.

Would I ever get to meet my human counterpart, or was I destined to go through life only linked spiritually and never physically? To find out at forty-six years old that you have a soul and then to just as quickly realize that you share it with someone still amazes me even now, as I'm writing this. The only times I got to see her face was when she came down from the sun; one night where I was shown my higher self and my twin flame dancing in a hall of lights; and when she went into the palm of my hand. On all three occasions, I never got a good look. Just enough to see she was the prettiest woman I had ever seen, even without fully seeing her. Maybe that's a bit hard to make sense of, but it certainly was how I felt. There would be times I would begin with my thoughts to fantasize about her and then would have to stop myself physically from going through with it.

It was hard at first, but when I was lying in bed that morning, the sexual human way of my mind and its ego-driven thoughts really began to change. I'm not saying they have gone away; they haven't. I have just become more personally enlightened about the importance of the spiritual side of this extraordinary connection that I feel very deep inside me about my twin flame. I knew nothing of this about a year and half ago, but here I am now. I'm just trying to show you, through my words, how intensifying my awakening was. I am still me, but I just look and live my life in such a different and rewarding way. It's not easy at times, but at the same time it is also exhilarating.

Ellen Redd of Twin Flame Initiates recently put up a caption about fake twin flames and the damage they do with false teachings, and the impact it has on the spiritual realms. I can't sit here and say I know that much about it yet, only enough. A lot of it has come from Ellen's knowledge on it all.

My perception of it is that I live my life opposite from what I did before. I live with truth, honesty, integrity, peace, love, tranquillity, faithfulness, and happiness. The list goes on, but the meaning of all these is, I try so hard to be as authentic as I can. That is so much easier said than done. Ellen has taught me that this is the basis for what you need to even begin to have a twin flame reunion, and I have learnt it's such a lovely, kind, and rewarding way to live your life day by day.

When you look around, most people are the complete opposite—all in competition with one another. Over half of them don't even know they are it's just the programmed life they live. No fault of their own, as they don't know the truth of how life really works. So, part of the driving force behind me writing this book is to make the collective consciousness wake up to a more truthful and fulfilling life to live in the here and now, to become fully aware of who and what you really are.

Just to wake up that morning and open the curtains and see that the sun had come out filled me with even more excitement. I can only say that I shovelled my breakfast down so fast, my mind will not let me remember what I had that morning. There is in the corner of my mind a snippet that remembers Coco Pops, but I can't be sure, as my thoughts were focused on going out the back of my house and having a look at the early morning sunshine. I was certainly eager to see if she was going to appear again. I didn't have to wait long, as I quickly looked up and as my eyes began to adjust, *bingo bongo*, there they both were, shining as bright as the sun.

I started looking at the man, and my intuition told my mind straight away that it was me. So early in the morning, and here I was already having a magical experience with the sun. Excitement filled my stomach. It felt good, and with the sun being so bright, I really was mindfully spreading their/my light across the sky as much as I could.

It didn't take long for my stiff and now sore neck to begin to grab my attention. I ended up being thankful for this, as due to the pain, I tipped my head back and rested it on my hands, which I was holding up behind my neck. When I did this and rolled my eyes back, as if looking upwards to my forehead, I realized that the two images crossed over enough to come together and touch each other.

I thought how amazing this was, and to know inside that I was helping to make it happen filled me with so much early-morning joy. I have been looking up at the sun all my life—here in Northern Ireland, in Spain, France, Switzerland, Scotland, it didn't matter! I had never ever done anything like this in all my life. Sore neck or not, I kept going until time caught up with me, and it was time to get my children up for school and then go to work.

I wanted so much to tell my youngest daughter, Ameila, what I had been doing before I woke her up, but I knew deep inside that she probably would have told me to "Wise up, you alien." Of that I had no doubt. So quickly

I knew to say nothing. I thought back to when I was twelve, with my dad telling me the same. So yes, it probably was the smart thing to do.

Even so, what an amazing start to the day that was for me! I happened to be working inside that day, and every minute of every hour I wished that I was working outside. Just to get outside to the sun that day, I would have painted an oil tank, a skip, or a line of wheelie bins. Anything to be out in the sun. But it wasn't to be. I would have done it for free and all.

What a gift to have received. This made me feel great inside. As soon as I got home and cooked dinner and cleaned up, outside I went, and off I went with my newfound amazing connection to the sun. Amazing, amazing, to be doing this now in my front garden.

I'll admit, sometimes my emotions would get the best of me, with my thoughts of the magnitude of what I was doing with a celestial body of light and so much of it. I really began to think to myself, *who else would be doing such things?* Or was this a journey I was personally on? I did keep asking my angels and guides and would get synchronicities back in numbers, and when I read them, the knowledge I began to gain about divine connection, the divine realm, blew my absolute mind. It was all about how I was right where I was meant to be.

If it was only one time, yes, it could have been taken as a coincidence. But with the repeated times it was happening to me, I had absolutely no doubt in my mind about what was happening and who I was becoming. There's no such thing as coincidence.

It was more than visions. It was a trail of deep thoughts and feelings that came in waves. If that is what unconditional love feels like, all I wanted was more and more, to help in such ways and not feel egotistical about it. A feeling of love was such an emotional high for me. No drug in the world could surpass this feeling.

When starting out on this journey, I couldn't have foreseen all these things happening. You come to experience blind faith, a state of always being mindfully hopeful, a determination of trusting all the things that are being chucked at you. You take in all the new information about an unknown series and levels of dimensions, the seamlessly infinite already-known knowledge flying around about chakras, Kundalini awakenings, meridian lines, earthing, races of beings, karma affirmations, energies, vibration, Mother Earth, enlightenment symbolism (good and shadowy), destiny, enslavement divinity, quantum physics, electricity magnetism, black holes, quantum entanglement ... the list goes on, but even those couple of lines are topics that had never entered my life.

Dolores Cannon to me was like an angel on this earth. I don't know for sure whether angels reincarnate as a human beings, but if there ever was one who could modify that belief, it surely would be her, as the dedication and knowledge she worked on, the healing she provided with her angelic work, and the writing in her books opened everything for everyone everywhere to get a glimpse of the subconscious universal soul, with a mind-set to help earth itself and those who dwell in it.

For someone like me to be witnessing this firsthand, I felt like it was my chance, my opportunity, my purpose, my reason for being and living at this time. I was embracing my divine purpose, using leadership skills already built inside. Not only did I believe that I could change my actual DNA by living an honest, truthful, loving life (thank you, Billy Carson), but I learned that we have all been capped at number two, and that the other ten, which they have called junk DNA, are really untapped and unused, a full ten more to receive downloads of retrograde ancient DNA codes, leading to your divine blueprint, ancestry, cosmically, universally. There is so much I still must learn, but I have tunnel vision that it's not about the end; it's the journey you get to experience traveling and living, creating as you move along on all the present guided moments.

I know all this might be too much information packed into a small page, but it reminds me of what it was like when I was learning how to meditate properly. To get awoken the way I did—and I'm only speaking for myself—meditating basically was, I don't want to say *easy*, but the quickness of how I was able to see and experience magical moments was breathing a couple of times, closing my eyes, and away I went. As I began to settle down a little after what I believe was the changing or receiving of a contract, I really had to learn what true meditation was.

I was always thinking of something and found it really hard at the beginning to block out all the brain chatter: bills, worry, fear, weight, health, money, food, not enough guilt, all the controlling thoughts, house, children, fuel, jealousy, paranoia, envy, distrust, aggression, consumerism, dark dilemmas, and judging things that hadn't even happened, and here I was playing out different scenarios in my mental state as if they had already happened, manifesting the negative into my own life by my own self.

So, to master mediation, to sit there and be at one with yourself and think of nothing, just to be, was so much harder than I ever anticipated. This is where your connection is made. This is when you give out and receive help from unforeseen knowledge, answers, and true manifestations. Each time, it is different—physically, spiritually, emotionally, mentally, visually, and positively.

Detachment is not that you own nothing.
Detachment is that nothing owns you.
(Thank you, Jay Shetty)

CHAPTER 19

Intuition

TO FIND THE courage within oneself to begin the journey of writing a book, having no prior knowledge or experience in the field itself—the publishing, marketing, editing, and finally production—has been a big eye-opener for me. Somewhere along the way, you begin to gain much more wisdom on the internal workings of the process as a whole, and somehow you find the mental fortitude to keep going, combined with an inner desire to globally get as many eyes and earthly minds to process your thoughts as words on paper and spread spirituality in your own unique way of the truths as they began bombarding my life on a daily basis.

I have come to notice about myself that constantly and continually, my thoughts run in one ear, but just as fast, they sprint out the other, chopping and changing as fast as a Formula One pitstop. To have been awoken to something that was so new to me, and to have such an unwavering drive and a belief deep inside on a divine level, I decided to embark on a spiritual awakening and discover what that entails daily to live your life of truth.

I want my readers to not only experience what I have gone through on my personal journey, who I have become, how I choose to live, and the knowledge I have gained, but also to inner stand the upheaval of all the lies and deceit showered upon every one of us. I want to lift the dark veil inserted into our minds at such an early stage of our lives and reveal the ignorance of all the very intelligent programming stuffed and packed tightly into our early fragile minds, to begin the onset of a fear-controlled existence. It is done so well; it is so carefully planned and intelligently executed, since the day your unknowing parents or parent signed your birth certificate in whichever registry office that is strategically placed up and down the country in every city, town, and village.

This is the day you became a commodity, bought and sold to a corporation and secretly swindled from that moment on until your timeline is up, and your usage is no more. Or maybe it's the beginning of another cycle, when the real battle for your energy truly starts all over again. The known name for this earthly process is your *strawman*.

Intuition—what is it really? This is something that everybody uses, knowingly or unknowingly, consciously or unconsciously, in their daily lives. I have used it throughout my entire life so far, and with so many moments not under the knowledge of doing so. It's that feeling when you walk into a room and upon entering, you seem to know straight away that you were the topic of conversation. It's being in the middle of a packed pub/bar and getting the vibe that something is about to kick off. It's your body's way of telling you to either get ready or get out of there as quickly as you can, just giving you enough time to evade the situation. It's receiving that strange and sometimes dirty look from a man or woman, as if in some way you have done them wrong in another timeline but knowing you have never clapped an eye on them. It's knowing whether to back out of that business deal at the last minute, and just the same, to seal it, knowing that potentially in the future it could work out well.

Intuition is what tells you to go for it, and just the same, to run from it, to say yes or no. They call it "that gut feeling," but is that where it comes from, amongst your breakfast, entwined with the bubbling acid in the middle of breaking it down to filter the good and create the waste? Personally, I don't think so.

Intuition is your direct connection to the divine and holds all the answers you need for personal growth and spiritual development. It also encourages you to be brave, follow your passions, and stay true to yourself, not swayed by others' opinions. Those are outside noises; intuition is your inner voice. It's a feeling of soundless words, a churning feeling from within, and at the same time instantaneously sent to your cortex. Only then does it become a sound through your verbal actions, a yes or no on the subject matter.

It's an inner voice sent from the metaphysical universe that not only lies within you but *is* you, a consciousness using your biological voice box as the sound to move you forward in life, to protect your physical body from within. Everyone has it, but not everybody uses it. Simplifying it down a little, as a person, you know when you are doing things to your body that are good and healthy alongside the bad and unhealthy. Eating too much or too little, either way, you will have that little voice relaying the need to change your eating habits. Too much junk food and not enough fruit, or thoughts of enrolling in a gym, but mindfully creating setbacks and never getting round to making the plans, constantly putting it off till next week or next month— but always there's that wee voice telling you to get started.

You may naturally stop paying attention to the stream of thoughts running through your active mind. This is when you are not listening to your intuition, knowing what's good for you and at the same time avoiding that one thing you know deep down is right for you. You are intentionally not listening to yourself, while most of the time you accept the onslaught of outer voices telling you the best course of action, what they think is good for you.

It's in the word: *intuition*. It all comes from with*in*. Too many people look for outside remedies to their inner problems and the voice that's trying to help them mentally from inside becomes quieter and quieter. As much as you think, it never gives up, because it always wants the best for you, it may be considered unheard, unthinkable, unrealistic, unrational, unresolved, uninhabited, even unruly at times. Nevertheless, it is always there seeking your mindful attention for your greater good.

Maybe it's the body that gets to live as a spirit, the biological body controlled by a mini universe that lies within. There's a magic to getting to live as a human in this extraordinary body of bones, blood, organs, cells, atoms, and DNA itself; the physical hardships, the pleasures, all the emotional ups and downs. The human body is quite amazing in how it all works in cohesion for itself. If treated right, it should never get sick or suffer diseases in any way, shape, or form.

As a being of light, it's a celestial gift, a heavenly holy saintly honour to live as a human. To live a life in the third dimension could be seen as a great achievement, a recognition of reaching a milestone in your soul's journey, because it is so hard. Maybe it's not just an honour but a universal honour to live as one. To achieve enlightenment and ascension as a biological human being—is this why your intuition is constantly teaching you to evolve to a higher importance in this dimension? Always striving to become better and better each day.

I feel sometimes that some souls who have awoken, raised their awareness to a higher level of consciousness, know they are beings of celestial light having a human existence, and that somehow this is the gift. To live your life out as a human being individually and collectively on your infinite soul's journey, you get to learn just about every lesson that the earthly school of life throws at you—even to the point that it is your deep self sending everything your way, good and bad, to learn and experience all the lessons that get weaved into and unto your path.

On a more humanly raw note, I truly have started to inner stand that inner feeling of intuition, the nervy electromagnetic interactions of atoms and molecules vibrating together in such a way to produce what we call a gut feeling. Not enough people trust this feeling, whether you are instinctive of it or not. You maybe get the feeling but fail to act on it, preferring instead to listen to those outer voices of family and friends, depending on where you live and your present and past social cultures. Most people are probably reading the different situations well, but they are unwilling to partake in the changes required to trust in the opposing outcomes.

Are you deeply in love? What is it that you see as love? The feeling you get from it—what is it meant to do for you? How do you personally react when you find it? Is it pure or even what is seen as pure love? Will it last? Nine times out of ten, your intuition will send you signals when these emotional experiences enter your life, but in the end, it is up to you as an individual to internally perceive how you feel about it and how you felt after going through the emotions attached to the feeling themselves. Everybody has intuition. The difference is that as much as we all feel and hear it, some people not only listen harder to it but act on the feelings it gives them and trust more in the outcomes. Especially at the times it's given, it seems so far from your day-to-day reality that you are constantly and continually living by.

It seems a bit like a computer program, a hard drive implanted somehow, to a reality you believe is totally you and totally true. Preconceived thoughts are already being played out in your brain under a form of controlling. A preset program is downloaded over time that sets everything else in motion but love itself cannot be implanted in a program.

This programming is the only thing that prevents you from fully loving not only yourself and others but the world itself—the grass, the sea, trees, waterfalls, animals, the sun, all things, and sadly, sometimes, life itself. As much as computers can be infected with viruses, the same way a good story can go viral, you cannot infect a computer with love, not even artificially intelligent love, as it does not exist. Only unconditional love exists, through everything for everyone from everywhere, as it is the most abundant frequency in the whole of the universal cosmos and cannot truly be faked.

Yes, some people do manipulate others to get their own way, but in the end, the emotion itself can't be faked with lies and deceit. Intuition will always confirm and relay the truth, if you only slow down and listen to the gentle inner calling of your being. That's where all the answers you seek will be waiting indefinitely to be found by you: your soul.

Is it an easy task to be open to it, continuously listening out for it? No, because the safekeeping egotistical mind instilled throughout your thoughts over your lifetime relates to these newly formed thought patterns and tells you that they're unreachable, unattainable, and even if you could, it would be so hard, take too long, and in the end, you'd be safer just sticking right where you are, never moving forward, never evolving, stuck always in one easily controlled state of mind, stagnant, glued to the spot, feeling secure with yourself, and letting the fear of change control all the ways you view your life. You're left always wanting more but too scared to listen to your intuition, drop the veil of fear, and just go for it.

Begin to rewrite your journey just as I am doing this very second as I write the words on this page, with my mind on autopilot fixated with trying to write something that will help somebody somewhere in the world start listening to their intuition and creating their own heaven on earth. Begin your own journey of diving into the abyss off all the unknown forbidding truths that are hidden in plain sight. Everything you see was once a thought in someone's mind. Change your thoughts, and you can change the world.

The path that I have chosen allows me not only to partake in but to fully immerse with my soul's purpose and live side by side within myself, with an unwavering belief guided by my intuition, my direct connection to the divine source of everything, where all my love flows from. I will forge my own path and help heal not only myself but beyond even what my mind thinks is impossible. I am willing to trust the gifts bestowed upon me for a higher purpose, an inner knowing beyond the realm of human construct. I can consciously manifest and combine with my higher self biologically, metaphysically, emotionally, and visually for the greater good of all with love, pure love. I let go of all fear that has festered over my lifetime, with an open and loving heart radiating it in all directions: north, east, west, and south.

That's what the NEWS stands for. And for too long now, they have spread fear to every part off our globe. It's time to renavigate that compass and use it to spread truth, love, peace, and harmony.

Is listening to your intuition hard? Yes. Can it be confusing? Yes. Is the path always clear? Far from it. Sometimes it takes blind faith and hard-fought trust. You have to forge your own path, for it is a path never travelled, but every journey starts with that first step and learning to listen to that inner voice probably at times screaming at you, roaring from deep inside your heart to just let go and find your soul—to awaken to who you truly are and why you are here at this special time on earth, to join the universal consciousness with love and truth, which is just as important as each breath you take.

From the very first moment you are born it is fifty-fifty with your intake and outtake of breath—fifty for truth and fifty for love, the spirit within, the working art of spiritually itself, and the strength and endurance of a beating heart. Yes, your feet get to rest, your ears, hands, legs, and inner organs all at some time or another get a little rest, but your heart never stops. If it does, your energy was needed for another purpose.

I have tried to show you just how much more there is to that gut feeling you get at times when a sticky situation pops up, but it is always showing and wanting the best for you to evolve. Having gained this knowledge myself, I want to share it with as many people as I can who don't innerstand, just like I didn't. I know how confusing it can be to an unawoken conscious mind. At the same time, allow yourself to begin to explore your own intuition. Have the awareness to work out for yourself what it is trying to tell you.

Start your own journey of truth and begin to live a life worth living. Inspire yourself; find courage you didn't know you had. Put no limitations on the potential you can reach. Self-leadership means overcoming obstacles. A new self-driven determination of personal belief in achieving great things for yourself and all others around you is reinforcing an inner wisdom of universal oneness from the source of love itself, expressing compassion for all life. The greatest and most noble work you accomplish is achieved through love. Zero is an unbroken connection to the divine, to infinite potential and evolution. Listen to your intuition and heed its call.

It's such a great personal achievement to live by truth, and this is why I'm writing this paragraph, as *heed its call* were meant to be the last words of this chapter. As I finished writing, I turned on my tell-a-vision set, and the time shown to me was 2222—twenty-two minutes past ten. But when on a spiritual awakening, it is a synchronicity sent to you from your guardian angels, and what an amazing moment for me personally to get as I was about to wrap up for the evening.

This number represents adaptability, balance, and harmony. Duality comes from the fact that 22 is repeated. Adaptability is the result of the mirrored image of double 2, which holds meaning in finding your divine purpose. The number calls forth confidence to fulfil my true purpose and bring balance into my own life.

Another meaning is that of peace and love, which are sure to be a part of my own future. This is a good sign that I will find my match soon. The 2222 twin flame meaning is one of healing and ascension. According to numerology, it's a message sent from my spirit guides to balance and harmonize my energies with that of my twin flame so the two of us can embark on this journey together. To discover and begin to immerse with angel numbers and your personal connection to them its hard to fathom that I went through my life up to this point and never noticed nor had the knowledge to even be looking out for them. Numbers are a language all by themselves, and I certainly will begin a personal journey as I know they mean so much more than just a set of numbers and to educate myself and the connection they have with words.

I do love my angels so much. Not only that, but to share your soul with another who can never be truly separated indefinitely—*wow*. You can see how fully engrossed in my journey I am every day, and how amazing this alone makes me feel. It's beyond describable.

I have yet to meet my other half in this world, but I trust in divine timing. I'm where I'm meant to be, and doing exactly what I'm meant to be doing. The plans I have for my life are truly exceptional, and for one who has barely prayed for my entire life, there's no more being hard on myself. I don't go through any one day now without saying a prayer.

Another exciting reason to see this number is that my soul brother Colly B has always told me he has seen that exact number all his life. He just didn't know what it meant for years, just like me, which gives it even more significance. Colly, here's a little message for you: "Eternal is not that it's everlasting, it's that it's ever present."

True growth requires the courage to release the past and step into the unknown. With truth, love, and light as your compass, your energies will navigate an unknown part of your heart, embarking you on your own journey of your soul's purpose, expanding in every direction, gaining knowledge, weaving a momentous path of wonderment, planting seeds, and sprouting roots in your once dormant consciousness. Evolve your physical being to not only help yourself but to introduce unawoken souls to their true essence, because at the centre of all life lies truth, love, and happiness.

CHAPTER 20

Walking Shadows
Seeking Light

THE OLDER YOU become in life; the simpler things become of greater value to you. Walking is just one of them. So many different reasons behind this simple act: going for a quick stroll just to take the dog for a walk (poo bag in pocket for all you poo leavers); taking a walk in the sun and in the rain; trekking up a mountain; taking a dander through a forest to be amongst and closer to nature; walking with a friend; taking a walk just to get out of the house for a bit of clean air or to clear your head; walking to the shop, to work, or just around the town; taking a stroll along a beach. Maybe you've had an accident and it's the simple part of a program to help build strength and heal whatever needs fixing.

Which brings me to the walks I love the most. I do love walking through the forest alone or with my children, but as they've grown older, that happens less and less, and as much as I'd like them to go for more with me, I can't force them. It's the walks I get to do with my father that I love the most. He's seventy-eight years young and never really walked that much throughout his life until he was seventy-seven. Me and my brother take turns taking him for his walks, but with work commitments can't do it every day, only as much as we both can.

There have been a couple of different reasons he started to try to walk more. Being seventy-eight, his legs were getting that bit weaker. He was also just a tad overweight. But the main reason had to do with his breathing. He smoked for much of his life, but he has now quit smoking for over fifteen years. You can still see it shortens his breath a little, and he can be a wheezy at certain times. It's for this reason that the walking has become so important to him.

At the time of writing this, it's around Christmas, and I'm still on my holidays. So, I'm getting to do it daily with him. Deep inside, I know that when I go back to work, I will miss our daily routine of slabbering and walking with one another.

Just to spend quality time with him and watch him grow old is a gift, as I know plenty of people with not only one but both parents who have already moved on. It's become quite clear to me how much some of these people truly miss them after they are gone. All have tears in their eyes, some feel sorrow and pain, but so many after reflecting on lives spent with their loved ones always end with a smile.

I keep telling my dad that he is the Trojan of the family, and he will live until he's a hundred. Personally, I want him to live until he is a thousand, but as we know as human beings, that will never happen. (Seems at one time it did, until they capped our DNA, but that story is for another time.)

When you go on a journey of not only a spiritual awakening but to begin a discovery of the truths and the deep knowledge you gain along the way, through research you begin to discover that death is non-existent. Everything and everyone is energy, and a transition takes place of your energy. As much as the human body goes back to Mother Earth, the spirit lives on. To know within yourself, you begin to innerstand that another cycle of your soul is just beginning.

When you truly innerstand that it's just another start, reflecting on your life becomes a source of happiness and joy from that point on. You begin to rejoice that you got time to spend with them. You got to love them for all the good and the bad. Then you begin to realize deep inside that everybody's perfection is all their imperfections. You begin to fathom the bigger picture, that the endless void you thought could never be filled is now so full, it's overflowing with memories, love, laughter, and pain, because that's what is real.

When you see it for what it truly is, that's when you begin to emotionally attach your feelings to it all. The restriction you have put on yourself mentally begins to lift and is exchanged with happiness and the knowing that in your time on this planet, you got to love and spend all those precious moments with them. It fills my heart just writing about them. So as much as it is only taking a walk with my dad, I know I will cherish these moments for eternity, and forever they will be implanted in my infinite memories.

From as early as my memories allow me to recall, now as an adult looking back, you begin to realize all the hardships you've gone through, the toughness of your upbringing—not only within your own homestead but culturally too. It was not only myself but my brothers and sister who were alongside me when starting this journey of life. Through the struggles and troubles, you begin to see the creation of all the bonds that now lie within, the deep emotional attachments that reside in the core off your being, implanted unknowingly at the time. As the youngest, you get that innocence stripped away rapidly. Certainly, you grow up much faster, as you are introduced into the adults' way of living.

Maybe you have just one parent at home, but sometimes never at home, as the need for money always keeps them at work to provide. This is when as brothers and sisters, you begin to look out for one another, like an invisible survival mode kicking in. You don't see it at the time it's happening because that is what's normal. You know no different, as being so young you have nothing to compare it to.

The need for this thing called *money* gets impregnated into your mindset. This is the beginning of getting it welded to your thoughts as you realize that everything costs something. The hardships families go through just by lacking good amounts of this commodity, which at the end of the day is just pieces of paper made from trees with ink displayed on the faces. Same as the three-sided coins made from metals, such as nickel, copper, and zinc—just like trees, all natural, made from Mother Earth.

When living this life, you see past money's actual function of buying and selling and begin to see that it's the control that's really displayed on its face. At least that is what you can see with your two eyes. Deep behind it all, it has thousands of faces within its inky covers—the making and breaking of people's lives throughout the entire globe.

We live in a materialistic world, and that is not actually a bad thing. The problem is all the misconceptions, educational lies, backroom cheats, sneaky systems put in place to control every ounce of its distribution, starting with the fundamentally wrong strawman. Forcing their swindle, adding to the common practise of lies and deceit to the ordinary folk who are left with the acceptance of lack to fulfil the money-spinners hierarchy, of the carefully planning and controlling pufferfish elites.

This is a big part of the matrix—the manipulation totally designed to make the rich richer and the poor even poorer. Struggling in the quagmire of scraps, feeding on only titbits, being kept busy enough to not see the enslavement program, never becoming self-aware, truly never knowing who you really are, you are left with the blinding theft and usage of your energy, indoctrinated into a society that has been shaped and structured before you were even formed in the womb—I would even go as far back as before you were conceived as a thought.

This has been going on for so long now that they are masters at it. The deception has been practised and practised by generational designers and refined to an art so that you'll never figure it out. Even your own thoughts are not your own and never will be. Only when you release the fear and educate yourself will you gain the knowledge that all the bullshit you've ever been told is a downloaded biological and holographical matrix system, built and perfected over an extended period, and done so intelligently that the lie itself makes you not even question it. You believe everything with a logical mind, never entertaining or having the flexibility in your mind's eye to even investigate for yourself the mysterious, mystical, and may I say supernatural aspects of this earthly plain.

To begin to decode the very intricate platforms of pending magic in all things, the quantum magic of the so-called nothingness, the whole English wording system was carried throughout time to every corner and nearly every nation of this globe. This is why it is called *spelling*. It was constructed into a system of magically dumbing down the masses, so that the normal global energy workers never awakened to the magnitude of the global swindling that plays out in our daily lives.

We go through life as soulless avatars, never ever catching on to how everything is done with words. Written words, verbal words, the block capitals in your name on every utility bill and every bank statement—this is the twin you never knew you had, but the one person who has invisibly been with you from the start.

This is the one the elite pufferfish use to gain all their global ends, and the real ones, which is you and I, are left in the pits of struggles, manipulated, abandoned, taxed relentlessly, yet through all this, the more you suffer, the more money they make. The magic of it all is if you don't awaken, you will never know.

If you put an *s* before *word*, you get *sword*, and that is what they are chopping you down with daily: *words*. Everybody is under the same magical spell, an illusion of trickery done relentlessly with your own verbal actions, whereupon it is you harming you. How smart is that, to fool the nations of this world with the old magical ways of wands, druids, and of course, the generational infected sick, murdering, sacrificing, banking pufferfish.

Licences, passports, certificates, insurance, securities, loans, debts, leases, inflation, taxes, legislation, courts, judges, currency bonds, banking orders, constitutions, congresses, parliaments, cheques, fixed summons, mortgages, cardinals, priests, ministers, capital benches, cells, networks, valid birthing canals—this is but a small fraction of the words manipulated in order to hide the true aspects of proper global money laundering on a vast scale, with magic trickery done so sneakily and within an earthly set of laws so deceptive. It is all designed and doctored by and to suit the elite pufferfish of the world, by themselves and only for themselves. Universal law is the law of one, and the only real and true law of this realm.

The world is changing, whether people like it or not. There seems no doubt that it is going to get a little worse before it gets better. It's a known cycle from the beginning of time—a bit like the bush wildfires in Australia, done in such a way that when it is over, the true growth can begin. What we have is trillion-dollar businesses tightening their grip globally, resisting on all fronts, infecting themselves with more and more greed with pufferfish oil, electricity, homes, fuel, water, and food. While behind multiple slammed shut and locked doors, or deep underground there is something that would probably discard most of the high cost of these natural commodities.

People have forgotten that a government is set up in the first place to *govern*, which means *control*. The best way to control is through fear, and that is exactly what they do. It's all a façade to give us the impression we live in a democracy. It reminds me of Punch and Judy, puppets on a string. You begin to see that the things run by the banks for the governments and done to the people are proactively set up to relieve you of your hard-earned money—annually, monthly, weekly, hourly with the relentless taxation of your pay, designed so darkly behind so many closed doors to a level beyond the mortal mind. The weaving of money into are modern society and the daily need for it, seems purposefully structured for not only people to love it, depend on it and the lengths not only socially and culturally but globally people go to get it is where the actual control lies. I have written a list as to the things that can be done with it, what can be done for it and what not only people, but businesses, financial institutions and banks about how far they will go to get. Yon can make your own assumptions behind each individual word, but in the end, you will find this is where the real control lies.

It can be, saved invested swindled stolen robbed spent taken offered banked loaned blocked hustled seized stashed concealed distributed manipulated circulated scammed calculated extracted demanded hoarded doctored displayed supressed hedged won overcharged tolled conned levied deceived snatched extorted hoodwinked blocked mugged cheated manufactured claimed pinched pillaged materialized grabbed plundered looted consumed engineered fleeced micro managed dodged exchanged masked donated and burnt, but most of all it can be taxed value added tax private tax inheritance tax fuel duties corporation tax income tax capital gains tax stamp duty wine duties beer duties cider duties landfill tax aggregates tax climate change levy insurance premium tax betting and gaming duties and air passenger duty. You get the point its relentless and endless. Change is critically needed to free us of this barbaric controlling system which has been fundamentally from its onset planned down to every minute detail to cause global suffering. The whole system is to make every one of us conditionally dependant on money. Pieces of paper made from trees coloured in with" DARK" ink that can be burnt with a "LIGHT"er.

To be a conspiracy theorist, a critical thinker, a theoretician or an unwavering determined truth seeker is to not only receive the knowledge but to know that it's the true reality. Fake reality is so darkly constructed by the cabal, the deep state, so vast, so organized, and so evil that you are deemed mad to even think such a poison could be real. I can innerstand to a degree if you're not remotely woken in any way shape or form, how you could not see through the veil, the very thin veil, because they do it in our faces now. That means you are still living out your program of this matrix, never realizing you've never been aware.

I'm writing this in such a raw and inexperienced way of my truthful thoughts with the hope of awakening as many unawoken souls as possible to the discovery of the truth of how, why, and who really runs this energy-sapping program. I seek to not only raise awareness but to deliver a higher level of consciousness to each reader of the truths behind anyone's spiritual journey. Awaken to the fact that we have all been fooled into living this way, to hide from ourselves who we really are and where we originate.

I hate writing about the brutality that is going on in our world, but deep inside, I have a inner calling to inform everyone of the truth, a reality so disgusting that the agenda is the control of every single being through a barbaric system, with its only design to create total anarchy on an unprecedented scale never before reached. In its rawest form, not money itself but the control of money is run by murderers, rapists, molesters, paedophiles, and devil-worshipping sacrificing pufferfish, and it's time we as the true people take back ownership and begin to turn the tables by simply saying no to it all.

In every government in this world, there is a system that has been in place for many years of either a purposely selected candidate put forward for the person-elected route or a person strategically positioned by the inner unknown (the show-running pufferfish). There is an invisible line, a level of hierarchy, in the echelon of the hidden power structure. This is where only yes, men and women are allowed to rise through the ranks, and the knowledge they have, which is on a need-to-know basis, would determine which level they get to reach. No outsiders are allowed. If they did sneak in through by some miracle and disagreed, they would be sacked, disappeared, or replaced by others who could be bought to keep their mouths shut and their accounts full. It's run like a cult, and the higher up you travel, the more you will become entwined with the bloodlust of the innocuous rituals carried out in either the back rooms or the underground dungeons to feed their demonic energies and appease their evils.

There's not that much changed from the Romans' bloodlust in the ancient elliptical amphitheatre known all over the world as the Colosseum. It's just been hidden from public view, along with your fate already sealed. It has become a private incessant degrading and humiliating of fellow humans, male and female, young and old, even to the sacrificing of newborns.

To some reading this right now, it will seem so far from your reality, but not from theirs, as no one lives to tell the tale. I certainly don't keep banging on about it for nothing. It is a true reality hidden in plain sight, though you certainly won't hear or read about any of this on the most popular or most viewed media outlets. They own all that too, along with their intricately designed propaganda, which the common person thinks left this world when Joseph Goebbels popped his overly deserved pill in 1945.

We are treated shamelessly on all fronts: promoted injections of the healthy, excess deaths within all ages, and now they want us and our children to comply through an invisible brainwashing tool, artificial intelligence. That's the only thing in your house that you can't see with your own two eyes—the Wi-Fi—but only to us because we are of human construct. They see everything, invisibly invading our so-called private homes, with one purpose: to de-create your whole family and sever the bonds; to steal all faith and belief in the greater good; to harness your energetic soul under a matrix blinded by the ignorance of the unknown.

As you have read up to this point, you'll agree that my awakening was intense and informative, surreal at times, uplifting at others, magical and thought-provoking. I was left with the unbelievable shocking truths of my inner soul to become a wayshower, a truth-talker, and a light worker, to tell my story and get it out globally, get it out to as many people as possible. I've had to financially sacrifice all I have for the greater good of all, as I now know for sure that we are all one.

If there was a way to flip that hive mind around to that of oneness: one soul worldly consciousness combined all together, working on a global tandem, seeking love for one another, with every heart beating to the same rhythm, helping raise everybody's vibration. At the same time, that would be it, game over, the real and raw shaking frequency of everybody's body and soul to the truth of how things on *Earth/Heart* really work.

For all the abhorrent and disgusting things, I have written about, when you dive deep into your spiritual awakening and finally realize what you are capable of, the happiness, goodness, and joy that surround you is palpable as you connect with the divine, alongside your angels and spirit guides. You can achieve greatness beside your highest self, whereupon your connection becomes only one, one love, oneself, a bond never to be broken, a path never trodden, and a love never felt: unconditional love.

So this message goes out to the bartender in Germany, the shop assistant in Leeds, the joiner in Poland, the process operative in Sweden, the chef in France, the policeman in Holland, the lifeguard in Spain, the goat herder in Tibet, the milkman in Peru, the electrician in Australia, the pilot in New Zealand, the lorry driver in Kenya, the beauty therapist in Norway, the taxi driver in America, the singer in Greece, the train operator in Dublin, the doctor in Morocco, the van driver in London, the dancer in Japan, the greenskeeper in Nairobi, the tour operator in Sorrento, the athlete in Romania, the publisher in the Philippines, the painter in Scotland, the DJ in Lurgan, the recovery man in Northern Ireland, the secretary in Liechtenstein, the soldier in Ukraine, the shopkeeper in India, the boxer in Malta, the janitor in Switzerland, the office clerk in Russia, the window cleaner in Argentina, the footballer in Kosovo, the lab technician in China, the jockey in Chile, the surgeon in Ethiopia, the builder in Iceland, and the park ranger in Canada. Whether it's the multitude of different jobs, the vast numbers of people involved, or the navigation of the infinite mathematical formulated structures that shape all spaces in which they are contained, numbers themselves emphasise cycles, and they carry profound symbolism rooted in numerology, where the repetition of numbers holds significant meaning, especially when embracing all the elements.

As so many already know, there are four elements: earth, fire, air, and water. Only now do I now know there is a fifth: ether, the upper regions of air above the clouds.

Fire is the element of power. The people of fire have desire and will. They are bold and ambitious, full of vitality, charismatic, passionate, fun, and lively. Driven by their heart's desires, they can achieve what they set out to do.

Earth is the element of substance. The people of earth are go-getters, creators, and organizers. They are artistic, and their innovative capabilities are unmatched. They are rooted and grounded in their approach to life, diverse and strong, with a persistent and enduring attitude.

Air is the element of freedom. The people of air tend to be emotional and intuitive. Being the most feminine, they are the most receptive and the most hidden. The moon and water are inextricably linked, and this connection persists in almost every elemental system. They are deeply lunar and peacefully detach themselves from worldly concerns.

Water is the element of change. The people of water have a deep sense of community and a love that holds them together through anything. They have a proclivity towards sensitivity. They are heartfelt with family and home life, and mysterious. They easily pick up on others' emotions because of their caring nature.

Ether is both nothing and everything at the same time. It's a stillness, yet it is the very thing that makes all movement and life possible. So, to say that something is *in the ether* means that it is something being communicated from place to place but with no precise location. It is the material that fills the region of the universe beyond the terrestrial sphere.

It is important to draw wisdom from different people, young and old, different things at different times from different places. If you take it from only one place, it becomes rigid and motionless. Innerstanding others and all the other elements alongside in combination with spirituality will help you become an individual person. Fear, deceit, and death divide, while truth, love, and light unify. The heart is the key that opens all the doors, walks all the roads, and makes all the turns. So, when the manhole covers are lidless and the black holes exposed, although the many tunnels are long, twisted, and dark, it is your heart that lights your infinite path back to the divinity of the divine, so you can begin to live a life worth living.

I intentionally set out in the beginning of this chapter to be as simple as possible by the natural act of walking, with the reason and connection to the love I have for my dad, unknowingly but always shining his unforeseen light on me; to the bonds created within a family when starting out on the journey of life, traversing the controlled darkness of money on many twisted and barricaded roads of lies and deceit that gradually get darker and darker the more you travel; to the trickery, cruelty, and outright barbarism beginning to be more exposed at every turn. It is the beating hearts of life collectively combining as one that gives substance to all the elements of this world.

So, it is on this earthy plain, in the maze of life, that love blossoms and radiates out from the heart that will set you free. With each coherent beat, you choose the right path to begin your own walk, make your own turns, and find your own truths. It is my most honest way of portraying to you, the reader, that a spiritual awakening is not all love and light.

First and foremost, it is the recognition of not only the darkness of the world but the darkness of what you encounter within yourself. You must mentally go back to find that inner child who has subconsciously been hiding within your thoughts, and in a lot of cases, unknown to yourself, has been designing the path of how you live and defend your life. This is when you begin to find pieces of the puzzle that hold you to who you truly are.

Through lonely days and nights in a kind of hermit mode, tearfully, you begin to emotionally tackle your core beliefs and bring them up for purging of everything and anything that doesn't align with your truest self. It calls on you to rid yourself of what was, what could have been, and what wasn't. The multiplying of emotions keeps boiling over and over, bubbling to the top, overflowing to the point they begin to stream down your face in the form of tears.

Night after night, searching your life's journey, you mentally resurface and at times reenacting a new version of an old event, whether there is a need for an apology or simply just to become aware that it exists, which sometimes is disguised within your emotions. Spiritual human souls on many platforms talk about doing the work, the inner work, to heal every aspect of your life. At the start of my journey, it did not get fully instilled into my mind, but now I'm in no doubt as to its meaning.

In the end, which I personally know there is none, but let's say at the end of this cycle, you begin to strive for some sort of emotional equilibrium, and in doing so block out the negativity that's always trying to fill the missing pieces to your life's jigsaw. You begin to replace it with intentional positivity, always with an attitude, deliberately to yourself and all that surround you on your daily journey. Then finally in your life you come to terms with the fact that every day is a new beginning.

It's all about the love. It's always been about the love, and it always will be about the love. Intimacy comes in many forms: mental, physical, emotional, and spiritual. In a romantic sense, it's not just the sexual aspect, but a feeling of closeness, touching, and the combined connected emotions. A cuddle, a hug, the holding of hands, a desired look, a squeeze, and of course, different kisses at the right moments. There is the intimacy you have with your friends, your parents, grandparents, brothers, and sisters, then your own family, and now for me my soul family of spirit guides and guardian angels. Finally, there is the ultimate connection to the divine. As the divine resides in and embodies you, it is then that you begin to feel the intimate closeness with yourself. The spark lies within us all.

CHAPTER 21

Feathers Belief
and Two Ribs

FIRST AND FOREMOST, never did I think I would be writing a caption of my life with feathers as the topic of conversation. White feathers, grey, black, yellow, pink, and brown, never meant anything really in my life, although I do have lots of memories of coming across them at different times.

About a year ago, it all started when I was lying in my garden and a black feather landed right in front of me. I remember looking up at the sky to see where the bird was, but there was no sign of any, which makes sense, as it would take it a certain time to fall to the ground anyway. I never thought too much of it at the time.

The next day, there was another in my front garden. As much as it jogged my memory as to the one the day before that fluttered just in front of me, I still didn't make any connection to them at all. It was the following day, and as it was summer, I was already lying down relaxing in the sunshine. When another landed right on me, I again automatically looked to the sky but saw nothing.

That's when I looked around, gathered up all three, and stuck them beside each other at the side of my front garden. These three feathers were all black and looked the exact same, only varying in size. Later that day I began searching to see if there was any meaning to any of this. As it so happens, if black feathers are found around your house, it means your family home is protected.

From this moment on, I started to become acutely aware of feathers. I didn't go looking for them, but when they presented themselves to me, my mind was beginning to become connected to their presence.

A week or so later, when I was taking a stroll around the local forest, I began to spot the odd white feather. Although I would look at it, recognize it, and relate it to myself that it was there, I'd just keep walking on. It began to happen so regularly that my intuition was probably screaming at me to acknowledge them a little more. Finally, I made the connection to my spiritual journey. The now new researching side of myself kicked in.

I found out that a white feather symbolizes a connection to your angels; to purity and clarity; and to gratitude and trust in the divine unfolding of your journey. At the actual time of finding a feather, you come to realize that your thoughts are reminiscing about something or someone—maybe a friend, a relationship, or a dilemma of some sort.

Darren Rooney Jason Carrol, and Mark Dover were three close friends I had the privilege of spending different times with throughout my life. Sadly, all three had already moved on. It was these three I remembered the most, and with the memories of times spent, they have never really left my conscious mind. When walking through the forest by myself, I was reminiscing about all three, and I came across three pure white feathers right in front of me. They were so close to each other; they were practically touching. I lifted all three, put them in my pocket, and kept walking.

At the top of the forest, there is a clear open expanse of grass. Back in our younger days, we called it "the green." So, I planted my bottom down on a summerseat that overlooks the green and has the best and most clear view. I took the feathers out of my pocket and laid them down beside me. This is when I truly began reminiscing about all the different recollections I had with my three friends, thinking back to different stories at different times that we had experienced together—the good, the bad, the funny, the mischievous, and all the adventures we used to go on, sometimes within myself getting carried away and reaching back and reliving the past.

Darren and I were taking turns shooting his father's shotgun out the back bedroom window in the same forest as his house at that time was on the edge of it. Then, quickly putting it all away, running to the tree, we were shooting at to see who the best shot was. Only at this time, the Troubles here was at its height, and with the army camp within earshot, as we stood discussing which one of us was going to pass sniper selection, six soldiers just appeared out of nowhere. All they had to do was look up and the game was up, but when they asked us if we'd heard any gunshots, Darren being

Darren pointed in the opposite direction and said it came from over there, and off they went. That was a close one.

Weeks later, we sneakily climbed over the same army camp's outer fence beside the helipad and played in its outside swimming pool. Eventually we got caught, turfed out, and sent out an almighty security alert that probably echoed around that whole camp.

Jason was a master with a pencil and at building go-carts for racing. He used to do my art homework for me, and if he didn't get ten out of ten, he got a nine. The only thing for me was that when it came to drawing something in class, I was exposed as a fraud. My art teacher knew it but kindly didn't say anything. When he got detention at school, they had to take his shoes off him, because he was known for climbing down the drainpipe and away.

Mark came along a bit later in life. I knew him from school, but it wasn't till we left that we started our escapades together. We started raving together, joined the same band (STORM HQ) as dancers, and I doubled as an MC. This is when we got to travel and perform at some of the best clubs in Northern Ireland at that time. We even tried our hands at becoming DJs. The thing was it was at a party. The real DJ went to bed and left his gear with us. We realized after destroying half the records that we just weren't cut out for it. I could probably write a full book on all the shenanigans we got up to in our journeys of life.

As I was having pleasant feelings of nostalgia, these experiences triggered so many emotional responses, and I could not do anything for about ten minutes but remember and cry. Speaking to them all felt brilliant to me, and my recollections certainly brought a smile to my face. There was a hole at the bottom of this summerseat, and this is where I stuffed the feathers. I have been doing it ever since. They let me know that day that they are in heaven and have successfully crossed to the spiritual realms.

On a different morning, I walked down my garden path where my car is parked parallel to my home, and there stuck on the driver's door was a white feather. If it was on any other door, I wouldn't have seen it. The lightbulb went straight off in my head, because the night before I had been thinking deeply about Granny and Granda Kirk and my Granny and Granda Graham. The feather reminded me of my thoughts the night before. It was like a gentle nudge from my angels, only this time, it was from loved ones. I instantly remembered apologizing to my Granny Graham for stealing her milk money years ago when walking home from a band parade.

The way the feather was stuck right in my line of sight on my door meant that one, I was supposed to see it, and two, my apology was accepted. I knew some things in this world now work in mysterious ways because that feather physically wouldn't have been easy to not only get stuck to the door but to where it was on the door. Then again, I don't want to figure it out. Some things are just better left to a divine interconnection, to the influence or the personal collaboration of a metaphysical note of gratification—a verification you are in safe hands, just to let you know you are not alone when reshaping and reshuffling your life and soul, find your light that lies within and let it shine.

I have surprised myself at times how I interpret my reactions to finding these feathers and having that moment of just the simple beauty and wonder of nature interpreted as encouragement on my journey, the benevolence of an angel, and the sharing of a privileged moment. I get such warmth and comfort just sharing it within myself. You don't see these trails of thoughts coming; it's more like they slowly creep into your mind, reforming your heart, from stone cold to the mushy red-hot magma flowing slowly but at the same time unstoppable.

There's a saying, "When feathers appear, angels are near." In my late years, upon receiving the wisdom that somehow all these feathers that came across my path throughout my life meant there was an angel close by, every time now feels in some way like a meaningful occurrence, even a feeling of a connection to who you truly are and the worldly gifts that come from a heart disguised as an organ.

A grey and white feather comes and finds you in times of change, or periods of making transitions in one's life from living in fear to finding love, from living bad to living good, and from times of dishonesty to finding truth. Stay committed to your values, walk the path of righteousness, and let your actions reflect your authentic self. The importance of being true to ourselves is the rewiring of how you perceive and how you begin to read your own inner thoughts. Rather than sitting in the waiting room of your mentality, hold faith with yourself, give and receive compassion, and let the light find you and lift you.

Which brings me to the biggest feathery-ist moment I have ever experienced. It was six thirty on a Sunday morning, and I decided to go to the forest for a walk. Cold and frosty was the morning that greeted me. The ground was filmed in a sheet of white.

As I was approaching the pond that lies at the bottom of the forest, what met my eyes was such an array of feathers that at first, I couldn't take it in, there were so many. There were four big grey feathers, and the rest were smaller white ones. I could see that the leaves had frosted to the ground, but none of the feathers had been there long enough for this to have materialized.

That let me know that what I can only describe as a fight had taken place between two birds, one grey and the other white. With the white feathers being so small and numerous, there could easily have been a couple of white birds, although I don't know for sure. As I began to count the white feathers, I stopped at forty-five, as the tiny ones got so hard to count with the frosted ground.

Maybe to anybody else, that's exactly how you could have interpreted the scene—as the aftermath of a fight—but for me, after my spiritual awakening, it was as if the universe had moulded this scene for me to come across, and Mother Earth had sacrificed the justification of the fight for me to witness the feathers right at that time, first thing on that morning. This is what my intuition was telling me, like a universal blessing in some way.

When I got home and investigated the meaning of this, it said that finding loads of white feathers signals something beautiful to come into my life—a connection to the spiritual realm and to divinity. I'm the first to admit, it certainly evoked my emotions. The world is overflowing with signs and synchronicities, messages and meanings to comfort, reassure, and guide us. It is up to us to decide whether we wish to cherish the moments and let them pass as memories or hold on to them as dreams. Even if the world is against you, stand with your dreams and aspirations, because at the end of the day, this is your life.

You do not owe an explanation to the world for your actions and decisions. Begin to groom your own mind and focus on communicating with your soul, because therein lies the source of true wisdom. Fill your heart with love and satisfy your soul. It's the flower of love.

At that moment, on that morning, I truly felt I was surrounded by a legion of angels, physically seeing nothing, but with an unwavering belief, an emotional connection to the spirit world signifying happiness, compassion, gratitude, unity, kindness, and peace. I was just living in the present moment with myself and the beating of my fragile loving heart.

Red feathers symbolize power and vitality. Yellow ones, at least in most cultures, mean happiness and positivity. Pink ones symbolize love, compassion, and healing. I've yet to find any of these, and although I'm not actively searching for them, I'm sure someday they will cross my path. Maybe a red one from a chirpy rooster, but I can't remember seeing any pink flamingos flying about Northern Ireland. The most sacred feather is the eagle's, meaning bravest, strongest, and holiest. Same again, not a big pile of eagles about here either, so any of these would be a rare find indeed. Probably nearly all would relate more to the traits of magpies and robins having their own little ways as to what they do when they come across them.

So, everybody reacts in different ways to all these moments, while others don't bat an eyelid to any of it. All of this is about personal perception, depending on your beliefs. That's how you will read each moment as it presents itself to you.

The frequency at which we vibrate is what holds the key to our spiritual resonance, and as you elevate your vibration, a profound transformation unfolds. It's a connection to nature on a soul level never experienced, although it's always been right in front of you, above you and below you, unseen to your natural vision but felt on an energetic level as you move towards a more advanced stage of awareness and consciousness.

Grounding happens when you just take off your socks and shoes and connect to earth itself. The electromagnetic field that has always been there is waiting to recharge and heal you from within. Mother Earth is real and alive, waiting to help, waiting to implode you with her energies and establish the connection she has with every soul on this planet. Mother Nature, Mother Earth, Gaia, and Mother goddess are all common personifications of the earth and its biosphere as the giver and sustainer of all life.

Growth, all growth, should it be volcano eruptions; the flow of wind, or the currents in the rivers; the rolling waves of the seas; the air we breathe; the growth of greenness; the forming of clouds; and the birth of all seeds— she enriches it all. Awaken to the fact that she is a living embodiment of everything that grows, from the hidden flow of lava to honey for bees, the caterpillar for the butterfly, the crunch in a biscuit (Audrey), the hot soup you slurp, grass, snow, and the rain. You truly could fill a whole book on just that alone, because she is everything, everywhere, and everyone good and bad. She is forever holding space for the growth of all life.

Earth is Heart and Heart is Earth, always evolving within the magnetic quantum field, bringing everything from the universe within the cosmos and through the heart. Which brings me to the removal of my two ribs and how the reality of quantum entanglement universally links and connects in one's personal life for a higher purpose of serving others, especially in their greatest time of need. This surpasses life itself and a conventional innerstanding of space and time, suggesting a fundamental interconnectedness that exists throughout the universe, promoting the concept of oneness and unity.

At the time of this experience, I had absolutely no knowledge of this at all, nor of the surrounding factors that had led me up to this very moment in my life. Only in hindsight have I gained the wisdom of its personal entanglement with me. When I was a tree surgeon, I had a bad accident that eventually brought me to lying on a hospital bed with a booked appointment to get one-and-a-half ribs removed. But as the MRI scan didn't show all, when the surgeon got eyes on it, he told me it was so twisted and unjoined that he had to remove the full two ribs.

As the procedure was close to my lungs, it was done by a thoracic surgeon. So alongside me on this ward were three older and might I say wiser men than I. All had breathing difficulties: one had a collapsed lung, another had only one lung, and the last one, who had smoked all his life, was getting one bad lung surgically removed for the other one to function better.

It just so happened to be a weekend that I was booked in to have my operation done, after my first appointment was cancelled for an unforeseen and unknown reason. Back then, I was a die-hard Formula One fan and would never miss a race. As it worked out, it was the Formula One Spanish Grand Prix, which did not start until two o'clock in the early hours of the morning. I was granted permission to watch it in my bed by the night nurses, if I turned the volume down and pulled my curtains around my bed to cut out the glare of the television's bright lights.

I set my alarm for one thirty and, at about ten in the evening and high as a kite on morphine, went straight to sleep. When my alarm goes off, I'm normally up like a shot. But under the circumstances, I was up and taking a shot, or should I say a click, of my personal stash of morphine to numb my pain every five minutes. That's twelve hits an hour, and I needed every one of them.

The older man opposite me was the guy with only one lung, and he was getting it serviced in some way to make it function better but ultimately to keep him alive. That day we had chatted away, and although I had never met him before, in some way I thought that I had, or at least had met someone who looked like him, but I didn't know who.

So, I'm sure at some time in your life, you have watched a medical series or at least a movie with a scene in a hospital with a patient lying in bed with a heart monitor at the side beeping away to the rhythm of their heartbeat—*beep beep beep beep* and so on. As I'm watching the race begin in earnest, it wasn't as if I was actively listening to the monitors beeping away, but it was in this moment that I heard that distinctive noise of one of the monitors when someone's heart stops beating: *beeeeeeeeeeeeeeep*.

I quickly sat up—painfully, may I say, as in that moment I had somehow forgotten that I'd had two ribs surgically removed and, in my panic, moved far too fast. I pulled back my curtain, and it was the man opposite me. I could not only hear the beeps but now see the continuous line on his monitor lit up.

So, I hit the red alarm button at the side of my bed, and within five to ten seconds, two nurses appeared, running into our little cul-de-sac and straight over to me. I quickly pointed them over to the man opposite. After a shot of morphine, I watched the panicked look on both nurses faces.

One nurse stayed with the man, and the other disappeared. But within one minute, there were seven or eight men and women all around his bedside. That is when they pulled the curtains round his bed. After about ten minutes of working frantically, they wheeled him away. I personally thought he had passed away, and although I had only known him for about two full days at this stage, I shed a tear for him. Not only could I not watch the race, but I had also forgotten all about it with all the goings on. Eventually, I must have drifted off to sleep.

When I awoke the next morning, the spot where his bed had been was empty. Right at that moment, the two nurses came walking round our little corner, and both were smiling from ear to ear. By the look on their faces, I knew he had pulled through. They really couldn't thank me enough for what had happened the night before. They told me he would be brought back up to our ward later that day. So it was in this moment, as they served me breakfast, that a thought bubble must have burst above my head, and I decided, as we say here, "to jump on the bandwagon."

I don't know whether it's the hospital toast or just the fact that someone else is making it, but it always tastes so much nicer than if you had to make it yourself. So, I asked the nurses could I have a little more as I took another hit of morphine, and not only did I get more toast but another cup of tea also. Under the surgical circumstances, I was as happy as a pig in poo.

It was about two hours later that the man was brought back up to our little recovery suite. It was only then that I began to think that I'd probably played a big part in saving that man's life the night before. There and then, I decided to keep it to myself, as I didn't want the nurses to get into any kind of trouble. Then again, at the same time, I wanted a good breakfast the next morning. So, it was a click on the morphine and lay back down content within myself that I secretly helped save a man's life.

Later, that day, we chatted as if he had just gone to sleep for the night and awakened after a nice dream. So happy that the Spanish Grand Prix was on that night.

After I came out of hospital, I didn't know it at that time, but for about two years I was addicted to morphine, but through a patch on my back. Working with a pain consultant that whole time, I was getting steroid injections, electro-magnetic therapy, acupuncture, and a range of medications. Having two ribs removed meant two nerves were severed, and what I was left with was what my thoracic surgeon called *chronic intercostal neuralgia*, which basically means neuropathic pain in the intercostal nerves that radiates throughout a person's rib cage and abdomen.

When something happens in your life like this, you very quickly become aware of your physical limitations, then the mental pain alongside the pain of being an active person having to somewhat live an inactive life. That was probably the toughest part. Slowly but surely, I have gotten off all medications, and with my spiritual awakening, I also no longer smoke, drink, or take any substances for recreational use. But if I was to, it would be a South American psychoactive brew called *ayahuasca*, traditionally used by indigenous cultures and folk healers in the Amazon and Orinoco basins for spiritual divination. But that's maybe for another journey.

Fast forward to my orange poofy night, and although not straight away, this is what set me on a clear path to my spiritual awakening, and eventually my connection to Mother Earth and to earthing (grounding) itself. I was gaining so much wisdom along the way, searching my inner self, and healing so much toxic trauma. This is when I researched, studied, and learnt more about the quantum field—what it is and how it works. I began to connect and combine my thoughts emotionally, physically, and cognitively, forming the associations with highly concentrated thoughts mentally, and at the same time using my personal resonance to try to heal myself. You could say it was like your own personal alternative form of medication through deep meditation. I called it *quantum prayer*. I hope that makes sense, as writing it as words is a bit harder than doing it all.

As my breath is my truth, I must honestly say that prayers never meant that much to me for nearly my entire life—at least, that is, to the time when I call myself to be *wide awake*. It's something I'm not proud of now, but that's just the way it was for me. With the roads that I once travelled, some not having much choice in doing so and at times being forcibly made to take certain detours at different junctions in my life, praying had never entered my reality as something with a function that was there to help in a time of need where indeed sometimes your life depended on it.

Imagine being on the front line of a Spartan phalanx waiting for the battle to begin, or in a foxhole surrounded, a bayonet charge to going over the top in World War I, leaving the safety of your trench knowing full well that flying lumps of lead of all sizes are going to be numerously propelled your way and the percentage of surviving so low. If you somehow did survive, surely you would feel like your prayers had been answered, but what if you didn't make one? Could you put it down to luck? Or could it be a destiny to live, or a belief with foresight that you told a loved one that you would make it home?

I will admit, those are somewhat extreme cases, but there is so much more one can pray for: a new house, help with your bills, the bullying to stop, a new car, your health or that of another, forgiveness, strength, protection, wealth, abundance, courage, wisdom, confidence, closeness, love—the list is endless. It depends on what your perception of *belief* is, or if it is something you've been taught to believe from such a young age already planted in your conscious mind, never having the courage to question it. Whether it's yourself at the end of your bed on your knees, hands clamped firmly together under your chin, alone and in the dark, or in a church alongside a congregation praying as one—that could be seen as worshipping as one and at the same time listening to someone telling you the way it is.

For me, praying has been different from what I've known as prayer all my life. With what I have experienced in my living room alone, I cannot think otherwise. Whether through difficult situations or heartfelt ones, angels speak to you through signs, energy, and symbols. When asking them for assistance in answering, sometimes (not all) your ears gently ring or there is a prolonged buzzing in the skull, neck, or even tickly parts around your face and body. It's like a metaphysical *yes*, depending on your perception and how you mindfully relate to the energy that surrounds you.

I know some will innerstand, and just as many won't Those on the path of true awakening will see it as your angels strengthening your resolve to prevail. Your line of communication is opened to source, and you realize you are a fractal of that praying as a heavenly assistant to serve your purpose in the helping of others. Nothing feels better than to be surrounded by angels every day. It strengthens your resolve and deepens the bond you have with the creator of all life, and your search ends, as the spark has always been within.

In truthfulness, I cannot begin to fathom the vastness, the cosmic reach, the length and breadth of the universal love that lies amongst the quantum field. To receive, perceive, or conceive—either through sound, vibration, frequency, matter, and light, biological or holographical, maybe the combination of all, even still another element yet undiscovered, I just don't fully know. I don't think anybody truly will ever know.

What I do know is that quantum mechanics is more than a fundamental theory. For me, it's about my personal experiences with the metaphysical energies and having my twenty-year old Malteser removed from my physical body. Something magical lies beyond my known knowledge or a scientific breakthrough that nobody has broken. Truthfully, I never had an option, due to the intensity of what has happened to me. I just can't explain it all, but having dived into this feet first, I'm still not fully immersed. I was as raw as one could ever have been and believe that's the way it was meant to be for me. I'm left with thinking nothing else unless my memory re-sparks itself.

The belief I have flowing through my veins, my view on life and how it has changed so rapidly—there's a small part of me that thinks, with the things I've seen, that at least some secrets of what is unexplored or hidden from the masses have been shown to me. It's been impregnated into my mind somehow that the universe is moulded with the energy of love, compassion, forgiveness, gratitude, and honesty. Whether my story makes sense or not, the wisest course of action is to at least always act with honesty, because so much dishonesty has entered the majority of everybody's daily lives on multiple layers and on all levels.

The struggle against immoral behaviour is not simple, but my overriding belief is to share what I know and to tell the truth, even to those most resistant to it. So be it, because no matter what I say, if you're not ready, you're not ready. As long as I get it out there and sow the seed, those who are ready to embark on a journey of truth—the revealing of secrets, lies, and deceit on a global level—and begin to see for themselves the lengths that have been generationally taken and then hidden within the matrix, will find that they possess their own resilience and perseverance to not only awaken their own soul but to begin your connection to their true spiritual self and who they really are.

Maybe this is on a personal level, but to the collective it's what a quantum prayer entails: a whispering of your soul formed from above, connected down through your spinal cord, your thoughts, beliefs, feelings, emotions, affirmations, and manifestations entwined through a specialized coherent heart having the scientific magic-making of something out of a nothingness, bridging the invisible gap to the divine dimension and floating on the waves of cosmic energies. This is where your prayers are finally answered and divinely returned to sender. Even now, my mind is constantly being blown in my own welcoming enigma of existence.

CHAPTER 22

Your Heart Is Amazing

SO, YOU SEE, there is a lot to take in. It's kind of like starting your life all over again, but this time based on the truth, the whole truth, and nothing but the truth. For the first six months off my awakening, I believed that karma was all bad. I had created at different times of my life karma for myself and had become mindful that, that's where I now was in my life. I couldn't have been anywhere else or doing anything else up to that point.

This is when I consciously started becoming aware of getting off the karmic wheel. I now realized that what you put into this world is what you get out. So, I set about trying to create good karma and was fully accepting of my bad karma, which with my new knowledge I fully deserved. I looked inside and dug deep to apologize for all my wrongdoings, and I truly meant it, too. There seemed to be quite a lot, and as I was doing this also, I realized I had created a lot of good karma for myself. At that point, I mindfully was balancing it all out. From that moment on and to this day, I have created no bad karma for myself. At times, it's not been easy.

What comes to mind was a situation, I think a test, that I just about scraped through. I was out playing golf one day with my father, brother, and a good friend. As I have always been up for the crack all my life, slagging one another has always played a part of that crack. So it was at this time that I was being mindful not to create any bad karma for myself. You could say I was right in the middle of trying to teach myself to respond to things rather than react. There is no way I can stop trying to have a bit of crack, slagging, and the first (I know, at it again) couple of holes the crack was mighty.

Then I became acutely aware that the joke was on me. It started out O.K., calling me Moses, asking when I was going to church, Sunday School, and things of this nature. It got to a point where I asked our friend to stop. Enough was enough. My intuition told me that a lot of talking about me was going on, so this was when I said no more. It fell on deaf ears.

It was when driving off at the next hole that the Moses thing popped up again. This is when the Mad Morph came straight out of me. I swung the driver full power and just stopped myself inches from his head. So glad I did, though. But it was then I knew I was reacting and not being responsive. Deep inside, I knew I had work still to do. I regretted it instantly, and in my mind for the rest of that day I made a promise never to lose it again. Only in the defence of my family and myself will I ever become physical with someone, as it only creates more and more karma, and you end up on the vicious wheel always repeating and never learning anything from the lesson itself.

I think my friend knows how close he came to getting split open. I could have killed him and would never have been right here, right now, writing and telling this small story about my early days of trying to get off the karmic wheel of life. So yes, I just about scraped through that one, but looking back, it's the one from where many of my lessons sprouted. In the end, I'm thankful I did it, but even more grateful I stopped the swing in time. Sorry again, buddy. You know who you are.

So, it's time to get back to my magical experiences I was having with the sun. I was interacting with it daily if it was showing itself, which sometimes wasn't all that frequent in this country. Since I began having the experience, I'd thought about what it would be like for me to go to Spain on my holidays again, with the sun out early morning to late evening all day every day. How much light would I be able to spread? Then again, I could need neck surgery by the time I got home, so it's like everything in life: ups and downs, highs and lows. But deep inside, I think I would have sacrificed and accepted the sore neck, and the magic would have taken the front seat for me.

How could I even have thought about not writing about this truly magical gift? It's like straight out of a sci-fi movie, only for me, this is as real as the air we all breathe, the water we all drink (not tap water I hope) and the sun we all see. I for one couldn't dream about it getting any better—when that's exactly what happened next.

When experiencing this with the sun, I truly felt blessed in some way to be doing something so magnificent and hadn't really come off the high this had given me when I spotted something for the first time (I never quit with those firsts, but I'm sure you innerstand). I couldn't believe my eyes, I truly couldn't. I never even saw it coming. I had been doing this for a while now, and absolutely loved it. It was connecting to me on an emotional level, that is of no doubt.

What I felt with my heart was a sense of belonging to the earth itself. I know what this must sound like, but I wouldn't write about it if it wasn't true, and through my writing about it I don't want to try to normalize it in any way. For me, it was the most magical biggest thing I had ever done and am still doing in my life.

I had caught a glimpse of a beam of light coming up from the bottom of the sun. I had never seen that part until this very day of doing this inspiring work. I still don't know if I'd ever looked down so low to the ground or if it hadn't shown itself to me until this day, but once I saw it, there was no getting away from what I was witnessing with my own two eyes. I went into slow-motion mode and watched from start to finish and made sure that what I was looking at was real.

I only had to dip my head forward and down a little, and as I slowly raised it up, at the same time tilting my head back, I could clearly see the start of the light coming straight out of the centre of my chest and up to the bottom of the sun. This is when, if I kept going, my twin flame and higher self would come out of the top of it, always bronzy goldy twin flame to the left and my higher self with diamond white light to the right. It was always this way and still is to this day.

It hit me like a ton of bricks. There's a saying that "once the penny drops …," and for me, it really felt like the whole ton of those bricks dropped onto me, only with emotions, and ones that I couldn't put into check. To realize in that very moment that what was coming out of the top of the sun was starting its journey from me, and not only that, but it was also coming straight out of my heart!

This is another moment in my life that I have never forgotten, nor ever will. I knew for absolute certainty now that it was my twin flame. To do what I had done throughout my life, all the relationships I had been involved in, from my first puppy love to my last relationship with the mother of our three daughters, I felt at that moment that I had been forgiven for all my wrongdoings—and believe me, this is something I had been asking the Most High for, and at the same time I also had forgiven any wrongdoing for their part unto me.

I had spent time apologizing to all their souls, and I truly meant it one night. But this is the moment when not only did I know my words were being heard but my lessons had been learnt. Never again would I do wrong or disrespect a woman, as without them, there wouldn't be nothing nice in this world, and us men would be a lonely bunch. Then there is the small point of us all reproducing together, lovemaking, sex, being sexual, horny, passionate—there is so much more to this single act than most off us stop to give a second thought to, "the gift of life itself."

Sometimes what you write on one full page with words is a split-second emotional reaction in your mind to a string of experiences you have had in your life, and only by stopping, thinking, and living in that present moment do you realize how important they are to you in your search for *true love*. In my angel synchronicities, with the multitude of numerical numbers I've received, I'm always reading about twin flame reunions and how rare they are. No one for sure will find the other half off their soul that split into two upon entering this world. Even if you do, it is not written in the stars that it will last, and separation and difficulties are never far away.

Imagine someone mirroring your soul and bringing to the fore all the good and all the bad, who you truly are, with a connection so strong, a vibration so radiant, the love so deep that you can't measure it, it's infinite and never-ending on the metaphysical side of life. I for one look forward to accepting the challenges that comes from such *pure love* from *one being to another*.

I have thought long and hard about how this could happen to me, and I believe if I knew all the answers, it would be too overwhelming. I just couldn't handle it. I truly believe that this is the reason; you'll probably never know them all. For the light to go out from my heart as one shaft of light, but then go through the sun and come out the top as two shafts of life that turn into brightly different-coloured arrays of radiant lights and then into human forms, turning then into angels with clearly both hands and arms straight in a cross position and stretching over the atmosphere—how magnificently magical is that? The gratitude I have is abundantly infinite and fills my heart with unconditional love.

Through my inner work, I had what I think is my twin flame enter through the left palm of my hand, and my higher self, who reminded me of Legolas from *Lord of the Rings*, entered through my right hand from the Pleiades. I have no memories of them either earthly or metaphysically leaving me. I can only think they have left a spark of themselves inside me. It's either that or they have always been there throughout my whole life, letting me live with my free will. Only now that I am wide awake are they showing themselves to me, because they are *me*. What lies behind us and what lies before us are tiny matters compared to what lies within us.

I have thought long and hard: Should I get a one-to-one reading done on myself to try to gain more knowledge about what I was doing and the things I was experiencing? At the same time, I've concluded that I don't think I'm meant to, as all I need to know is etched deep inside me. As much as I crave to find out more, I believe it is all part of my journey, and bit by bit, as I choose to live my life as my authentic self, it will be revealed to me in divine timing. I also have a strong belief that going within with my angels guiding me is all the outside help I need.

If there is one person, I would take a reading from, it would be twin flame initiates Ellen Redd. If she lived in Northern Ireland, I truly believe I would have already got one, as her knowledge and willingness to help the truth-bearers and twin flames is second to none. To know you are a light worker, a star seed, an earth angel, who was destined to be on earth at this exact moment in time to help raise the collective consciousness into the fifth dimension and onto the new earth, is a very hard thing to let enter your human mind. I still didn't fully know what I was, but what I do know is that I'm destined to help in some way, because if you've been on the journey with me by reading my book thus far, there's so much that I have gone through on my journey, so many out-worldly tasks and yet I truly believe I'm only getting started.

To fathom it all in my mind and live and raise my children alone, work every day, and keep it all together, deep inside I now believe that I have at least made a conscious choice to partake in a mission with my soul on a divine purpose to help, if only to write this book and tell my story. It means sending out more awareness on a global scale and encouraging everybody who is on the fence to jump the right way. People who are caught up in the program of this matrix must collectively wake themselves up and seek the more truthful and rewarding life that each one of us deserve by right.

So here I am now, with everything coming within myself and up to the sun. Some readers probably are having a niggling thought, *is this guy on magic mushrooms, or whacking LSD into him every day and then at weekends a couple of blasts of DMT just to top it all off?* But the truth of the matter is, my body and mind are somehow tapping into my ingrown DMT, and my pineal gland is working on automatic for me to see the visions I see, and so clearly, too. As much as I have been blessed in a way to have this gift with the sun—I can do this at any time as long as the sun is out, as if it is now either built into me physically or implanted in my mind—it's something I'm taking very seriously and trying to light this world up each and every time I do it.

It does get to me emotionally sometimes. I can't help it. The belief I have inside that I'm helping feels so real to me. Then, when this happens, the detail I can see through my tears blows my mind every time. To slowly watch them go up from my heart, go through the sun, then split in two and go out the top—you need to innerstand, this really is instantaneous, so quick, so magical, so bright, so clear, with so many patterns—I nearly cry every time. If I don't, I certainly feel it every time.

I love doing this. It gives me a sense of belonging and fills me with such belief that we truly are all *one* on this planet. *We are light energy.* There is a magnetic field around every one of us. They call it your aura, but I believe it is so much more than that.

The earth itself has a magnetic field just like us, and *earth* jumbled around spells *heart.* I truly believe that your heart is the key to everything. Inside each one of us, everything is working in tandem for our highest good, and if it was allowed to flow naturally the way God intended, life for everyone would be so much more peaceful, loving, and fulfilling. It is the pufferfish that upset all this balance in such degrading ways, globally. We are poisoned daily with everything, and when you look for help, you are poisoned a little more.

I have concluded that at this moment in time, humans aren't running this planet, and the ones who are seen and believed to be running it are just being used. "The root of all evil is money" is a long talked about saying, but it's not the actual money, as lots can give you so much, not only desired pleasures but security in trying for a life of harmony and bliss.

The word *evil* spelt backwards is *live*, and that's the one thing they don't want us to do. The work that goes into keeping the matrix programming going on to the masses every single day lets me know that those at the very top of the pufferfish elites know exactly, down to the last microbe, how spirituality works, why it works, all the dimensions where they are working tirelessly to prevent a mass awakening, but deep inside each and every one of their souls, they know they can't stop it.

It's like check in a game of chess. It's only a matter of time until it's *checkmate*, but if they have a couple of moves left, they will use them, as pufferfish do, until we are all awoken and relieve them of their positions so they can puff no more. In the end, it is so simple. It's all about *unconditional love* from within. It's so easy to go off on a rant when speaking about such things, although it sometimes is called for, because the more it's spoken about, the more people will get awake, which then in turn will gain the knowledge about all the lies and deceit for themselves.

Throughout this year, I have to give a big shout out to Rebecca James and her posts on Facebook about all the astrological things that happen, not only with planets, stars, portals, moon, and eclipses, but also all the emotional phases that come with it—including all the positive energy that comes from within her posts and all the timings of everything's life path and the alignments that come with it all. There are things I wouldn't have had a clue about but for her posts, so thank you, Rebbeca. So much of it resonated with me daily when I was searching for truths and trying to come to terms with all my inner work and all the healing you must go through when you're becoming one with yourself.

I followed Rebecca to find out about eclipses, lion gate portals, openings, and closing different energies. It helped me more than she could have ever known. Equinoxes, different planets crossing over and giving different energies—these are things I had absolutely no clue about when I first started on this journey. At that time, I wouldn't have even called it a *journey*. It was more like a call to arms for me.

Astrology, the universe, the cosmos—I truly did learn a lot at this time. Believe it or not, with what I was doing, I really didn't have much time to learn all the details myself. That's why I am so appreciative of her blind help on all the workings of everything. It helped me make sense of things nearly daily. Most recently another woman popped unto my feed, and again I believe she was personally weaved unto my path cosmically. Her name is Gypsy Rose Connection to Spirit from Australia and is a professional psychic, tarot reader and medium. She has also written a book "Healing with the Stars 2024". This book has been a great source for not only knowledge but like Rebecca talks about the emotional energies that match all the harmonizing qualities. The daily struggles and the daily joys that lives alongside us every day. So thankyou ladies for all your loving energies they have meant more than you could have ever known.

I had started to follow blood moons, blue moons, eclipses, portal openings, and it was on one of these nights that I got overwhelmed even more. There were so many different things happening throughout the year, but every time something was happening with the moon, I would always go outside and search for it. But it was always cloudy, and I never got to see the moon. Only once did I see one, and it was what they call a *blue moon*. I went out my back door to go to put some rubbish in the bin, and there it was, and as much as it was cloudy, I could see it as clear as day.

I went back inside and grabbed a chair. This was about eleven in the evening, and as I was sitting there just looking at it again, it was so bright as I stared at it. *Bingo bongo*, I couldn't believe my eyes. I mean, what I saw, I wasn't even trying to look at it in this way. It all happened so naturally.

This just keeps getting better for me, every time something new like this happens. I didn't get emotional, as I was in shock for about ten minutes. You could say I was in awe, as not once in my thoughts had I linked what I was doing with the sun to the moon. I just couldn't believe it. Now here I was spreading light in the night sky through the lit-up moon. An unbelievable magical feeling came over me. I truly was blessed. My mind took off at a million miles per hour thinking, *Now I can do this at night.*

I had learnt quite a lot at this point, but I knew there was still so much unknown to me. The people I was following, their knowledge, what they could do, psychics, spiritual warriors, tarot card readers—they were probably years ahead of me in terms of not only what they knew but what they could do. A few that I took inspiration from were Ellen Redd, Rebecca James, Billy Carson, Alto Pianeto, Honey Dipp, Gypsy-rose Connection to Spirit, Deme B. Coach, Carmel Fuller, and Joanne Honey Thomas. These are just some of the names, but they are the ones I followed intently and felt I was part of their soul tribes and families. I took different aspects of all their knowledge and combined it somehow into a little spiritually mindful soul tribe of my own, so these different people I have unconditional love for from early on.

Their combined guidance has helped me with so much on my journey, and each one of them has helped me in a different way—emotionally, mentally, physically, spiritually, positively. Different posts at different times have popped up on my feed just when I needed them and helped me make sense of what I was doing in my intense inner work. I look back in hindsight and know my angels have synchronized these at just the right times for me, as they were all spiritually guided. Carmel Fuller is the only one who didn't send a lot of posts, but for me, she was the queen of queens when it came to sending a multitude of loved-filled gifs. A master at it really, and at that time I felt everyone. I truly took a lot of love out of all those beautiful small gifs with amazing massive meanings of love. My gratitude for all these is infinite, as they all combined to help me more than they could have ever known.

So here I was now, experiencing this with the moon. It was a little different from doing it with the sun. It was the same thing, but the shafts of light were so close to being the same colour. There was a slight orange, but not at all that much. Also, there weren't as many swirls of lights, but more of a constant beam. Even though it was the night sky, I could see more than when doing it with the sun, especially when tearful, though at night it was more like wave after wave of light.

Of course, it didn't take long before the emotional link to the magnitude of what I was doing hit me. It was truly, truly amazing what I saw. It wasn't like the sun, where it helped with the brightness, more like the thin lines and patterns inside the shafts of lights became more prominent to visually see. What another amazing night I was having.

Going with the flow of things was beginning to enter my conscious mind, and I felt inside that the light was somehow connecting to other people's light around the world as a collective. To feel you were playing a part in this was amazing—not only when doing this, but later lying in bed with tears running down your cheeks, and you know that you are smiling from ear to ear. There have not been too many times in my life where tears and smiles went together, but I was beginning to experience this a lot more often, and it filled me with even more love, as I was believing more inside my mind that it was collectively helping, like a small cog in a very big wheel, to share my light.

Truly, at that moment, as much as I had heard it on a multitude of posts over quite a long period of time, I knew I was a light worker to be able to do this in the day and do the same at night as well. It felt so special to me. To gain the knowledge that I am one who can form the light blew my mind that little bit more, and I couldn't stop doing it either.

I know I will never have all the answers to all the questions that I ask, even to myself. I believe this is the way it is meant to be for everyone. My own thoughts begin to go back to the start of my journey, when all the amazing things were happening to me, and what is it even gonna be like for me to go back and read what I have written about myself?

When I started writing, I did not go with the intention that down this road, I would begin to have such a connection with my spirit guides. Then, I was progressing and having such blind faith that my guardian angels were guiding and protecting me daily. It's not only that they have been there all my life, but also not even about me believing anymore; it's about knowing. Walking with angels is something I had to put into the title of my book, as they have played such a big role in not only showing me what true love is but also compassion, honesty, integrity, purpose, self-reliance, guidance, creativity, ambition, belief, inner wisdom, wholeness, coming to terms with seeking my higher self, and connecting the way I had by changing my life completely.

My spirit guides filled me with spiritual intuition, knowledge, courage, and ambition. They showed me unconditional love and how to love myself, who I really am, and what I really am. People can say what they want; they always have and always will. To be experiencing all this on different levels, there is nothing that could make me change the journey I am now on—a journey of ascension, enlightenment, truth-bearing, my soul's purpose. This has connected me to the divine realm, to truly inner standing such things as the law of one, the reason for DNA itself, the cosmic blueprint, to allow an infinite soul to experience what it's like to live an entire life as a human being. It is truly a gift, and boy, has it been a hard gift at times, but it is a gift all the same, as tough love is still love.

People around the globe I have seen cannot come to any such agreement as to what the creator of all is called God, the prime creator, the source, the one, the beginning, the maker. For me, I have come up with something so much simpler: *love*, earthly, universal, cosmic, galactic love, just love, the most abundant vibrational sound and frequency. It's all love, conscious love. The quantum field is love. It's everywhere; you just must go, find it for yourself and begin your own journey from within yourself.

CHAPTER 23

Truth Love Life Source Light

THE LAST CHAPTER of my journey has finally arrived, and I have put so much thought into it. I really haven't a clue how I should start it, even to the gathering of my thoughts. At the end, it is beginning to rattle my brain, excuse the pun, "but to no end." I have a feeling it could be a long one. Safer grabbing yourself a cuppa before you begin.

When starting to put pen to paper at the very beginning, I will admit I found it very difficult, as it was something I didn't have any prior knowledge of doing, or even what my writing style would be. I hadn't written since school almost thirty-two years earlier. Certainly, I knew early on I would need help with my punctuation, paragraph splitting, this is when I found Microsoft word existed So, a very big thank you to whoever read my manuscript, as I was never a good writer. If I had to use a typewriter, I'd only be on about chapter three. So many thank yous. I know how difficult it would have been, so I am abundant with my gratitude.

My life has changed so much over the past couple of years that some people might have to get to know me again. Don't get me wrong: I am still me. But now I live my life in such a simple, beautiful, spiritual, loving, and hard-working way. Compassion is one of the great many things I have learnt on the road least travelled, and I am such a better being because of it.

Unconditional love was maybe the most difficult for me—to try not only to fall in love with myself but to do it unconditionally, my experiences helped me greatly with this. Just to get out of my own head, my analytical mind, and bungee jump into my own heart for the very first time in my entire life was an amazing achievement for me.

For years, I only saw my heart as something that beats, and with each one pumps blood around my body at least that is what I was taught at school, but I have come to realize it is so much more than its physical function if that's what it truly does, I even feel myself starting to question this. It is the centre of our very being, and through my research I believe it has an actual separate brain of its own, which has links with the universal cosmos itself. It has 40,000 specialized cells that stay within, and each day now I give 5,000 each to my three children, 5,000 for myself, 5000 split between all my family, 5000 to my matey Enzo 5,000 to my soul brother Colly, and the last 5,000 to all the metaphysical beings that walk, guide, and fly with me every second of every day and from every year since I was born.

Your heart is a gateway to the divine realm, but the secret has always been that your heart is the divine, and always that is where the spark lies from within. Until it takes its last physical beat on this earth and your cord is dissolved, this is what connects your body to your soul.

I have done what you could say is a lot of soul-searching, and this has led me down many untraveled paths. For the first forty-five years of my life, I never thought about it at all. I never knew I had one. But by Joe, I know for certain now that this is the real me. It took some digging and forgiving for all the things with my free will I have put it through, but the thing is, it's been waiting on me all this time, and not only that, to let me connect with it in such an immense and intense way.

It put up with everything I threw at it: smoking, drinking, drugs, aggression, violence, ignorance, hate, fear, every low-down thing you could possibly think of. Yet here it is, an unconditional forgiving loving soul that gladly and happily reconnects with my purpose. It's truly, truly amazing. If you had the experiences I 've had, would you gladly give up everything that was bad for you in a heartbeat? That's something my guardian angels and spirit guides have made sure is still beating strong. As I write this, I feel it pounding.

I have changed as a person so much, and not from the outside in but from the inside out. Still, my life is constantly evolving every day, don't get me wrong sometimes, it's the seemly small insignificant annoyances that troubles me, it comes up so quick and so fast within my egotistical thoughts at the time I don't even realise I'm self-sabotaging. So, it's not to later do I make sense of it all and begin to intentionally redirect my thoughts and take positive action towards deprogramming my mind from the built in negative matrix channelling already imprinted into my sub conscious over my lifetime. This is something I'm getting better at transmuting with greater speed and now don't give it my energy long enough for it to seed a root within my thoughts. Since becoming personally aware, sometimes I still find it difficult to control a tendency, to be impulsive causing some instability, in losing the importance of keeping my integrity intact. This is something in my life that I had desperately tried to uphold, but many times in vain. This is when you can demonstrate your potential and start to consciously make the right decisions, emotionally moving forward without hindering your personal advancements, as you are free to live your life with truth as the foundation of your freedom, continually and consistently upholding your moral principles. To attain true fulfilment ultimately depends on you achieving wholeness and oneness within yourself regardless of the external outcomes. You could simplify it down to say I'm finally after so many years that I'm attentively beginning to learn from my lessons.

Just the other night, didn't my magic rekindle itself with another amazing gift either bestowed upon me or given as a reward for all the inner work I have been doing for the benefit of the collective consciousness as a whole?

Then as you begin to delve deeper, I think I have volunteered to the divine to be here right at this time, right for this purpose. For me to even write such things lets me know how much I have changed. There are two ways to take such thoughts: one is to say, "Loopy loo his head away" and then there is number two, those whose consciousness is more highly developed and more in tune with the workings of the universe, who think something deep is happening within this person. This is when you begin to interpret an inner standing of the divine challenges that arise, then as an individual taking that inspired action within oneself you embark on the limitless possibilities that await you on your cosmic journey.

You see, it is better to be hated for what you are than to be loved for something you're not. To truly have made peace with your past and heal all that was broken, some known and some unknown, to be awoken and receive gift after gift, help after help, light after light, and light after so much darkness—the doors aren't just opening, they are being blown off the hinges, never again to slam shut on the collective. For me on a personal scale, I feel special that I have made the choice to help, fostering a deeper inner standing of who I really am, and with a newfound determination even when confronted with constant adversity, I have a new resilience to overcome all obstacles woven onto and into my path.

So, this country is not known for its long spells of sunshine, nor is it known for showing you the moon on a regular basis, and certainly not the one you would get to see if you were living in the Australian outback. More like a dented 10p piece. The clouds win nearly every time. So, I was sitting out in my small front garden barefoot earthing, with blanket, coat, scarf, gloves, woolly hat, long johns, the whole works just to stay that little bit warmer.

Earthing was the reason I was there in the first place. I'm beginning to love sneaking these firsts in now. As I was doing this, I began to see the light from my chest go straight into the lamppost outside my house, and upwards it went. At first, I don't think I fully grasped the situation, but then I tilted my head the exact same way as I do with the sun and the moon, and *boom, bingo, bongo, bang,* up it zoomed like some super-duper highly volted torch (probably German made). No way I thought of this happening.

When I say I was evolving daily, I didn't mean things like this. What I meant was the person I was becoming because of the daily life struggles that I was bringing up and dealing with. This was something else. This was the evolving of what I was finding I could do with light. Right there and then, I started to smile.

I mean, I smiled so much that my emotions got involved somehow, and tears of joy began trickling down my face. When this happened, all the lights began to shoot upwards, from all the lampposts that I could directly look at and some indirectly. Even people with a living room light on or a bedroom light on would beam straight up, with each one of them having a beam running to my chest.

What was happening to me? Somehow, I was evolving with light itself going through me. To me, it seemed that the deeper I went in dealing with doubt, lack, resentment, greed, fear, judgement, gluttony, envy, etc., and how all these things had mentally been addressed, they just didn't affect me. They were not a part of my everyday life anymore. Gifts were being created for me.

Light bearer, torch bearer, light worker, light houser—I couldn't think anything else. I can't stress this enough. I truly believe my DNA was changing because of living by truth. It's such an amazing way to live day by day. You get to the point where you can't even lie to yourself. What a feeling you get from that alone! One of the biggest lies people live with and defend is fear itself. Nobody wants to admit it, but there it lies, festering and controlling how you react to others.

So, no moon, no sun, and still, I can form this light. With these tears, I could see the little formations of my twin flame, our higher self. I didn't know which one, because with the lamp lights, they were all the same colours. To this day, it's amazing every time I do it.

I now know I'm meant to do it. Sometimes there are about twenty going up at the same time, and every time I feel *wow wow wow*. Deep inside, I know I'm helping, I just know it. Your gut feeling, your intuition, it fills your stomach with it. So, I began getting my many layers on a nightly basis and started doing this regularly. It was when I was doing this that, yet another amazing sight came to pass.

When doing this with the lampposts, it would be the same as the sun and moon. My neck would get sore and stiff. But when earthing and sitting at the same time, the back of my head would be the same level as my outside windowsill, so I had gotten good at resting the back of my head on it to ease my sore neck, using my woolly hat as a go-between cushion. It was when doing this motion that up high in the night sky, over to my left, I began to see about six or seven lights all in a row moving across the night sky. As I knew very well, the stars' alignment outside the front of my house came from the direction of the Pleiades, even though I couldn't see them. It was right on their directional path.

As I started witnessing this and the line of white bright lights got even longer, I made a diamond-shaped hand telescope and watched them get longer and longer. I unrested my neck very quickly, as I had never seen anything like this before. It was like an unbroken chain of them, and it just got bigger and bigger in length. Some were bigger than others, but only in length, not height. They were the same height as they traversed the dark sky. I could see them as plain as day illuminated above me to the left. This was nothing like the orange poofy whatsoever; this was up much higher than the orange poofy. Like a set of train carriages of white luminous light, with a destination unknown to me and at the same time using to trackless night sky as its compass.

As I watched, mesmerized by this sighting, the front of the line began disappearing. They were disappearing at the exact same spot as all the lights that were still coming forward. It would also go black until I saw the last one disappear.

In the line of lights, you could see the darkness between each one, which I thought at the time that they were all separate, but I don't fully know, as they could have been joined. This is something I couldn't make out. The one thing I could see was that they were all separated by the same distance between each light. To this day, I don't know what it was that I witnessed, or even if they disappeared at all.

Being so high up, they could just have easily turned the lights off. If this was the case, they turned their lights off at the exact same spot where they all began to go dark and disappear. Truly a magnificent thing to watch with nothing but my own two eyes. I've never seen anything like it since, and I have done a very amateur diagram to try to show you what I mean, just as amateur as my orange puffy diagram.

I didn't know what to make of it in my mind at the time; I only knew that I had witnessed something extraordinary up in the vast night sky. I have asked people from around my hometown, and nobody has seen a tap, only me. Was it for me to see? I probably will never know in this lifetime, and maybe then, when my timeline is up and my spirit and soul move on, I will get to answer that question.

Writing this has reminded me of another massive thing I saw in the middle of the day with my youngest daughter, Ameila. I do have a photograph of it and a video, so I might just include that in this book. I truly had forgotten about it all, so happy to have kept the picture and video though.

I have written this book with the intention of not knowing everything. With so many firsts happening, it really is *raw* and *real*. As much as I have gained a lot of knowledge about it all since. I have tried to write it from my perspective with the knowledge I had at the time and not from what I gained along the way. What I mean is, I have written it in a way, from the visions I was having, through my interactions with whatever came across me in my inner work, the experiences that I went through.

I've probably left out the sweating, the shaking, the shock I experienced. How I felt after it was done each time and then eventually being awakened is when I truly began with the lessons it was teaching me about every single humanly possible thing in my life, and to face it all head on. I believe at the earliest moment of finding and experiencing these magical things, it took a good while to get over the shock of it all and to begin to evolve emotionally. The connection was being shown to me. I felt like a yo-yo on a rollercoaster in one of the biggest spaghetti junctions not even in this world but in the whole of the cosmos. I was being shown so many magical moments, and at the time, I certainly was in awe of it all.

It was then as a soul having a human existence that got awoken inside me, and the journey of learning, the knowledge, the *truth* began flooding my mind. This is when the path less travelled truly began in earnest for me/ soul/spirit/higher self/twin flame/divine. It took so long to work it out mentally and spiritually that I am all of these, and so is absolutely everyone else, because we truly are all one.

At the beginning of your awakening journey of truth you quickly realize that all your struggles, your losses, the drama, the dilemmas and all the pain of suffering somehow you find are welded to the fabric of life and accepted on a global scale. You begin to discover a deeper purpose, amplifying your relevance to matters of the heart that sparks of a spiritual awakening. To then an expansion of your consciousness to a higher level, offering solace to a version of yourself beyond the mortal realm, deliberately seeking a connection to that infinite part of your soul that metaphysically has little concept of the physical normalcy of time.

From being awoken to becoming wide awake, you see things more clearly. Intelligence is something that should be used for the benefit of all, but I have learnt that this is not the case—far from it. Words are more powerful than the common man and woman could ever imagine. In the secret societies of this world, very intelligent souls use the spellings of so many against the masses to benefit only themselves and their hidden greedy deadly agendas. Pictures, shapes, and colours, and all the hidden symbolism that comes with them—once you see through it all, you can never not see it.

This has led me to believe that as much as sacrificing was done many years ago in its rawest form, publicly beheading people to offer blood to these so-called gods, it has never stopped; it has only evolved. It is done more sneakily but on a grander scale and over a longer time. Wars are only one way they do it. Food for thought when one country invades another in times of war the first thing, they do is capture the TV and radio stations, I wonder why that is. Then there is smoking, drinking, poisoning, pharmaceuticals, drugs, work, murder, and it's all done through the back door, privately, so as not to reveal the true agenda of the depopulation of the 8.1 billion people off this planet.

The pufferfish are the darkest of all and are unknown to us all, and even the puppets who serve them don't know them or how intelligent these dark pufferfish are. Alfa- Draconian Jesuits secret societies illuminati knights templar allied masonic degrees secret orders freemasonry, there is so many built in orders, a countless amount some benevolent, some malevolent and your insight into all their true meanings would depend on the wisdom you receive, and how far up the ladder you become as it would be on a need-to-know basis. You can be sure that behind the financial institutions of this world a lot of its members if not all sit on their hidden seats at the very top. Of this I have no doubt. This is the secret system with all its coherent mechanised parts working together to make it seem so natural, but from the inside it is a very highly established procedure perfected over the years. Engineering a process and transforming from the inside with a desired outcome to a world order of control. Resulting in a monopoly of money and death.

From darkness comes light, and this is what they know will be the end of it all, as the unhidden and untwisted parts of words and symbolism are of light that will not stay dormant for too much longer. It's a bit like a cold sore; it's always there, you just can't see it, but when it appears, you cannot hide it. You can try, but it always comes back.

I'm not going to write any more of this, for it is my last chapter. But it had to get a mention just to tell the reader the lengths to which the pufferfish elites are willing to go and the endless amounts of our own money they put into hiding all of this and the dumbing down of the masses, because when in this state of mind, control is so much easier for them. Wake up, dear souls, and gain your own knowledge about it all, and once you see it all, you can never unsee it.

I'm so happy you have gotten this far in reading my book and have surely come to innerstand the journey I have been on and what I have gone through. Everybody deals with their emotions in different ways. When I began my healing, I certainly hadn't counted on going underground to some very dark holes to bring things not only to my attention but to transmute the darkness through my very being and eventually get rid of the ones that don't serve me anymore.

I have witnessed entities coming up to my face and dealing with them head on. I must tell you the story of the first two that came up to my face. They were both old menacing-looking greys. The first one came up close, and I believe I might be the first person to metaphysically give him a Scottish kiss (a head butt, for those who don't inner stand this terminology) and off he went. The second one came up even closer, with his hand up to his face, using his finger in a *shh* fashion, as if telling me to stay quiet, with a menacing look to his big eyes. This one, I chased just using my eyes. I hope this makes sense, but I looked at him and leaned forward, not blinking once, and off he too scooted.

After this one, I remember thinking that I felt like Mike Tyson giving the terrifying stare-down he always gave to his opponents before his fights. Don't think he ever lost one of those, but he certainly won a lot of fights before he had even thrown a punch. (A hero of mine, too.) So, I will thank Mike for that one. I did have the pleasure of meeting him alongside my brother Stuart when he made a very rare appearance in Dublin. (That's another story, bro.)

So yes, you could say it sounds a bit mad as to how I got to deal with some of my emotions, but that's just the way it was for me.

Today we live in a generation where dishonesty is widely accepted alongside a dog-eat-dog cultural mentality, with no relevance to the matters of the heart. Were sneaky agendas, systematized broken links and subdivisions of society are immorally promoted to the public continually adding to the individual servitude of today's modern living, spawning an acceptance of daily enslavement. Rigorously motivated by media outlets on a multitude of social platforms to the young, beginning an indoctrination process with an agenda of separation hell bent on opposing unity, and strengthening the development of societal division with the love of nothing bar how easy the digital money is to use. Yet behinds the scenes, lies the unseen meticulous planning of daily manipulating control within every exchange of the monopolistic internal and hidden power structures, of the modern combination the governments have alongside the agreeable cohesion of deceitfulness and trickery of the banking systems. It just seems so easy for me now to go off on one, because when you not only live by truth, but find the reality hidden within and behind the thin veil of lies a non-fearful awoken soul can't miss it, Just in the same way I cannot miss an opportunity when the information as a bombardment of thoughts flows within my mind, which I then in the moment display as words on paper for you the reader to consciously become more aware of what is truly happening around us every single day.

Dolores Cannon once wrote, "We are all unique and have our own path to follow, so it's important to trust ourselves and not compare ourselves to others."

How many people reading this right now when told about spiritual healers, empaths, psychics and reiki spaces automatically think of people in a tent with a picture of a flower on it sitting crouched like a Buddha, wearing funny bright colourful clothes, piercings everywhere, tattoos on show, Caucasian men and women with dreadlocks smoking weed, humming, eyes closed, swaying their bodies around. Quite a lot, I'd say. For me, this is a good example of the matrix programming that has infiltrated the masses of people who have a built-in perception, and the secret to it all is they don't even know it's merely a form of unknown ignorance.

For me, these people are the heartbeat and fabric of all true beings, the planned societal ridiculing stigma that is pushed onto them. It's about time it stopped. There is going to be a massive U-turn on this earth, and these are the souls the freshly awakened will run to for guidance and knowledge. All they have ever wanted to do is help. They have never seen themselves as more highly evolved souls, only ones at the core of their being because of the inner truth they possess, the spiritual knowledge of how things are and came to be. They want to spread the *truth*.

On my journey, I have not yet found many like-minded people, as I had no clue of it at all. Only my soul brother Collin Brown has been my rock, and hopefully in writing about my awakening, I finally will get to meet people on the same soul level of innerstanding as me. I certainly am not what would be known as a hippy (which is yet another matrix stigma, by the way), but a normal guy who loves painting and decorating, but with an extraordinary awakening to put myself—gladly, may I say—into the firing line of the spiritual warfare that has been upon us for countless years.

Small minds can't comprehend big spirits. To be great, you must be willing to be hated, mocked, and misunderstood, and so it is! There is no turning or looking back for me. It is onwards and upwards. There's that old cliché saying *the truth hurts*. Well, so be it, because it is spoken from the heart.

Spiritual warfare comes right before unprecedented seasons of *love* and blessings. If you are experiencing unusual adversity and things seem odd as you are simply trying to make an impact for the kingdom of *love*, be encouraged that *love* may be about to bless your efforts significantly. Often, spiritual warfare is the enemy's attempt to steal our happiness about what *love* is doing in our lives. Don't take the bait. Double back on your peace and joy in *love* and sovereignty over every situation in your life. To finish this little paragraph off, every time I mentioned *love* in it, you can substitute *God, Source, Creator, Most High*, and *Maker*, but in the end, you will find that they all mean *love*. Everything resonates it everywhere for everyone. You just must reach out and grab it with your heart. Loved this when I read it just changed the words a little to doctor it to love. I have searched high and low for its author but to no avail so thankyou for your words of wisdom it resonated with me daily.

About 90 per cent of the time, we are listening to our logical fear, and ego-filled thoughts rather than our dreaming pulsating hearts. If you want something you've never had, you'll have to do something you've never done, and for me, it is the writing of this book. If you were to ask me a year ago about writing a book, I can honestly say I would have laughed quite a bit, but here I am, an evolving awoken soul living for each present moment.

Yes, I have problems just like everybody else, only now I see them as challenges. That makes a bigger difference on not only the outcome but how I feel reaching that outcome and thereafter.

The synchronicities that have now entered my life daily are so frequent and so numerous, it feels like my angels are shining a torch on every one of them. Each time I think I am writing the last paragraph something comes and grabs my mind and says *no*. One thing I do know is that my angels never sleep. I'm sure of it.

Two of the most recent synchronicities I have experienced came when my father got a new car, I honestly never looked at the number plate until the other night. That's when I delved into the meaning of its number. Then the very next morning, I went to the forest for a walk, truly expecting myself to be the only one there, as it was bucketing down with heavy rain. As I parked my car in the car park, there was no-one there, and as much as I didn't see anyone out walking, there was a Jeep parked beside my car when I got back. That's all the vehicles there were in the car park, and on its number, plate was the exact same one as my father's.

Before my walk, I had just been on the phone with a publisher for my book, which I had rejected, not fully but was going to pursue another avenue. When I read my synchronicity message that was guided to me, my stomach turned, and my intuition told me to go for it without delay. That's exactly what I did. Unbelievable that this could have happened so close to those conversations. Everything has happened in my life for a reason, and I wasn't going to change that now.

The other one was even more amazing. My daughter Ameila's tablet played a crucial part. I could see that some sort of dim light was coming from her bed, and as I checked, she had falling asleep with her tablet still on, and not only that, earphones still on too. As I went to turn it all off, I saw that the time on her tablet read 0606 and, on my phone, it was 0610, so either my phone was fast or hers was slow. It worked out that mine was too fast.

So, I checked the number and what I found out absolutely amazed me to the core of my beliefs. You see, I had been asking my angels, spirit guides, cosmic birther, soul family, archangels, teachers, ascended masters, even my twin flame what my soul's purpose was. You have an inkling but truly do not 100 per cent fully know.

With what I had been going through with my spiritual inner work, and on a highly deep ongoing emotional level, I really had been asking a lot, truthfully daily, just because every day some small part of me was changing. They call it *the shift*, but its symptoms were vast. My skull would be vibrating and tingling constantly; it is now as I'm writing this. My ears are ringing and buzzing like a comfortable form of tinnitus.

The only reason I say *comfortable* is because I have experienced this for quite a while now, knowing it doesn't last. It comes and goes in snatches, at times highly concentrated, and at other times a little more subtle. The effect on your body could get very intense at times also, but it was a bit easier to adjust and get on with your daily routine of living and loving.

I was searching for this answer, but at the same time emotionally connected to the search for it. I would become tearful at times because of it, but always with the belief that even the unknown was for my higher good, so the tears themselves weren't of sadness but of the unknowingness, as my deep connection to finding out as a truth seeker really meant the world to me on my journey's path.

The caption I read was that my angels had sent me a message that I was an *empathic light worker,* a beautiful soul here to raise the vibration of earth and its environment. My life had already changed so much, but this was a moment it changed to yet another level of consciousness. Another nice moment came over me, wave after wave of tears, so much so that in the end, the sides of my face began to tingle and sting slightly at the same time. It's as if it went straight into my heart, personally an amazing moment for me to experience.

Angels—I want and need to tell you how much I love you with every beat of my heart. After so many years of free will and not even knowing yous were there, guiding and guarding me from when I entered this world, my deep pure love goes back to the very first beat of my heart, to the ones that are now with me as I write this in bed at this very moment, to my very last one that I take on this earth and beyond, because I now know that this is when we will meet and, armed with earthly memories, will begin the next journey. I love you all so much, with all my being.

"Patience isn't just a card game, it's a virtue" is a saying I have been using all my life, just because I thought it sounded cool. It has taken me up until now to realize the true meaning behind it. As I've said in this book a couple of times, as a human being, you want to find everything out yesterday, whether your mind can comprehend it or not. I now know that this is part of your ego. The ego itself is not 100 per cent bad; it's only trying to look after you in most cases. It is the way it's being corrupted from outside programming that dismantles its true purpose.

Tomorrow will go better if you use today to make a difference. This might seem a simple thing to say, but it's not, as today we live with a mind-set that you can never have enough. Even when the bottle is full and unopened, you want another one, and if you can't get it, you would be willing to smash one to receive two back. Until this mind-set changes of never being content with having enough, you yourself and as a global society will never change. Only by going within will the process begin to change.

Silence is like oxygen for me; it's a must. I love connecting with people, but I love reconnecting with myself even more—getting back in the flow of my own rhythm, my true authentic self, without anyone else's energy influencing me. It has never been personal; it is always about self-care. Thankyou Honey Dipp another caption I found on your site. If everyone practised this in only a small way, you would find that even that one act alone would prevent the active mind from exploiting itself so easily and at least slow it down enough to become aware of your present.

Sometimes we unintentionally get entangled in other people's energetic webs, which sets off a chain of tragic events What is not meant for me will leave me. It's O.K. if your heart needs more time to accept what your mind already knows. Just don't let that uncomfortable energy drag you down forever. Forgive yourself and all others and move on.

What holds people down is hatred, resentment, violence, greed, envy, jealousy, revenge, judgement, lies, adultery, cheating, omnipotence, ill will to anybody, and fear. Some of these are very easy to recognize, depending on your character and how you live your life. Others are automatically programmed into your thoughts, and only by going within do you become self-aware.

What lifts people up is love, truth, honesty, peace, compassion, gratitude, integrity, oneness, forgiveness, faithfulness, honour, closeness, unselfishness, kindness, respect, unity, and trust. Seeing those all written on a page together, it shouldn't be hard to see which list of things you would want in your life to make it better. You just must learn how to control how you respond to things sent to destroy your peace.

The cosmic birther/prime source creator is the life force energy that exists everywhere and within everything in the universe and relates to *love* and *unity*. Life is not about dividing; it is about unifying. Only you can make that choice. It is not my job as the writer to save you; it is your job to lead by example and show everyone how you saved yourself. To align yourself with the divine flow of the universe, culminating in a life of love, truth and fulfilment in all you do.

By learning the universal laws that control everything, we can tap into a potent force of personal strength. This force has the potential to lead us in the right direction, helping us to take charge of our lives and accomplish what we truly want. Everything is a product of the mind. What we think, believe, and perceive can shape our world. Think of yourself as a human magnet constantly attracting what you speak, think, and feel.

Like attracts like. The vibrations or energies you send out are made up of your conscious and unconscious energies, and you attract into situations, experiences, and people that have similar energy or vibrations. The universe provides a mirror so that you can see the reflection of the energies and vibrations you are emitting. Ensure that these energies you project are loving and uplifting, as your presence can be a healing force for others. Upon hearing this on my Facebook page I fell in love with its words. I have searched for the author but cannot find them anywhere on my page so thank you for its wisdom.

Manifesting, affirmations, and reality all go hand in hand. Dream big, think big—so big at the start that they seem so far away and unreachable. It is not until you become the woman or man worthy of them for them to become true. You set yourself goals to get there, and you set mini goals to get to your own goals. This is how you reach for your dreams and earthly desires to create your heaven on earth.

Believe in yourself and put the hard work into achieving your own personal success, whatever that may be. To most people, this will be monetary wealth, but there is so much more than just money, and when you go within and search your soul, this is where your answers will lie. There is no doubt money will be a very big asset because of how modern society has been set up and how all is revolving around money.

For me, it's the journey you go on and who you become when striving and changing as a person when achieving and reaching your goals. That's what will make you happy when you get there—content and joyous with not wanting more and more, where your mind doesn't fall into that infected-with-greed mentality, only wanting your bank account to build in such a way that you only want to hold onto it and watch it get bigger and bigger, and forget why you set out on your journey to gain it all in the first place. Scrooge McDuck out of *Duck Tales*—that's what and who you will become, metaphorically speaking.

When you reach a point in your life when you can look back and see integrity, truth, honesty, and hard work, then deep within yourself, you will truly be happy. There are so many people who get rich off the backs of others, and when push comes to shove couldn't give one toot (wanted to use another word there, but I refrain) about the individuals whose hard work made it happen. Enslavement comes to mind—modern-day enslavement.

When you go through your life up to forty-six years old and only then find out about manifesting and setting positive affirmations to create your future, you realize that unknowingly and unintentionally, you have been harbouring and manifesting so many negative thoughts that align with the reality you have made for yourself. You couldn't be doing anything else but what your day-to-day gives you, because all along, you have thought it into your existence, your reality, your present life.

To think that pufferfish have known this and have for years kept it to themselves, manipulated billions with it. If you look up the meaning of *manipulated* in Google, it says "(a tool a mechanism information used in a skilful manner) to control or influence cleverly or unscrupulously: 'the masses were deceived and manipulated by a tiny group.'" For me, personally, that group is *pufferfish*, very intelligent dark *pufferfish* that relish and enjoy the suffering of the poor, like sacrificial lambs to the slaughter. They should be disgusted with themselves, but it's quite the opposite. Through researching and decoding all their information, which by universal law they must tell you about, they're quite proud how they fool the masses. The technical meaning of *sacrificial*, as found in Google, means "designed to be used up or destroyed in fulfilling a purpose or function."

Arbeit mact frei is a German phrase the Nazis used at the gates of Auschwitz. It means, "Work sets you free," but as we all know, it was a complete lie, and this is what is happening on a global scale. To simplify it, what you see is not what you get. Everything is downplayed with lies and deceit, when it should be played with truth and honesty.

I know I have repeated myself a few times about the total influence the pufferfish have globally over us all, but I only say this because I have come to learn, with my affirmations, that if you say something so repetitively, a reality can form. This is what I want to get through to the people who are snoring just like I was, to at least begin to recognize how this world really works. Everything you've ever been told was built upon a bundle of generational lies, because to fool someone is quite easy but to teach them how to un-fool themselves is so much harder, and all ego defensives will come out fighting.

You see, that's how well programmed we all have been from birth. If you can educate your way past this, you'll never unsee it ever again.

I am not writing this as the bearer of all knowledge—far from it. But from my perception of the truth and my inner wisdom of learning to demystify the mysteries and seeing through the now very thin veil with the help of the groups I participate in, on several platforms, I have drawn my own conclusions based on my truths of not only the dark workings but the workings of light.

The true celestial beings of this world can be seen through astronomy and numerology combined with spirituality. Therein lie all the different codes of life: the DNA itself, earth codes, universal codes, cosmic codes, everything is inside each one of us.

The intensity of my awakening has truly put me on the path of not only writing this book and searching for the truth, but knowing that I truly have a special purpose, a divine connection to want to help others who are just like I was. At the beginning, I trusted with blind faith, but the unforeseen belief I had has now turned into a knowing of the truth. I know that I not only volunteered to be right here at this very moment but made the choice to do so. "We are all loved, many are called but few are chosen." This is a caption I've seen a lot. I like what it says, but I disagree with the last three words, as I believe we all can be chosen. It's about personally making the choice to do something about it.

To even comprehend this in my mind from where I was two years ago is still hard to fathom in its entirety. To go head to head with your own ego about matters that have been spoken about from early indigenous tribes right through to modern days, to come to terms with the magnitude of emotions and that you are here to help raise the earth's collective consciousness and heal generational wounds that go back to a time the world has forgotten, when I myself still have healing to do, is a blessing. On ancient knowledge alone, there would be thousands better equipped to carry out such a worldly task, but here I am, with a self-belief beyond anything I have ever thought possible.

To be at times living a somewhat normal enough life, now thrust into a life that is filled with magical moments beyond human construct. I have a newfound passion that wasn't there, a heart that I've found to be pure, a feeling given to me or bestowed upon me to help all the neglected souls of this earth. It's a direction I didn't know I would be taking, but I now have the wisdom and driving belief that somehow, I was destined to do it.

To be happy in all you do is half the battle. I have realized that happiness is not what your house looks like but how you love the people within its walls. Happiness is not about finding success at a certain time but finding something you love so much that time itself seems to disappear. Happiness is not about thinking you have earned the world's approval but waking up each day and feeling at peace in your own skin, quietly anticipating the day ahead unconcerned with how you are perceived. Happiness is not about having the best of everything but the ability to make the best of anything. Happiness is knowing you are doing the best you can with what you were given. Happiness is not something that comes to you when every problem is solved, and all things are perfectly in place but in the shining silver linings that remind us that the light of day is always there if we slow down enough to notice. Loved that caption from the first time I read it. I just want to thank The Daily Coach which was presented Blinkist and to that of the author Brianna West "The Mountain is You "for those words of wisdom.

Slowing down is the opposite of what is truly happening nowadays: speeding up full-throttle ahead, pedal to the metal, no rest for the wicked, all guns blazing, never slack her till you wreck her, go, go go go, more more more, and by the time you awaken from this pace of life, you'll realize that you are too old to enjoy it. For the hardworking rich, financially no worries, yes, but physically and mentally you can be spent. Then the hard workers who have paid tax all their lives working the same nine-to-five job retire with a multitude of health problems. You collect two thirds of your pension, but the government still unscrupulously takes a third of it away, for there is no end to it all.

There's that saying that keeps popping up: "You will have nothing but be happy." When the reality is soup in a can with a glass of unfiltered probably warm water, having to live off the state and right to your end be still fighting for finances, maybe at this point is when you finally awaken to the programming you've been under, and your usefulness is no more to them. It's such a sad thing for me to write about, but for many so true. This bull crap about having nothing but you'll be happy is a figment of someone who has everything for themselves bar their *soul*. A soulless being, remorseful of nothing, regretful of nothing, skip loads of material that eventually becomes nothing even to them. Material life is a simulation to innerstand the existence and deserve eternal life.

A poignant saying I hear a lot and believed throughout my life is, "You come into this world with nothing, and you will leave with nothing." I have found this to be untrue. You are a being of energy of light, destined for a path already chosen by you. You choose when and where you want to be born, and you choose your predestined end. But what you do with all that time in between is up to you. You have free will the whole of this time. You also always have one guardian angel with you, and that angel stays with you your entire life, ready to help you with anything and everything if you but ask. You could have loads of guides and angels, but always you have one.

Your angel cannot interfere with you physically, but when asked for help metaphysically it will heed your call and do what it can, always for your higher good. This is who will be there at the very end, of at least that I'm sure. Throughout your life, everything is set in motion from a very, very young age to try to dim your light, and if successful enough, to even try to put it out fully. Whereupon there is only darkness.

I have thought long and hard about maybe this is the time where you leave with nothing, or even you don't get to leave at all because you are held down so low by the dark forces. There might even be a time when, if you are so dark that you practise the darkness, the only thing that leaves you is the one angel you've had all along, and back down you go consciously or unconsciously to begin the lessons of learning all over again, forever trapped in your binding agreement to that one contract that never expires.

Only through enlightenment and eventually ascension can it truly expire on a world that has become an invisible open-air prison. Through darkness can only come light. You cannot have one without the other. And always remember, it's your free will as to which one to choose.

For a while now, I had thought this was a good ending for my book, until I read over it a few times. There are too many gloomy bits by which to end on.

First and foremost, I would like to thank my best matey, Colin Brown, who has been on this journey and now his own journey, with me and supporting me throughout. In so doing, he has become my *soul brother*. Never once has he questioned me or doubted what I told him I was going through. To now see Colin beginning his own journey fills my heart up with not only abundant love but a ton of gratitude for him always being on the other end of the phone listening to my evolving experiences, sometimes on a daily and nightly basis. I now have come to innerstand his wife, Jacklienne, called me his second wife.

Truly, all jokes aside, we also got to experience some magical moments together. That's when he became part of the spiritual awakening that has now really begun to pick up a lot of pace globally. To tell someone that you're seeing all these visions daily and then on one of his visits for him to experience it alongside me was such a euphoric moment for both of us. He has never looked back since. You can't when something magical appears in your life right in front of you. The only explanation is that we certainly are nowhere near alone.

I remember with the knowledge of knowing beforehand he was coming, I had asked my angels so much to show him something, and they answered my call. The jumping around in excitement and the look on his face has forever been imprinted in my mind. I have told him it will be his turn to write a book next. Though he might have to hurry himself, as there is one thing I personally have kept out of this book: my dreams.

Throughout this book, if you think what I was experiencing was otherworldly, my dreams have risen to a level so crazy I'm nearly afraid to write about them. The one thing I will say is that as much as we are moving into the fifth dimension, in my dreams, there is quite a lot more. I had never thought too much about the lower ones, like one and two, but my dreams showed me stuff that makes the third dimension we are all living in look like a paradise world. I felt sometimes that maybe there was a zero dimension out there also, but that's all maybe for another day, depending on how this book gets viewed by everyone and hopefully everywhere.

To get a calling to write a book is something all by itself. I believe deep within me, I was advised to write about my experiences, maybe because they were so crazy. That's how I felt at the time. Going through all of this, keeping life normal, raising my three children, knowing full well I couldn't tell them but at times desperately wanting to. They would have thought I was loopy loo, so I resisted. They could certainly see that I had gradually changed over time. Even my youngest daughter, Ameila, said one evening, "It's O.K., Dad, you can get mad at me sometimes. I deserved it, because I was shouting and being cheeky to you at the same time."

Two years beforehand, there would have been no tolerance on my part. I would have gone berserk and punished her. Though the thing is, when you have unconditional love, or at least as close to unconditional love as you can get, you truly make the transition from reacting to responding. Writing those words is easy, but to master something like that, as I had reacted to every situation in my life for forty-six years, felt, from the inside, fantastic. I just couldn't show it to her at that moment or she would still be shouting at me.

I love my daughters more than life itself, and even today, I am as affectionate as I can get away with. Sophie and Jasmine, nineteen and seventeen, have grown past Dad fooling around and being silly. By now, they have realized, and told me too, "Dad, you're a real asshole at times." Deep down, I know they mean it, too, but even deeper I know they love me and that I'm always present, providing for and protecting them through thick or thin with love.

I made a vow to myself a few years back when I became a single father of three girls to not go chasing girls in any way, shape, or form. I knew from that moment on, I would not give them the time they would need to build a proper relationship, as my time and my mind would be on my children. One-night stands and casual sex just didn't appeal to me anymore, as I had been in a relationship with the mother of my children for about eighteen years.

Anyhow, my chat-up lines would certainly have been outdated. Don't think "Are you coming in for a quick coffee?" would have stood the test of time, or "My feet are killing me, because you've been running around my head all day," or is it "Are your feet killing you"? You see, I haven't a clue either way.

Over the years, it's not like I didn't have a few chances, but as hard sometimes as it was, out of respect, I always declined. I said I would wait till my daughters were all eighteen, but now I don't think they would hold it against me. I don't think I could have let another woman act as a mother to them, because I want their own mother to do that. She left me and not the kids, so I thought that would be unfair.

I have never broken that rule once and am quite proud of myself for it. Little did I know that the journey I was about to go on years later would give me the knowledge that there are twin flames. I never heard of them my entire life. To find out the truths of life has been the most wondrous thing, but to apply that to the way you live every day was little short of a miracle for me, as over the years I had put up with so much lying from so many people, and still, some of them don't know, I know.

It just kept getting better for me, as I had learnt how to forgive in the beginning. I thought I was forgiving, but deep down through my deep thoughts I had only done it verbally. This is when you must go inside and deal and heal with revenge, retribution, and that feeling of *I owe you one*. As much as some took longer than others, eventually I made peace with my past.

So, for me not only to have never met what I now know to be my twin flame but to not even know she existed at this point still amazes me even now, with all I have gone through. I began doing inner work, still in its infancy, when Ellen Redd and Twin Flame Initiates popped onto my feed. Just at the right time, too. It was in following Ellen that I began to see that still there were a lot of people saying they were twin flames when there were false. There seem to be a lot of egotistical people claiming to be ones, and here I was doing stuff with a metaphysical woman, not fully sure what I was at, a lot of the time.

This is when I started slowing my search, quieting my posts, and typically saying nothing of it. I didn't get that sense that I wanted to show off in some way by telling the world I had a twin flame. Quite the opposite.

I began gaining more knowledge on the ancient history of it all through Ellen's very honest and informative posts. Looking from the outside in, you could see people arguing between themselves and missing the point altogether about reunions, separation light codes, truth codes, masculine and feminine and the trails, and challenges, tests that you must do on the earthly plain to even begin to honour the other half of your soul. Metaphysically, you must go through so much more. It felt at times that there was a little sabotaging at work, and I innerstood sometimes why Ellen would close her comments section.

For me, it was about pure love, honest truthful deep love, and if you share half your soul, surely your heart must be vibrationally connected, along with your frequency being a match of unity. Alignment, healing, calibrating, union, forgiveness, self-love, and compassion are all linked to an unwavering love and innerstanding of harmony that's full of joy. It emphasizes the heavenly connection between two significant historic holy souls that are inner-woven as one from the beginning, split in two entering this earth, destined to come together as one to anchor their light and let it shine so bright that in some way, everyone can feel it, as we are all *one*—a universal consciousness aware of everything within everyone and connected to everywhere. A connection that cannot be broken, an everlasting bond, that even death cannot divide. In this world or the next your twin flame displays a reciprocation of love never matched, a burning fire that can never be extinguished. A light working twin that purposefully helps broken wounds with no fear or judgement. Your divine counterpart. To realize upon entering this world as one to the magnetic feminine going one way and the electric masculine going in the opposite direction, then getting to live for that day were your soul twin draws as one together to electro magnetically quantum entangle the bliss of divine love.

I allow myself to have thoughts that on a divinely guided path on a journey of lifetimes, maybe one day I will meet my human counterpart, and with the sexual chemistry of a universe, have a reunion that echoes across the cosmos. To simplify it a little, someone to hold and have a proper cuddle every night when drifting off to sleep. As beings, we need our sleep, but our souls can then go to whichever metaphysical realm they choose and light up the spirit world, on the pretence of being back in the morning so we can cuddle as beings again, and together create our heaven on this earth.

I'm not quite sure how I could write this one as an affirmation or even a manifestation. I think I will leave this one to my heart. It alone is a gift off all gifts, a divine of all divinity, a flame that never dulls, and a light that can't be dimmed.

Sleeping, snoring, unawoken, it is time to awaken and claim what is truthfully yours and always was and always will be. Grab your torch with your mind, body, and soul, and help light this world up with *love*.

My soul is a masterpiece, a work of art woven with the threads of my experiences and dreams. I embrace my uniqueness, for I am a kaleidoscope of colours, and each shade paints the world with love and compassion. Let the brilliance of my authenticity shine, illuminating the lives of those around me. My presence is a gift, a melody that resonates in the hearts of others, so I dare to be true to myself, for it is in this beautiful tapestry of authenticity that I discover the boundless potential of my soul. Let my essence bloom and inspire like a breathtaking masterpiece, forever leaving its mark on the canvas of humanity. I embrace my light and let it radiate, for my soul is a masterpiece that can change the world.

This is a caption that popped up on my feed on Facebook about a year ago, and at the time of reading it, I fell in love with the words. I have changed some words to personify and doctor it to myself, as it inspired me and resonated deeply and touched my soul. I have read it nearly every night for this last year of my life and would like to take this opportunity to thank the writer of such words of wisdom. They have been with me throughout my journey, and now I know it off by heart, as I have read it so many times.

The Source

A cosmic birther of all radiance and vibration, soften the ground of our bodies and carve out a space within us where your presence can abide. Fill us with your creativity so that we may be in power to bear the fruit of your mission. Let each of our actions bear fruit in accordance with our desires. Endow us with the wisdom to produce and share what each being needs to grow and flourish. Untie the tangled threads of destiny that bind us as we release others from the entanglement of past mistakes. Do not let us be seduced by that which would divert us from our true purpose. Illuminate the opportunities of our present moment, for you are the ground, the truthful mission, the birth, the power and fulfilment as all is gathered and made whole again, and so it is.

This prayer resonated with me when I first read it from a page on Facebook meant to be the ancient lord's prayer but have no information as to who put it up it just felt right to me

I have finally come to the end of my book, and my tenth ink pen doesn't want to set itself down. I have come so far in my journey, and always it is the beginning of another, a quantum leap of faith by following the path of my heart. To find your truth of not only love but divine love, know deep within your beautiful soul that as one cycle ends, another has been already mapped out for you, and with your free will, you get to choose which path to take.

I hope you have enjoyed my book. I alone cannot wake you up; that is completely up to you. If this book has resonated deeply within your soul, then it is the book that has found you. Sending light and love to all.

When you take the science out of it
LIGHT IS LOVE. CHOOSE LIGHT.

1111 9999 0000

THE END

Can't believe I just did this.

On my journey I have come across different captions at different times that not only inspired me but also give me the mental fortitude to keep writing so I thought it would be a befitting end to write one myself. "My life's perception is like a cosmic puzzle, always expanding learning leaving loving and compassionately placing all the spiritual pieces together to self-create my most beautiful life, before the deciphering of my deepest darkest struggles catch up to my bliss, my divine purpose in the opening of my heart and soul, to then the fitting of my last biological piece on my journey back to source. Only then to recharge in the incubational womb of pure love and begin another cycle of infinite unknown wonderment magnifying my movement in all directions as oneness, always one, we have always been one, there is only one and we are it" "What happens after you die" and "are we alone" the two most famous earthly questions receiving this knowledge is a "MATCH MADE IN HEAVEN"

A list of words that have entered my life after forty-six years of being in the matrix and under its program, and I've threw in some numbers too.

Love for All

self-confidence	desire	navigate	creativity	11	1
associated	abilities	special	initiative	111	2
personal	recognize	symbolism	pioneering	1111	3
authority	sacred	commitment	influence	22	4
receiving	scribes	significance	attributes	222	5
integrity	ceramics	faithfulness	humanitarianism	2222	6
reality	vibration	existing	benevolence	33	7
dependability	anonymous	consideration	altruism	333	8
self-reliance	sequences	encouragement	magnifies	3333	9
manifesting	purpose	perspective	destiny	44	
abundance	analyse	transformation	courage	444	so so
concept	compassion	meaningful	potential	4444	many more
resonate	adaptability	established	motivate	55	numbers
pursuing	passionately	imminent	illuminate	555	the combinations
instinct	consideration	expressing	solution	55555	are every
intuition	diplomacy	representation	definition	66	where
self-leadership	encourage	obstacle	notoriety	666	angel
ambition	divine	limitation	perseverance	6666	numbers
tenacity	balance	tranquillity	celestial	77	are
initiative	harmony	determination	cosmic	777	for
inspiration	eternity	selflessness	tribulations	7777	each and
assertiveness	infinity	stability	karmic	88	every one
belief	oneness	biblical	karma	888	of us, you've
significant	wholeness	happiest	resilience	8888	just gotta
circumstances	potential	closeness	retrograde	99	believe and
prosperity	universal	sincerity	obstacles	999	use your
affirmations	energies	represent	gracefully	9999	intuition
reinforce	enthusiasm	enlightenment	warrior	00	when looking
inner-wisdom	opportunities	astrology	guardian	000	for them
guidance	fruition	vibration	galaxy	0000	with faith
spiritually	numerology	uniqueness	enslaved	1010	gratitude and
			717	0909	love

1st ones [drawing] [drawing] (orange) Colour Different Direction

Going Straight motion different directions and different Heights but the same thing Minutes apart couple of

2nd [drawing] Orange in Colour also the little bits looked like it was turning up to go down

Turning angle up down and round

3 / 2 / 4 / 1 / 5

3rd [drawing] white Rectangle going on a upward angle Trails after and at...

4th [drawing] white going Straight ahead Trails after and at... Smaller one

5th [drawing] nearly the same as the 4th one with Trails bu... a different level and on a Different fast...

No shit this is feeling unreal Exciting ~~~

Happened 2:00 am

All off the above ~~~ only Seen for Split off a second if you wern't looking would never see it

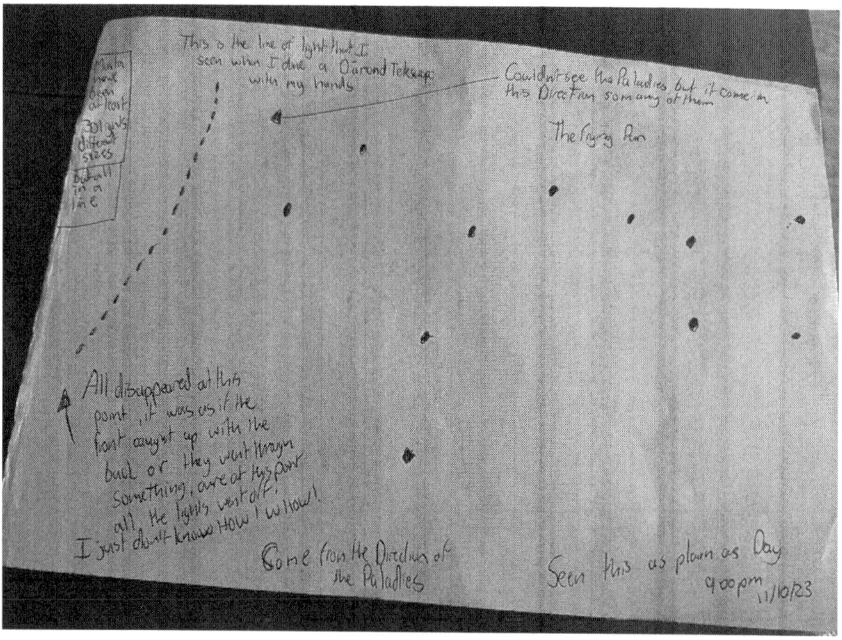
This is the line of light that I
with my hands
Couldn't see the Paladies but it come in
The Frying Pan
All disappeared at this
point, it was as if the
front caught up with the
back or they went through
something, once at this point
all the lights went off.
I just don't know How! w How!
Come from the Direction of
the Paladies
Seen this as plain as Day
9:00pm 11/10/23

LOADS OF ORACLE'S LIKE: (Nicky)

Loads of toyshop New Earth No Guns No Lie No Sewage
No Acid No Tanks No Jealousy No 3 D Poonami 10
No Money No Missiles No LSD No 3 D Poonami No AK 475
Free Energy love Hammers only If needed Crystal lme Poo
Crystal Clear Water for Everyone (C(lean)
No Bottled Water No Control Earth Act No money Loving DINASAURS
No Cocaine WEED Mak Mother Earth act loads FUN No Pee Pee
No Tree Surgeons loads DANCE No Toilets
No Jet fights No WARS loads DANCE No Toilets
No Chain Saws No Bombs loads MUSIC
No Jet Bombers No WAR ANGELS
No lawn Mowers No wke Cloud ANGELS
No Bombs Unitify with All
No Strimmers No WAR GODS
No Trenches LOVE LOVE
No Hedge Clippers No WAR GODS VIBRATIONAL LOVE
Trees that Walk & Talk LOVE Plenty of Respect LOVE LOVE
No soldiers No cameras VIBE
Trees as Big as Skyscrapers LOVE LOVE
All Animals talk No survovense Spirit Guides LOVE LOVE
Tons of Birds Guardian Angels LOVE LOVE
No Government LOVE FOR ALL loving Souls LOVE LOVE
Abundant Stars OWL!! LOVE LOVE
THE
love Energy PLENTOF START LOVE LOVE
Truth Energy No Alchohol LOVE MAKING DAY OR NIGHT LOVE LOVE
Massive FOREST'S OR MORNING LOVE LOVE
No Fighting FOR EVERYBODY TO FEEL

S   T   A   R   T   P   A   G   E

811	1920	122	3929	1441	2222	354	9966	777
3211	991	1555	5859	3333	4113	711	1090	11
8332	2121	3233	9199	1707	1114	1889	1771	11
444	717	8088	4141	888	1757	6001	8608	144
777	727	8888	2272	1818	212	6625	7112	44
222	2225	323	222	2111	4022	4400	2225	1000
777	2211	2221	0001	6366	66	5353	2332	6655
1909	2224	1441	711	2224	66	3937	9990	2200
4746	1111	4744	7177	909	8805	1000	2233	3200
2122	2222	2122	8889	2244	3333	6655	8181	9202
2101	33	2221	9060	2022	7444	7755	5958	3885
7998	0900	666	660	7373	2003	5335	3929	1110
2332	1144	919	1819	7177	7311	1717	8500	1411
66	144	1332	1717	4144	4446	1819	9311	777
66	333	1818	550	2922	2272	660	9867	8070
7007	1444	1909	699	5111	8828	9202	2201	9994
5553	211	3336	7554	1669	7717	2200	6001	7733
2243	0000	3332	222	7733	1221	7171	1155	5554
0744	1444	2277	433	911	7207	1144	3885	666
222	1133	7774	4575	955	2444	4440	2828	2071
1111	322	555	5554	1330	8999	222	574	0707
1111	2221	66	8882	2244	211	2272	3888	0808
1112	660	2011	4647	9929	333	8500	5353	3333
1414	2333	9876	533	3545	1555	9555	1909	0909
757	1144	1616	0533	2422	2002	555	7171	9555
1100	88	353	8686	1155	1333	666	1333	8881
1555	1433	2211	22	3311	2122	7701	111	4114
1111	1444	3722	06	2288	2327	7733	2212	177
599	1441	111	06	666	323	9994		

P
A
T
G
E
(2)

					4646	711	2022
77	444	122	2226	444	887	2255	2111
4440	2224	122	0002	2101	515	110	1337
4321	144	9474	0707	0044	2222	144	2141
144	144	1811	0901	1111	0707	444	1711
1330	1919	6161	717	1000	0717	2332	1555
1447	2222	7575	222	8889	0828	999	1916
4144	3222	999	444	8088	5656	2223	5355
3333	888	2210	2002	8818	2112	2221	2522
8880	727	611	2232	7071	2244	0727	888
6001	3313	711	2332	1555	9999	7077	1700
144	3534	727	0005	775	311	111	1313
33855	969	1144	0011	9696	1920	123	000
2133	1711	7434	0717	888	2115	222	1100
515	5551	4446	0818	1011	3553	3444	4221
2224	2332	2227	0919	0002	8088	2888	199
1919	1818	2323	555	944	6050	6050	2101
9099	737	2272	2224	9395	0004	737	2211
6878	911	2022	0717	111	0555	66	3007
2515	2297	1010	3033	111	0909	66	444
2121	1404	0002	1555	1858	0919	1177	2288
2233	1212	2221	1616	1909	999	777	2272
2313	1144	8088	2021	2121	7077	919	8088
0000	1636	1551	2229	2233	2111	7333	1122
2525	9000	1555	0717	0339	1616	4333	575
9919	2121	2228	1033	4447	7733	1113	343
5556	122	2330	1223	1441	7733	1717	2922
1000	311	2355	444	2220	4212	1646	111
9696	1100	1228	111	2323	6888	1212	171
9977	1117	0717	2112	252	222	1100	111
4447	1122	1338	2212	1117	444	1911	2118
4433	66	1330	2335	2020	8084	6556	2222
333	66	1111	1112	2992	9999	144	333
222	66	2222	444	300	8040	144	0117
111	122	1911	6677	300	687	144	444
699	122	2021	4343	1722			

						7979	7777	5332	(444)
	3121	4144	6266	33183	1441	8077	4444	9909	
	222	1221	9495	1313	1330	3999	9999	888	8558
	444	1442	4005	1919	555	2021	6565	9292	9292
	400	1010	5700	66	1611	555	7997	0939	1111
P	989	7272	1606	66	1000	5557	3222	6116	6666
	898	1919	8825	1441	2121	2202	3773	5888	223
A	9696	445	2244	1212	2202	2220	7977	3333	0755
	6006	494	2322	0737	2212	8889	997	333	0715
L	979	2227	0711	44	7575	7999	1133	111	77
	6050	0000	0747	2255	555	8000	1001	2112	777
E	2099	0707	444	0747	6776	33	1551	777	7777
	7222	6001	444	827	789	8848	66	1500	1808
	2112	6881	9555	66	3223	1515	66	2332	111
	1201	688	1661	66	9899	1909	661	2114	1818
	444	3888	8338	33	3344	5555	66	66	7707
(3)	4243	1442	4774	33	2525	6866	66	66	1909
	2928	8886	1555	1444	2111	666	6060	2323	1200
	221	1711	4050	1911	2114	1616	111	1414	1117
	122	32232	777	2547	6757	2222	111	1010	3336
	722	9777	6001	7713	1808	1555	112	1131	444
	8999	8111	2332	8228	2800	7700	4444	1155	444
	8884	7727	5557	333	7775	4474	2277	7727	4444
	7001	5533	7761	1331	8448	888	3344	2221	4444
	1133	944	9911	1808	7733	2207	0000	777	4434
	377	797	44	8808	7575	6665	555	2000	
	411	1700	44	8808	3344	2100	66	2020	3133
	77	771	44	7222	333	2222	7700	1909	1717
	77	1107	66	2111	333	200	6757	66	777
	727	757	66	2233	2727	323	7177	66	777
	222	919	8020	577	66	9299	7977	0000	555
	6333	111	22	7444	66	8880	4321	66	313
	777	111	22	5535	22	6066	8883	5599	313
	2777	444	22	1616	22	1300	6066	55	6676
	8088	446	3333	4444	5700	77	1221	007	373
	1666	8101	4744	7701	112		424		

006	1131	1119	0909	929	5959	1909	2000	(1111)	1440	1000
					9599	221222	669	(1111)	1303	4411
1333	888	0900	177	8811		1115	868		6566	4747
1221	3333	2002	1400	2000	1411	795	664	1800	7778	9811
6622	1447	2222	1117	8888	8989	7818	(9209)	(0000)	707	9339
3332	1552	1857	2121			2828	(9999)	0949	6566	550
0909	3443	1101	1100	(4144)	4646	1362	(6666)	0900	3555	799
010	2211	0000	2110	(1010)	444	1707	111	2121	555	
888	2100	6066	3636	(11111)	1551	1212		2211	144	777
555	2000	1411	1922	1313	5052	1119	2101	0909	1922	222
505	1818	9599	4343	7997	333	1122	828	010	3636	222
1101	2222	1117	1838	828	4949	444	1001	888	4343	8333
9559	0808	333	1909	1808	1113	2424	444	555	1838	377
3443	333	888	3309	122	1323	2300	666	505	0117	1411
8887	2131	211	1110	1881	1919	828	1717	505	0117	1411
8080	2044	7122	5757	6009	222	2772	2255	1101	3309	(6060)
1404	2212	0001	6866	4441	3933	0900	5999	9559	1959	(5555)
6016	6066	1922	199	8898	7979	449	0909	3443	3117	7077
6660	6066	144	9777	8088	8885	2011	7799	1221	1636	8188
505	2222	3555	7828	888	7778	1155	444	006	771	2000
333	9599	6566	22	515	2424	464	777	3332	666	3331
7711	2255	7778	66	6677	444	1112	777	1333	(4444)	1959
2303	1411	1959	06	2272	7997	1122	2276	6022	8797	1909
1707	8484	6566	66	808	7001	1333	9555	2044	2000	4343
2101	1161	1303	2272	2222	3888	0404	7717	2212	2000	3636
1222	3336	1444	1001	3030	1515	0808	1555	6066	2828	1117
477	1545	3309	7771	3331	1717	8033	(3333)	9599	33	1838
4101	8484	1822	3333	7700	2255	7151	(1010)	(2222)	288	3555
2023	949	707	2424	7755	3733	4117	(1818)	2253	2005	177
2121	222	6566	2023	8108	8727	2033	2111	1411	221	1400
2212	1141	3555	1661	1881	2424	1446	2223	222	2255	1311
0707	1221	1055	4244	8885	6010	1747	2246	1222	(0000)	1444
(55333)	6554	144	2121	1313	795	4343	0928	1777	0022	1959
0712	222	1311	3111	212	6888	4007	(1111)	0606	757	6566
0818	6534	1222	22	0188	1555	7999	1202	0909	833	707
0919	5685	0606	3331	0808	7676	3331	00	1446	(0909)	192
	1000									

	144	2151					1000	66	9939
	222	2114	3553	0444	115	1919	1000	66	9939
P	111	900	919	0737	1939	1909	424	33	4042
	7778	991	1919	600	1616	1808	711	33	3773
	1303	5155	1747	1444	1717	1010	727	33	333
A	2040	2252	1117	707	1919	1801	2922	33	222
	8886	2111	7007	707	1919	1909	818	66	4440
G	2121	2055	9499	233	1747	2101	88	66	444
	2202	494	4141	555	2006	2200	888	22	1111
	2228	3366	1666	777	1611	111	003	88	1111
E	8484	0929	1331	9999	337	2220	010	2222	1111
	949	9009	7001	2222	727	303	222	1717	2226
	222	8585	5335	4222	1717	911	500	2000	7044
	1141	0000	888	1616	222	334	3131	828	4445
5	1221	0747	77	1707	222	1800	1323	1122	9099
	6566	222	2101	77	0002	66	1100	5888	1616
	6566	144	2111	501	252	66	4111	828	9999
	0616	144	2228	707	3732	444	77	200	444
	0818	377	0836	959	9999	444	500	9129	333
		8484	0900	1909	9996	22	371	1000	777
	1222	1808	1414	1444	444	22	371	1303	33
	1010	3344	1101	2222	7770		2040	9969	33
	4044	2151	4040	22122	898	2030	444	2996	2112
	5655	2080	2121	2205	252	2030	2030	9906	2112
	7677	7009	1711	556	66	0700	0901	6090	1111
	1909	1777	3700	4131	66	111	1011	4060	123
	2110	1030	3330	2877	6566	0737	2121	7775	3343
	2222	2303	8989	4407	1222	0757	0022	3333	444
	0001	0333	2666	3100	9555	44	777	9999	66
	144	0626	4770	3666	4000	1808	7777	9969	66
	144	0722	337	1000	1122	808	7717	333	66
	1330	1711	1611	3737	7900	007	333	33	66

1?	8?7?	4??4	1??	??
1101	6229	(0088)	1616	2212
505	446	6061	1717	2222
555	1441	66	(0007)	1445
888	121	66	(0111)	8448
010	5565	66	(0505)	1010
3443	7707	313	22	2151
9559	(1010)	616	717	444
006	9932	0524	0922	444
1221	1111	(0808)	1000	7887
1333	1113	0744	2040	(939)
3332	0806	9.00	1040	555
(0606)	1636	0757	1238	(7778)
(0919)	(1010)	(0909)	6666	5131
	1322	(1444)	2244	444
(0909)	176		888	8811
(0003)	008	9696	2773	8811
(0303)	1515	7774	5335	800
2999	4447	6162	8888	800
9001	7444	115	88	8779
7001	1331	5115	88	1333
(0818)	7011	1330	111	2222
(0828)	3330	2626	444	2424
(1333)	(6666)	2555	66	555
515	616	8441	66	9938
7880	1144	1212	1404	0907
1222	(777)	6263	5556	2002
9966	2112	5556	8441	7221
(11222)	1707	515	6666	(0909)
(11333)	1929	4212	8448	(1010)
828	2001	4000	1???	????

PAGE 6

929	4244	111		88	22	1441	9998	111	2826
0001	2262	111	1414		82	5115	1919	2200	3336
2221	66	1221	999	0000	77	1511	911	1144	111
0011	66	1270	333	1555	77	9197	959	4334	2121
272	777	06	3221	77	334	919	2033	8811	444
533	777	1000	1010	1133		1000	123	5551	1909
0707	2229	4044	111	2000	477	1000	898	111	1808
5757	4040	4488	8488	1144	887	1000	0007	1313	4417
8828	2200	626	2322	2220	(881)	1000	1555	9098	1929
7616	2211	0000	2222	1203	8718	8011	1400	2117	222
9929	447	0033	222	9969	3100	7877	900	1131	1848
6767	1444	1001	2332	1133	3030	221	171	1911	6660
644	6666	2001	9279	6566	4243	8842	1313	115	1001
696	2222	747	9279	1220	8011	2255	1010	121	1001
9000	0000	2020	4044	222	6644	1424	66	111	4646
444	0808	1955	66	777	9109	1606	66	1515	7020
123	808	1111	1000	5808	3938	1919	66	2055	9095
66	808	88	1221	1313	4808	1177	22	9981	7180
66	0927	88	0929	1133	1848	9118	11	7677	9875
55	0818	22	111	2223	6959	3222	11	7700	1211
22	1171	2020	111	2110	222	155	11	7700	8031
499	777	1111	626	0808	999	006	66	7700	7077
1212	5252	9299	111	0919	9299	222	66	1909	7077
1191	8088	1010	7373	2020	797	7077	2212	1818	3993
555	2272	333	7474	1919	0919	6636	2220	3898	9599
2828	1001	555	6464	300	5838	060	555	9969	994
2121	0696	777	7107	303	929	4020	9969	2222	4455
406	1959	7777	919	3030	7575	2040	1100	111111	7711
1909	0292	2222	7717	1909	7444	2221	1100	707070	1441
999	6644	0055	9919	838	1050	5056	2442	100100	3232
414	2309	5155	9929	0909	7771	1001	8808	9939	1555
1311	3325	1077	9969	717	1331	1001	3113	9787	111
1808	999	7676	6001	0717	444	8000	2828	6444	5557
1333	111	6628	7227	2002	6626	4000	5111	555	666

PAGE 8

					2121	333	1717	898
4441	88	8884	8484	9777	11	6444	888	222
7557	88	1919	777	1444	22	1119	888	0013
0929	4040	4141	777	999	44	222	9299	1747
7999	1000	555	444	999	44	2881	4441	9778
515	7772	888	888	2272	55	555	222	955
828	9010	4422	1801	88	66	5255	7808	22
6888	333	949	1144	77	77	777	303	3737
5577	4440	222	404	99	88	9797	888	1711
755	545	888	222	3343	888	2525	0909	222
8533	4554	7733	828	8000	1666	6866	1115	22
5070	44	444	0009	6444	5556	9808	909	2002
5070	222	888	5999	888	6666	9808	2210	303
99	11	900	3733	1661	9770	3300	7799	332
22	11	8118	1313	3399	1404	4406		332
9599	7772	888	111	2220	7676	7000	2222	123
99	7772	737	1707	9969	969	6000	909	123
99	2229	7676	8180	3939	1818	6330	1010	9668
8878	123	22	2222	1119	1757	2040	1144	6666
555	808	77	0707	9777	1939	222	244	7737
555	4433	7788	9444	3303	2002	222	0304	99
1001	4545	555	003	3377	0502	222	2121	88
777	1212	7777	222	1881	0911	8885	123	77
777	2828	1010	1777	7979	1010	900	2002	7818
99	44	1001	8585	1222	0616	3131	2080	7777
99	22	333	969	5655	0525	6666	1515	9595
199	44	3733	999	9696	2121	1717	1818	444
5111	88	333	6363	444	2323	333	0909	1444
5588	88	333	7733	2288	111	8188	1808	929
44	4000	1010	1555	3399	3010	8818	1727	1515
11	4044	222	5551	5533	4010	2111	1515	8585
11	150	222	909	8683	4444	111	2111	3131
222	1911	7447	1929	4433	0260	1111	7878	222
8448	2424	1313	1444	808	202	33	99	222
9688	474	8680	1919	888	202	99	777	5255

PAGE 9

					22	1311	9790	4949
2002	1111	8488	1434	4744			2227	727
0717	66	5999	0929	202	4647	1201 99	22	3030
1002	445	4222	1404	202	444 8555	8818	22	222
2223	2223	555	1600	1911			33	1311
1929	2111	8886	33	989	8090	2922	33	1555
4441	1049	9777	1171	2222	9911	6699	33	333
777	717	3737	606	7722	833	88	22	333
9303	8448	222	9967	1440	4444	155	22	4433
1808	1111	444	9313	222	727	727	22	4002
1555	1233	3113	88	7700	7711	555	744	4744
1227	2233	444	88	8099	7979	3555	727	555
111	1133	0999	5464	3636	99	6666	333	777
1122	0003	888	1113	99	8879	9900	222	848
0717	0010	2828	11111	3111	222	3333	1311	656
444	6666	441	8484	3344	777	77	4744	880
444	1010	898	9777	1616	77	1555	0222	5755
2121	1111	5555	8222	8484	777	212	4544	6161
303	7770	555	444	4774	1911	4404	1000	122
303	4440	4544	111	4640	6166	777	8885	1133
0292	1001	2882	11	755	3303	1199	1010	1010
0929	881	9229	4488	2626	3303	6030	1010	1313
1606	8818	1119	11	9119	1212	2227	8020	111
404	6688	929	2332	884	1131	3737	3636	333
0906	1001	222	7771	6699	70500	33	333	202
1001	545	4477	8484	2220	77	8837	9899	1100
1919	123	6666	888	2121	22	5456	9699	1100
999	555	1999	3131	7700	6060	6556	6909	0003
0838	777	9009	966	5655	7373	8884	1717	2242
0717	7777	9919	555	6161	6665	888	7771	777
7887	777	2020	1110	1818	0004	2020	7771	444
7771	7770	555	3444	555	1333	377	444	0011
8448	7007	2828	1100	5655	222	8887	88	777
1144	3133	0292	123	9099	1911	8998	88	
							22	

444	3733	11	222	555	2382	828	8228
4644	4114	2100	1441	1441	1010	555	6767
1010	8083	7272	1404	144	1010	8330	3377
2121	3733	646	7799	505	1111	2828	222
2008	7007	7999	444	2122	707	88	0011
1818	7227	33	0909	767	919	33	211
1313	1114	77	2222	994	919	868	771
1331	8088	2232	1010	949	2112	7117	171
414	5656	818	909	222	1331	8884	9000
707	66	0838	0090	222	4144	2000	1112
567	22	0727	123	9889	6465	6776	44
8581	77	0304	33	999	1331	777	122
88	6313	0801	2626	777	1303	111	6111
88	1221	828	6262	4440	0911	1803	4455
99	1616	0838	1313	555	881	144	9000
22	9969	2252	2626	2277	2822	656	8188
22	8889	1144	88	9998	8077	7778	2040
33	7117	0010	88	333	9339	1110	2202
33	2120	141	88	1111	5557	2226	909
66	111	313	1411	1133	8484	1414	123
66	211	211	1141	882	1555	1117	414
66	626	202	8888	2000	9777	909	8081
2002	323	1101	333	277	1144	111	1122
2323	7799	1313	3333	555	8336	0909	233
6111	77	222222	3111	7595	66	0919	8181
1113	7777	33	77	202	707	2882	333
1555	7044	1080	44	7710	9071	3395	222
555	5000	2020	1618	1303	222	8333	123
414	9991	2020	6221	7799	444	5445	123
4111	0002	11111	1118	2233	5858	222	6776
2442	2242	2323	505	2094	9811	4446	909
414	1212	2202	929	4440	8778	6446	444
353	5999	1000	7775	9939	2441	656	818
77	22	1000	7778	5556	1919	4565	808

717	1313	222	6616	2222	1114	7177
919	11	7724	9997	2121	5000	222
313	88	868	5999	777	1414	444
455	44	999	2202	2232	1171	5535
2886	3211	333	1414	6666	918	1333
2828	7676	3333	1122	3313	4222	21212
3838	123	33	8188	4433	1133	222
727	5445	33	8088	1661	1114	7277
333	7772	5757	2332	1166	7744	696
878	6966	5454	909	777	9789	1666
898	8885	0799	2040	2999	88	5115
7377	7575	777	303	9991	88	1717
5555	220	777	233	9778	1155	4443
55	1221	777	6776	1616	1200	7799
3343	4433	7770	222	2000	9091	7779
6000	4433	7774	383	2111	1133	1011
2777	1616	441	123	2112	1221	3011
333	222	144	123	1907	4141	1122
222	222	888	8188	2121	1110	1555
144	333	9811	2208	6666	1144	1212
144	4434	3383	1111	4494	4040	1010
44	4434	9990	2020	3001	0000	8333
9909	555	5222	4343	4114	99	1555
44	555	7774	6226	1099	122	1919
33	555	1818	6884	777	33	1808
333	5550	9799	1111	4118	1115	1909
333	5555	7474	123	1339	5555	444
99	999	444	9444	5585	5555	2121
4346	2002	77	33	9984	777	2233
646	1166	2200	33	7870	777	5454
888	3333	9799	6977	2000	8844	5454
5335	222	4411	777	1886	919	3933
377	3393	4244	777	337	1000	1118

PAGE 12

177*

9899	0909	7728	2002	500	949	5655	4445
111	0909	123	1441	1001	7171	6898	9909
77	4440	7707	1001	123	1616	7878	5333
1111	4244	1888	949	123	1153	6616	7879
888	5551	7778	22	444	1441	333	1171
4646	6266	7778	22	00	1414	4447	1117
9337	4443	3366	22	00	4444	1211	7337
111	424	123	66	2200	0518	7878	919
4744	11	3833	222	2300	818	333	919
7333	33	171	1878	122	1701	2266	9919
222	117	9898	521	121	0818	1115	1313
2277*	303	1919	1111	6166	55	1010	1818
474	3232	7000	3332	7275	55	757	1010
666	1555	1112	4333	1929	1505	123	7227
4444	4411	1909	1111	8181	759	1010	555
1919	1717	88	8815	0011	1010	005	4444
77	1313	2022	818	121	2022	333	1118
77	919	66	777	4222	212	1010	123
2020	8886	4448	777	6776	446	3400	
1111	8880	6262	177	2800	1818	414	
2020	7979	66	505	00	1818	8689	
6888	777	66	1111	899	2404	6869	
9966	777	66	7222	711	212	222	
3773	8686	66	8005	994	949	2700	
7879	888	4448	9966 *	6660	9449	3200	
4222	1110	8886	500	2332	8911	424	
3878	1114	7888	777	919	1133	446	
8871	3311	5444	777	3031	333	4440	
5335	995	22	5999	30	199	414	
606	117	9008	6222	30	1221	252	
244	003	8181	4899	8228	2026	1140	
123	1002	6222	3636	33	3121	200	
7399	4414	1949 *	2424	1010	4447	4044	

Printed and bound by CPI Group (UK) Ltd, Croydon, CR0 4YY

30/04/2025

01857728-0002